A Dedication To

Difficult Dogs

A Heartwarming Tale Shedding Light
on Canine Mental Health

Dr Dennis Wormald

Published by ABAdog Pty Ltd
Melbourne, Victoria, Australia

Developmental and copy editing by Carla Wormald
Further copy editing by Sarah Newton-John & Stefania Franja

ISBN: 978-0-6457708-0-3

First edition: paperback 2023

Since 2018, ABAdog has been helping dog owners to understand dogs with behavioural difficulties by providing empathetic and actionable advice through their veterinary care provider. See www.abadog.com for more information.

For rights, orders or permissions inquiries, please contact ABAdog publishing at support@abadog.com

This book is dedicated to all the difficult dogs I have seen over the years, who have been misunderstood by the people around them. In particular, I dedicate this book to my own dogs Bunji and Oscar, who suffered from anxiety and taught me a lot about how I can help the other dogs I meet. I also need to thank the rest of my dogs and cats who have loved me over the years, and also my family, friends, and colleagues who supported me and believed in my vision.

Contents

Introduction

The average person's understanding of human mental health has increased dramatically over the last few decades. Thankfully, public awareness of the suffering that conditions such as anxiety and depression can cause is much improved. This has allowed for more empathy and understanding for those affected individuals from the people they live with, and from society in general. However, the dogs in our lives are not so lucky.

Most dog owners are not aware of the presence of mental health conditions in dogs at large, let alone in their own dog. The prevalence of mental health conditions in dogs and humans is believed to be similar. This means that if you know five or more dogs, you probably know a dog who struggles with their mental health. We need a significant improvement in society's understanding of animal mental health, so that we can better tolerate their behaviour and care for their needs.

As a veterinarian with a PhD in dog behaviour, I have made it my life's mission to help people to understand the animals around them. In my work I treat dogs with mental health conditions, but much of the struggle I face is around changing the human perceptions of dog behaviour.

While the story in this book is fictional, it is based entirely on the countless interactions I have witnessed in my clinical work. This book is not based on one true story, but on a mixture of many true stories that have been blended together. The interactions between the characters in this book are designed to highlight some of the most common dog behaviour misunderstandings that people have, and how these lead to problems. The story is as accurate as I could write it, including the motivations and body language of the dogs involved.

As a dog behaviour academic, I strive for scientific accuracy in my writing, as far as is available from our current research on animal behaviour. Useful information explaining the theory and background behind the story is provided for reflection at the end of each chapter. Gaps in our scientific understanding of dog behaviour are highlighted, and educated insights are offered.

When reading this book, it is important not to harshly judge the human characters. They are not uncaring people who dispassionately ignore the cries for help from the dogs around them. These are fictional representations of normal people who are unable to properly understand, read or interpret the behaviour of dogs. I see people like those in this book regularly, and they are well-meaning, good people that love dogs. Misunderstandings such as these can occur in any situation where a human is unable to read the body language of an animal. So long as there are people who cannot see the emotions behind the misbehaving or threatening dogs they encounter, stories such as these will continue to occur.

CHAPTER ONE

Puppy Troubles

The fuzzy realm of broken sleep and haunted dreams evaporated away as Allen looked up to see his two people watching him. They were a professional couple, well dressed even on their day off. They took pride in all things under their roof. Allen felt comforted by the warmth of their gaze as he lay next to them on the sofa. Hearing them start talking excitedly, Allen's focus slowly sharpened. He yawned widely and stretched out his legs, feeling a rising surge of curiosity at what the day could bring.

Allen had been walking for a few months now, and had quickly learned to navigate his home. Petra, his female person, reached down with both arms and lifted him up in the air. Feeling startled, he began to squirm and whine. Allen didn't want to be restrained at the moment, sleep time was over and now it was time to play. He twisted around in Petra's arms until he saw his favourite toy lying on the floor nearby, and then stared at it longingly.

'You really like this thing, don't you?' commented Petra, balancing Allen on one hip as she leaned down to fetch him his toy rabbit.

Nathan, Petra's husband, rolled his eyes. 'Obsessed! Totally obsessed, and he hasn't even touched that ball we bought him!'

Allen immediately put one of the rabbit ears in his mouth and started sucking and chewing on it.

Nathan peered down to inspect a dark spot on the carpet more closely. 'Looks like he's wet the floor again. Your turn to clean it up,' he said with a scrunched-up face.

Petra whipped her head back and slowly responded in a confident tone. 'We can't expect him to be perfect Nath, he's still just a baby.'

As Allen was Petra's first puppy, she felt secretly unsure of her ability as his mother. They had moved to the area for Nathan's job as a toy manufacturer, and it was isolating. Far from her own mother, Petra found herself pretending she had parenting all figured out. She told herself this was for Nathan's benefit, so he wouldn't worry. But acting the part also helped ease her own concerns.

Petra left the loungeroom and went to put Allen onto his puppy-pad in the laundry. 'Any left in there little one?'

She closed the door to the laundry, leaving Allen inside, and went to clean the carpet. Allen sat on the cold tiles with his bunny, looking up at the door. Feeling upset and a little fearful for being left alone, he burst out into a series of cries and barks.

'Shoosh Allen!' yelled Nathan from the couch. 'Just go to the toilet and then we'll let you out!'

At hearing Nathan's voice, Allen knew from the tone that things were not going well. He stopped crying and started chewing on the other ear of his bunny. When Petra finally opened the door, he ran out clumsily, stumbling over the rabbit he treasured so dearly.

'Hey Allen, it's walkies time! Want to go play at the park?' she bubbled excitedly.

Allen hadn't yet learnt what this meant, but the tone of her voice excited him. He vigorously wagged his tail and jumped up at her leg, hoping they might be about to play.

* * *

Once at the park Allen felt exhilarated, but also very nervous. A cool spring breeze combined with the warm sun caused the grass to shimmer pleasantly. Fenced inside an off-leash dog area with a childproof lock, he was free to run and play. Allen didn't run though, he stood still, staring in wonder at the sight of two white terriers and a large brown pointer chasing a golden retriever with a stick. They were more than twice the size of him, and very impressive, but also quite intimidating. Quietly panting with his mouth open, he moved to stand behind the safe legs of his person.

'It's okay Allen, you can go play too,' encouraged Petra, looking down from her conversation with another lady.

'Aww he's shy,' commented one of the other women, gazing over at Allen. 'What a cute little sausage dog! I love them when they're puppies, their short stumpy little legs and long floppy ears are just adorable!'

Petra lifted Allen up and carried him closer to one of the terriers, who had sat down in the grass to inspect a small white butterfly. 'Go on Allen,' she urged softly.

Allen gawked at the dog, unsure of what to do. After freezing for a moment, he looked around to see that Petra had moved back with the other people. Just as he was turning to follow her back, he felt himself get knocked to the side! The large pointer dog, with brown eyes to match his brown coat, had tackled him to the ground! Allen yelped in surprised shock and started wriggling to sit up. Just as he regained his footing, he was pushed over again by a large clumsy paw. His heart was racing, his mind reeling. He could feel his pulse beating in his ears and a tide of fear and adrenaline surge through his muscles. He needed to get away. This was not fun. Allen looked back towards Petra, seeing her and the other people smiling and laughing.

Petra paused for a moment, looking slightly confused before asking, 'maybe I should go get him?'

The lady furthest from her shouted in her direction so everyone could hear. 'It's okay, my one is just playing! He always does this with puppies. He loves them so much he gets super excited.'

The other ladies all smiled and laughed.

Allen was cringing, bracing on the ground for another attack. Next time, he would be ready. At that moment, the white butterfly took flight from the grass and fluttered past the pointer's face. Intrigued, he turned away and followed it, losing interest in Allen.

Meanwhile, the other white terrier had been off sniffing a dog poo next to the fence. Wondering what all the commotion was about, she surveyed the area and noticed Allen hunched down in the grass. Realising she hadn't met this puppy before, she inquisitively started to approach him. She was only slightly larger than Allen and walked up to him calmly with her tail wagging slowly.

Allen, shaken up from the recent tackle, wasn't about to be taken off guard again. He watched her closely as she continued to approach. Anticipating that this dog might also push him to the ground, another surge of fear spiked inside him. Rather than being caught off guard, he decided to try to take the front foot. Once she was a little closer but before she had a chance to attack him, he ran straight at her.

Seeing Allen charging in her direction, the terrier paused, unsure of his intentions. Moments later, he launched into her body and snapped his needle-like teeth at her legs. She yelped in shock and jumped backwards. Without wasting a moment, the terrier turned and fled to the onlooking people who were smiling and chuckling with each other.

'Looks like he gives as good as he gets,' one of them commented.

* * *

Back at home, Allen lay collapsed on the couch. All of his energy had been drained by his earlier encounters at the park. Nathan was resting his head on his arms, watching him sleep. 'See how cute he is when he's resting honey?' Petra gazed at Allen as she crept towards him, smiling adoringly. Being careful not to disturb him, she slowly climbed onto the couch by his side. Nathan turned on the TV to the lowest volume that allowed them to hear the words, and they all snuggled into each other.

Dreams of being attacked in the park soon woke Allen with a start. Feeling frightened, he looked around the room for a moment before realising he was not in danger. His muscles began to relax once more, but he forced himself up and slid off the couch. Focused on the television, his people didn't pay him much attention. Allen had the strong urge to relieve himself. He walked over to the laundry, having remembered that he liked going there. The door was closed; a breeze had blown it shut while everyone was asleep. Allen did not understand why doors were sometimes open or closed. They often surprised him when they suddenly changed state like this. Squatting in the hallway outside the laundry, he let go. A warm relief comforted him as he listened to the pattering of his urine hitting the carpet floor. But he wasn't done, he moved a few steps over and arched his back, relieving the other half of his urge. As he walked back down the hallway, he was not fully aware of what had taken place. The sensations of relieving himself were still new, and he was often surprised to see and smell the result of his actions on the floor.

'No!' yelled Nathan from the end of the hallway. He ran up to Allen and sharply tapped him across the side of the muzzle. 'What have you done? You are so naughty!' he exclaimed.

Nathan grabbed Allen and turned him around, pushing him towards the mess he had made. 'Look here, see what you've done? That is bad! Bad!'

Petra ran up to the hallway to see the reason for the commotion. Once she understood why Nathan was yelling, she joined in too. 'No! No!' she yelled. She picked Allen up and put him into the laundry, closing the door behind him.

'This is ridiculous, what is wrong with him?' she whined, 'we just took him out only an hour ago, why didn't he go then?'

'Well, he probably hasn't learnt yet that he isn't allowed to go in other places! So, we just need to keep showing him like this and eventually he'll learn,' said Nathan.

Allen sat next on the other side of the laundry door and cried; he didn't know why he was being yelled at, but he did know that it wasn't fun. He was scared and felt more alone than ever before.

* * *

After dinner that night, Allan was delighted to see his parents in a good mood once more. They were taking turns playing games with him and he was relishing the attention. Nathan shook the bunny in front of his nose and pretended to throw it down the hallway. Allen, anticipating where it might go, ran down the hallway excitedly as he frantically scanned the area for the toy. Confused, he turned around to see the rabbit dancing about in Nathan's hand once more. Allen ran back towards him. Nathan laughed, before finally tossing the bunny across the room. It bounced a few times and rolled along the floor, settling on its back next to the television.

Quickly changing direction, Allen's feet slipped on the floor as he sprinted over to grab it. Just before reaching the bunny, he stumbled on something and fell onto his side. As he looked up, he found the bunny conveniently lying in front of his nose. Before thinking, he reached out to pull the rabbit towards him. As he bit down on the toy, his teeth also latched onto the power cord for the television. Surprised, he stopped to feel the smooth surface for a moment. Intrigued by the novelty, he naturally proceeded to let go of the bunny and put the cord into his mouth. Like most puppies of Allen's age, he regularly put things he found into his mouth, much to the dismay of his people. This power cord felt nice to chew into, it helped to scratch his itchy gums.

Petra stopped what she was doing and stared at Allen, her eyes widening and her mouth falling open. 'No no no!' she screamed as she ran up to him.

Allen cringed and looked down, dropping the cord from his mouth. He felt his head lurch down as she gently slapped him on the top of his muzzle. It didn't hurt, but he understood the threat. Feeling a mixture of shock and fear, he instinctively turned away and slunk behind the television to hide. It had happened again; his parents had done that thing where they suddenly become angry. Allen had noticed this transformation in them many times before. They were mostly nice, but at times like this they would suddenly change. They would stay this way for a while, then go back to being friendly again. He had no understanding of why it was happening, and it worried and confused him. Looking at the cord he had just been biting, a surge of fear now welled up inside him. His brain had instinctively and subconsciously linked his fearful feelings with both the cord and his people. He looked away, avoiding the unpleasant emotion. Allen slowly crept out from behind the opposite side of television and kept his eyes fixed on the ground, too afraid to look up.

'See, he knows he wasn't supposed to do that! Look how guilty he's acting!' exclaimed Nathan.

* * *

At work the next day, Nathan was complaining about Allen to his friend Mick. They worked together managing different sections of a large toy factory. 'He just doesn't listen, but I can't stay mad at him for long because he is just so damn cute!' he exclaimed.

Mick was a large well-built man with a light complexion that was contrasted by his many tattoos. 'Sucks a million, hey' he replied, 'maybe you should go see someone who can help?'

Nathan looked down and sighed. 'Maybe, but I think he's just settling into our house. Or maybe he's going through a puppy phase. I'm sure he'll learn eventually. So, how's your little one going?'

Mick smiled broadly, his tongue pushing into the gap where his missing tooth would be. 'Tessa? She's going great, just great.'

* * *

Tessa couldn't contain her excitement. She loved going down the street to the shops with her parents. Upon sighting a small black scruffy dog ahead, Tessa ran forwards and started pulling on her leash to get to it. Olivia felt her arm lurch forwards and stumbled.

'Tessa, you really are determined aren't you!' cried Olivia.

Mick smiled and followed after them, shaking his head as Tessa continued to pull ahead on her leash.

Tessa didn't hear her mum. She really liked dogs and was too focused on this one to concentrate on anything else. As the other dog came closer, it noticed Tessa and stood up straight, barking a long warning in their direction. Tessa stopped and watched in stunned silence. She felt a shiver of fear and was terribly confused. While she knew she liked dogs, this one was acting strangely.

'It's okay Tessa' said Olivia, 'come with me, it's okay.'

Olivia picked her up and cuddled her close as she carried her across to the other side of the road.

'Some dogs are best to stay away from Tessa, it's nothing personal' she commented.

Once Olivia had placed her back on the ground, she stood and watched the dog, refusing to walk.

'Come on Tess, we'll be late for our dinner booking,' said Olivia.

Moments later, the dog and her owner turned down a side-street and out of view. With the strange dog gone, Tessa looked back at Olivia and started walking after her. As they continued walking, Tessa soon forgot about her fearful encounter. By the time they reached the restaurant, she had met three other dogs and her opinion of them was as glowing as ever!

* * *

Petra and Nathan were sitting down at a table outside the local Chinese restaurant, smiling at each other. Nathan broke the silence.

'Really nice to be out with just the two of us, seems a bit more peaceful without Allen, don't you think?'

Petra stuck out her bottom lip and whined, 'I hope he's okay at home all alone.'

'They're here,' said Nathan, smiling as he looked across the street.

Mick, Olivia, and Tessa had just arrived. They waved and made their way over to the table. After ordering their meals, the conversation turned to Allen.

'So Petra...' said Mick, 'Nathan tells me you've been having a few teething issues with Allen?'

Petra looked uncomfortable, shifting in her seat.

'Oh, don't be silly' she said, glancing up at Nathan. 'He's doing great! He just needs more time, that's all.'

Sensing that the topic might be a little awkward, Mick changed the subject.

'Well, we're having our own little problems with Tessa too. You won't believe what happened on the weekend. I accidentally dropped my fishing knife on the floor without realising, next thing I know, Tessa is running around with it!'

Nathan, looking relieved, feigned concern as he replied. 'A knife? Oh no! So what did you do when you found her with it?'

'Well, I didn't want to startle her in case she slipped and cut herself or something. So I was acting all calm on the outside, when inside I was freaking out big time!'

Feeling the mood lighten, the others laughed as they leaned in.

'So I started quickly walking over to her,' continued Mick. 'And I casually said "Hey Tessa, just hold still for a second"...

'Then she starts playing with it and waving it in the air! Somehow, I managed to grab her and take the knife away before she cut anyone. Very close call, very lucky!'

'So did you tell her off then, so she doesn't do it again?' asked Petra, shaking her head in disbelief.

Olivia and Mick looked at each other.

Nathan interjected. 'Yeah, I know he's a puppy, but when Allen bit the television cord the other day, we yelled at him! And now he doesn't bite the cord anymore. Worked pretty well!'

'Doesn't work for the shoes though!' added Petra sharply.

Mick looked puzzled. 'Well, isn't that just normal puppy behaviour for Allen to chew on lots of things?' he queried. 'We don't bother getting Tessa in trouble if she does something like pick up a knife, because really—it's our fault—we shouldn't have left the knife out in the first place! How can you blame them if they don't know better?'

'Okay, fair enough...' replied Nathan, pausing for dramatic effect. He put on a smug expression as he continued. 'But how would a puppy like Allen know it's bad to chew shoes or bite cords if we don't teach him?'

Mick frowned, thinking before he replied. 'Hmmm, good point, didn't consider that... On the other hand, we don't really want to teach Tess how to handle knives either. 'Not sure I would trust her you know? Best just to keep them out of reach. Same with the bleach and the power outlets!'

'Right...' replied Nathan, shaking his head slowly. 'So what you're saying is, we could just do the same with shoes and cords and stuff, just put them out of reach? Sounds like taking the easy way out to me!'

Mick chuckled, feeling a little awkward. He was unsure if they were having an argument or a discussion. 'Yeah, I mean, Allen wouldn't know that it's wrong to pick up a knife, would he? But I don't suppose you will start leaving knives around so you can teach him, will you?'

Petra tilted her head, frowning as she added her opinion. 'Well, I guess we could try that. We can put the dangerous things away—like toddler-proofing the house, but for a dog!'

'That gets me thinking,' said Nathan, smiling broadly with a glint in his eye. 'Maybe you guys should get a dog for Tessa? She really does love them!'

Olivia gazed warmly at Tessa, nodding in agreement. 'She does adore dogs! She even loves it when we use a leash on her for walks, so she can pretend she's a dog.'

The others all chuckled, and Tessa grinned back at them.

'It helps manage her safety too,' continued Olivia. 'So we love it! We do get a few strange looks though, but it attaches to her backpack so at least we don't put a collar on her!'

Tessa, understanding what had been said, looked up at Olivia and tugged on her jumper. 'I want a doggy Mummy, I want lots and lots of doggies,' she said softly with pleading eyes.

Anthropomorphism

In this chapter, the reader is initially led to believe that Tessa is a dog, because she is attached to Olivia by a leash. This blurring of the lines between children and dogs is not uncommon in society. Many people think of dogs as children or small people. It is only natural for humans, as a caring and altruistic species, to want to nurture our pets like children. It's understandable that caring for a dog as though they are a child might be related to believing that a dog thinks like a child. The belief that an animal's behaviours are due to human-like thought processes is called 'anthropomorphism'.

It is quite a common misconception that animals think about the world in the same way that people do. However, I don't think people make this error because they're stupid. I think that as a social species, we are designed to project our own emotions and motivations onto the actions of other humans. Our social brains aren't designed to cross the species barrier. If we like or dislike something, it's only natural to assume that other organisms would feel the same way. It also seems that people actually enjoy seeing examples of animals behaving in ways that appear to be explained by human-like thought processes. I have seen many examples of viral videos on social media where a dog has been trained to act in a human-like way. I have seen dogs trained to stroke other dogs with their paw, to hug other dogs with their legs, and even to empathetically copy a person who is limping. Just how children might enjoy the magical feeling of believing in the tooth fairy, I think many people also enjoy believing that animals really do think just like a person.

Anthropomorphism: the bad

If anthropomorphism makes us love our animals more, then what could be the harm in that? Why should it matter if the video of the dog wrapping its legs around another dog has been trained to do this and isn't actually displaying affection? By pointing this out, am I just trying to ruin everyone's fun? The answer is no. I will explain below how anthropomorphism can actually be really harmful to animal welfare.

Anthropomorphism has led many people to believe that dogs will enjoy the same things that people enjoy, but that isn't always true. As humans are related to primates, we like to hug and touch to display affection. However, dogs don't naturally think like that. Neither dogs nor their wild ancestors behave this way when people are not around. It isn't a natural thing for dogs to stay still while another animal scratches or hugs them. Therefore, it isn't surprising to me that many dogs don't enjoy physical affection in the form of hugging or stroking. I have seen many cases of this preference first-hand, and how sad it can make their owners. They often don't notice their dog is uncomfortable until I point it out, at which point it suddenly becomes obvious to them. Despite the unnatural nature of petting, most dogs do learn to enjoy it. Personally, I find cases like this the most surprising—where dogs can learn to thrive in the unnatural situations we put them in.

Anthropomorphism also leads many people to assume that dogs have a theory of mind. That is, they assume that dogs *know* that each animal has its own subjective experience of the world just like they do.[1] Because of this belief, many people also assume that dogs have morals, because they understand that making another animal feel good or bad is the 'right' or 'wrong' thing to do. This is an example of humans believing that animals are smarter than they really are. As humans, we learn our sense of right and wrong from a very young age, but we are not born with it. By the time we are adults, most people don't have to think whether something is 'right' or 'wrong', we can simply sense it. Given our ability to instantly decide whether something aligns with our morals, it's easy to assume that morality is a simple process. If we can do it without even thinking, then surely a dog has morals too! There has been plenty of research into this area, but the picture it paints is very murky. The problem is that it's easy to fool ourselves into thinking we are seeing a sense of 'right' and 'wrong', when really what we see is a dog responding to punishment and reward. A hallmark of humans displaying a moral decision is when they choose to go out of their way to do something because they believe it is the 'right' thing to do, and not based on their own self-interest. It is very hard to find a natural example of that in the world of dog behaviour. Simply training a dog so that it appears to act in this manner does not count. Many people also believe that they see their dog act guilty. However, guilt cannot be felt without a sense of right and wrong. Guilt occurs when you feel bad for not aligning your behaviour with your moral compass, regardless of whether your behaviour was intentional or not.

As children, we might learn that every time we touch fire, we feel pain. In the future, we learn to keep away from the fire. We don't learn to keep away from the fire because it is 'wrong' according to our moral compass. This is what happens to Allen when he accidentally bites on the cable. He reacts to the yelling of his people by learning to be frightened of the cable and keeping away. He also responds to the yelling by displaying fearful and appeasing body language, to signal he isn't a threat to his people. Because Petra and Nathan believe Allen understands the concept of right and wrong, they interpret his appeasing behaviour as a sign that he is actually feeling guilty. This evidence of guilt makes Petra and Nathan feel like the punishment is justified, because they think Allen 'knows' he did something wrong. Ultimately, this common scenario shows how anthropomorphism of dog behaviour leads to the use of aversive punishment towards dogs, as we attempt to 'help' our pets learn to have good morals.

Anthropomorphism: the good

Despite all the problems that can occur when you think of your dog as a small person, in some ways it can also do a lot of good. The key is accuracy. If we anthropomorphise a behaviour and it leads us to an incorrect interpretation of the behaviour, it can be harmful. However, in *some* situations a dog really *is* thinking just like how a human would, and in these cases, anthropomorphism is useful. It can help us understand how they're feeling; fostering empathy and improving their welfare. So how might we know when it's accurate to anthropomorphise an animal? It all comes down to the neuroanatomy.

Our human brain has a large, wrinkly, well evolved frontal-cortex. This part of the brain sets us apart from the other species on earth as it provides superior intellect and reasoning. The lack of an evolved human-like frontal-cortex in the dog means that we are likely to be wrong any time we anthropomorphise a dog's behaviour in a way that requires the dog to have complex ideas (such as theory of mind or a moral code of ethics).[1] This is one of the most common mistakes we make when trying to understand what an animal is thinking; we tend to overcomplicate their thought processes. Even though dogs are thinking simple thoughts with simple explanations, this does not make these explanations obvious to people, as our mind automatically overcomplicates them. Our natural inclination is to attribute far more intelligence and complicated cognition to dogs than they probably possess. One way to help overcome our natural bias in this regard is to consider how a six-month-old child might think about something. When thinking like children, we intuitively know that our grasp of concepts is simplified.

Throughout this book, you might notice that the explanations provided for the dog behaviours we observe are very plausible. The explanations are basic, and do not require the dog to have complex thoughts. This should not be insulting to their intelligence in the least, but rather ascribes an endearing child-like innocence to their character.

The frontal-cortex also allows people to think a lot about the past and the future, and to run scenarios through their mind. As humans, we can easily transport our thoughts backwards and forwards in time, momentarily ignoring the present. As the brain of a dog isn't well designed to do this, they spend much more time thinking about the present. They are living in the moment. When people think about a dog being 'smart,' this is usually what they are noticing. The dog knows what to do in the moment in response to something that just happened—and they are very good at it. This is like how we think when we play sport. We are often absorbed in the moment, acting without thinking too much. Even professional sportspeople don't often have time to plan what they are doing when they react to an opponent. As you will notice in this book, Allen and Nella are almost always thinking in the present. Their mind hardly ever wanders to the future or past.

Unlike the frontal-cortex, there is another section of the human brain that is relatively under-evolved. This part of the brain, called the limbic system, is used for emotional processing. The limbic system is very similar in all of the mammals on earth.[2] Our human limbic system is doing pretty much exactly the same thing as the limbic system in the brain of a dog or a mouse. As this part of the brain is responsible for feeling emotions like fear, pleasure, anxiety and pain, it's accurate to anthropomorphise these things! That is to say, that when you are feeling scared or worried, that's probably a similar experience to what your dog feels when they have those feelings. This is because the limbic system of people and animals is almost identical. If you see an animal that's enjoying some food, or fearful or in pain, go ahead and imagine how they might be feeling, you'll probably be fairly close! This will also help you to understand things from the perspective of Allen and Nella as you read through this book.

CHAPTER TWO

Welcome Home Nella

Olivia sat with Mick at the kitchen table, the morning sunlight streaming halfway across the room. She was watching Tessa play with her white stuffed dog.

'Tessa, I think it's time to wash Nelly again tonight, she's getting dirty.'

Tessa rolled onto her back and held Nelly over her head. 'Wash Nelly in the bath?' she asked.

'No, she's just a toy Tess,' replied Olivia. 'We'll put her in the washing machine. That way she'll come out cleaner.'

Tessa frowned, staring up at Nelly. The toy's button eyes and floppy ears were dangling down towards her.

'Dogs get washed in bath, not washa machine!' she whined. 'I wanna wash Nelly in the bath!'

Olivia giggled as she replied. 'Well, I suppose you're right. You can have a bath with Nelly tonight and help wash her, okay?'

Tessa smiled, still gazing at Nelly. 'We gonna have bath tonight Nelly, okay?'

A few seconds later, she turned to Olivia and continued. 'Mum, Nelly says we can wash her!'

Meanwhile, Mick was sitting at a table across the room with his laptop. He stopped scrolling through the website he was browsing and clicked on a link.

'This one looks good…' he commented.

Olivia walked over and started inspecting the webpage over his shoulder.

'Ooh, a Staffie!' she said grinning. 'I heard they're good with kids!'

She reached out and pointed at a picture of one of the puppies on the screen.

'That one looks so cute! Let's call them to see if it's still available.'

As Mick started dialling the number, Olivia excitedly read over the details. It had only been a week since Tessa had begged her for a dog, but she felt like the search was taking forever.

'Oh—and they're available now! Can you imagine how excited she'd be if we brought one home tonight?'

Mick smiled back at Olivia, zipping his finger across his lips as he held the phone to his ear.

'Hello?... Yes, I was ringing about your Staffie puppies advertised on puppydogs.com?...'

Mick spoke in a hushed tone, turning his head away from Tessa.

'Oh wow, ready this afternoon? That's great! What's your address?... Okay, 3pm sounds perfect, see you then!'

Tessa looked up, frowning with curiosity. 'Mum, who's Daddy talking to?'

Olivia smiled to herself as she replied. 'Just someone from work honey. He has to go meet them soon, so we'll wait here, okay?'

* * *

A few hours later, Mick pulled up outside a suburban house with an unkempt garden and peeling white fence. He turned off his GPS and eagerly exited the car. As he walked down the driveway, he folded open a piece of paper where he had written down a list of questions to ask. He stepped up onto the creaky wooden porch and knocked on the screen door expectantly.

'Coming!' he heard from the other side. It was the same foreign accent he had heard on the phone earlier.

The door opened, and he saw a young woman with black hair in a tracksuit holding a small white puppy in her arms.

'You're here for the puppy, right?' asked the woman.

'I sure am!' replied Mick, smiling warmly.

Then, before Mick could start to read his list of questions, the puppy was thrust into his chest. Mick looked down with his mouth open and eyes wide. A tiny, warm, snuffling puppy with a soft white coat had suddenly appeared in his arms.

He forgot he was holding a list of questions, and leaned in as the lady started talking.

'Here's his vaccination card from the vet. It's $900, six weeks old, last one left' she said abruptly.

Mick went to reach for his wallet, sliding his hand into his trouser pocket. At that moment he realised there was still a piece of paper with questions sitting in his hand. Mick paused, realising Olivia would not be happy if he didn't quickly ask at least some of them. He clumsily unfolded the sheet of paper with his one free hand and started reading off the list.

'Just have a few quick questions first,' said Mick. 'Um... Can I see the parents? Like to see what kind of dogs they are?'

The lady suddenly looked sad as she replied. 'Oh, I'm so sorry, they're at my mother's house. She bred them, but here's the photo.'

She turned her phone around to show Mick, who recognised the same photo of the parents he had seen on the website.

'Oh, they don't live with the puppies?' he asked. 'It said in the ad online we could meet the parents with request... How long have you had them here away from their mum?'

The woman looked confused, and then smiled uncomfortably as she replied.

'We had them here since they were born.'

'Okay,' said Mick, tilting his head to the side. 'So you took them away from the mum when they were born…

'And have they been wormed?'

The woman looked at the vaccination card and pointed. 'Yes, see they got wormed here. The vet signed.'

Mick looked at the card, stating the date of vaccination, then down at the puppy that had fallen asleep in his arms. He continued onto the next question.

'Um… okay and how often have you been worming them?'

The woman looked confused again. 'I can't remember it's so many times, we wormed them whenever they need it.'

Mick heard a man's voice from inside the house yelling something. The woman turned and shouted angrily back in reply. Something didn't feel right to Mick. He was a good judge of character, and was sure the woman was hiding something she didn't want him to know.

'I feel like I'm being a bit rushed into this,' he said. 'If you wouldn't mind, could you just hold her for a minute while I go to the car to call my wife? I need to check if there's anything else I forgot to ask.'

The woman's face soured as she replied. 'Okay but be quick, my husband needs me for something.'

Mick handed the puppy back to the lady and walked back out to the car to call Olivia.

'Do you have the puppy?' asked Olivia as soon as she answered the phone.

'Not yet,' said Mick. 'There's something a bit strange about the lady selling her, she seems really nice but just super rushed. I just wanted to check with you again before we get her.'

'Did you ask the questions I gave you?' said Olivia.

'Yes, she said the pup is vaccinated. I saw the card, and she's wormed too. But she also said that she had the puppies living here with her since they were born, but not with their mother.'

There was a pause on the other end of the line.

'What? So she couldn't show you the parents?' exclaimed Olivia. 'It said on the ad we could see them!'

'No, the parents live with the lady's mother, and the puppies live with her.'

Olivia felt a sinking sensation in her chest. 'I'm just a bit worried Mickey, what if it's one of the puppy dealers like in that article I showed you?

'It said the puppy farms have really bad conditions for the parents, and they just breed puppies all their lives in cages. The puppies from those places often have diseases, and bad behaviour too.

'Remember they said that meeting the puppy's parents is the number one rule for avoiding these people?'

'Well, the lady does seem a bit off,' pondered Mick. 'Like she's hiding something. And she doesn't seem very attached to the puppy either, now that I come to think of it...'

Olivia gasped, then replied with a sceptical tone to her voice. 'And now that I come to think of it, she said the puppy had been living *away* from its mum since she was born, didn't she?

'Puppies drink their mum's milk! How have they been feeding it? That's very strange. Her story doesn't add up Mickey... I think she might be a puppy dealer!'

Mick looked at the ground, frowning and pacing as he spoke. 'Okay, yeah, I don't want to support these people either. I guess I'll have to let her know we aren't interested.'

* * *

Tessa was sitting in the bath that evening, her head tilted to the side as she rubbed suds through Nelly's fabric fur.

'You're so good at looking after Nelly,' said Olivia, smiling. 'Would you like to get a real dog one day Tess?'

Tess looked up and grinned back at her, this wasn't the first time she had been asked this question.

'I want a dog, Nelly needs a friend, she told me.'

'Oh really?' said Olivia. 'A boy dog or a girl dog? What would you name it?'

Tessa thought to herself for a few moments before responding, this was an important decision.

'Nelly! I want to call the dog Nelly.'

'But won't you get confused Tess?' replied Olivia, frowning. 'You already have a dog called Nelly, we'll have to come up with another name.'

Tessa dunked Nelly under the surface and then pulled her back out, watching the water stream off her legs into the bath.

'Okay,' said Tessa, shrugging. 'We can call her Nella.'

Olivia burst out laughing and leant over to kiss Tessa on her forehead, then turned to the doorway and yelled out.

'Hey Mickey, Tess just said that if she ever gets a dog, she wants to call her Nella!'

'That's a great name Tess!' he called back. 'Liv, I found something just now I need to show you later, I think it might be the one. I'm going to meet them tomorrow.'

Once bath time was over and Tessa was asleep, Olivia popped Nelly in the washing machine and then snuggled in next to Mick on the couch.

'Here's the puppy I was looking at before' said Mick, showing his laptop to Olivia.

'They look like lovely parents,' she said, sighing deeply. 'But I hope we can actually see them this time.'

'Yeah,' agreed Mick, nodding sadly. 'Are you sure an Irish Wolfhound isn't going to be too big for us though?'

'Are you kidding? You know I've always wanted one,' said Olivia. 'We have the room, but we just have to teach her not to jump up on the couch!'

Mick continued, 'and she'll be a bit older than the other one we almost got. The breeder said we wouldn't get her until next week, when she's 10 weeks old.'

'Well, if the breeder says it's best to wait, I think we should trust him,' said Olivia, sighing. 'She'll still be super cute at that age, and might be a bit better at dealing with Tess too.'

'Well, that settles it,' said Mick. 'I'll let him know we can get her next weekend!'

Olivia suddenly sat up straight, gently clapping her hands together a few times as she grinned at Mick.

'I have a better feeling about this one,' she said. 'And he asked us so many questions in his email before... I can tell he really cares about the puppies and wants them to go to good homes.'

'Yeah, he does!' agreed Mick. 'I'd do the same if my dog had puppies. It was so strange how that lady today couldn't wait to get rid of her cute little puppy, she didn't seem to care for it at all!'

* * *

The following weekend, it was cold and drizzling when Mick arrived outside the breeder's house. He zipped up his jacket and walked briskly down the pathway to the front door. As he rang the doorbell, he could hear the sound of two children playing inside. A dog started barking, and before long the door opened. A tall man with long sideburns and a moustache stood inside, smiling back at Mick.

'Hi, I'm Jason. You must be Mick? Here for the puppy?' he said in a friendly tone.

'Sure am!' said Mick, as he reached in to shake his outstretched hand.

'Come on in, it's cold out there!' beckoned Jason.

As Mick followed the man through the house, they passed a room with two boys playing on a game console. He felt like these people were more trustworthy than those at his last puppy experience. They made their way into the lounge room, where a large slender grey dog was staring at them. It barked twice when it saw Mick, with a worried look in its eyes.

'Shoosh girl, it's okay, this is Mick' said Jason in a calming voice.

'She's a bit protective with strangers, but if you let her sniff your hand, she'll be fine,' he explained.

As Mick walked closer, he could see a section of the room had been fenced off, where the dog was standing with four puppies fast asleep at her feet.

'Her name's Sharpie, this is her second litter. The dad lives at my mate's place, you're welcome to go visit him too if you like.'

As Mick stepped closer, Sharpie looked up at him and started panting. Mick was a little worried, this was a very large dog! He couldn't remember seeing many larger than this in his life. At the same time, there was something magnificent about her presence, she was an impressive-looking dog.

Mick slowly took another step closer then stopped. 'Maybe I'd better sit down, and let her come to me?'

'Nah, she'll be fine, she's a big sook!' said Jason, affectionately slapping Sharpie on the rump.

Mick took another step forward to where he could reach out his hand and offer it for Sharpie to sniff. He felt the worried sensation of rising anxiety in his stomach. Mick was a tall man, and wasn't used to putting his hand out to a dog without having to bend down. Sharpie's head was at the level of his belt when she stretched her head out to sniff the tips of his fingers. She sniffed Mick for a few pensive seconds, then slowly but surely her tail started to wag. Then she looked up at Mick and made direct eye contact, before stepping forwards to lean into his body.

'There we go!' said Jason, grinning. 'Now you've got past the vicious guard dog, you can come look at your puppy, if you still want her.'

Mick felt very relieved. He started stroking Sharpie on the side of her head as he spoke to her.

'Aww you *are* a sweetie, aren't you?' he coaxed. 'You're just protecting your puppies. Good girl Sharpie.'

The four puppies were lying in a heap on a large pile of blankets. Their fur was short compared to Sharpie's wispy coat. Two puppies were grey, the other two black. As Mick stepped over the partition and walked up to their bedding, Sharpie turned around to follow him, her tail slowly wagging.

'They've just eaten lunch and were racing around playing only half an hour ago, I think they've tired themselves out,' explained Jason.

Jason bent down slowly and then sat down on the blankets next to them. The grey puppy closest to him sensed the movement and looked up with a sleepy half-squashed face. It started trying to get up, and in doing so managed to stand on two of the other puppies sleeping next to it. These two puppies both lifted their sleepy heads and started yawning and rolling over to see what was happening. In doing so, the final sleeping puppy was knocked, and it too was roused from its slumber. In a matter of seconds, there were four puppies up and about, tails waggling, exploring their world. As each puppy noticed Mick, they all had their own unique reactions.

Mick bent down to sit next to Jason, and the first puppy that had woken looked at him and froze, shocked and excited by the presence of a new human. Mick put out his hand towards it, and it sniffed him briefly, before walking towards him and proceeding to lick his leg as he sat on the floor. Mick felt a twinge of embarrassment as he realised that the puppy was licking a spot on his pants that looked like some of Tessa's porridge from that morning.

The second puppy that noticed him was a grey puppy with streaks of black on her muzzle. She sat down on the spot and regarded him with an inquisitive look while slowly wagging her tail.

Jason pointed her out to Mick. 'That's your puppy there, she's the shy one.'

The third puppy waggled his way up to Mick and started trying to climb onto his side and lick at his face. The last puppy to wake, a smaller black female, started running towards Mick and tripped on a blanket, rolling over and sliding into him, legs first. Mick laughed and started trying to manage all the puppies at once, unsuccessfully. As he pushed one off, the others would jump back onto him, seeking more attention.

'Looks like you're pretty popular with this lot!' said Jason, 'here, let me grab a few of them so you can meet your one.'

Jason slid two of the puppies away from Mick whilst the third one started to chew on the sole of his boot. Mick looked over at the shy, grey puppy sitting at the back of the enclosure in her bed.

'We're going to name you Nella' he said, smiling as he watched her.

Nella stayed still, regarding the unfamiliar man that was now reaching his hand out towards her. She had only ever met two other men before, and while she liked them, this one was different. She was unsure. As she leaned forward to sniff his fingers, her opinion started to change. She liked what she smelled. There was a calmness in his scent, and odours of food and children were present too. Nella liked children. The two boys she had grown up with had been given the task of feeding the puppies, so there was a particularly positive association present.

Nella looked up at Mick's face as he spoke to her fondly. 'Hello Nella! Aren't you a cute little puppy dog?'

Nella could hear the soothing tone in Mick's voice, and her slowly sweeping tail gradually sped up. Then before long, her whole body erupted in a wormy wiggle. She stood up and walked towards him, his shape in her vision blurred as her head moved side to side in sync with her winding bottom. Nella pushed her body sideways into Mick's lap, where she collapsed and looked up at his face. As Mick smiled and leant in closer, she started trying to lick towards his face. This was what she did to all her carers in her life, and it had been particularly successful with Sharpie. Two days prior, when Nella had been licking at Sharpie's lips, Sharpie had regurgitated some food for her and the others! Mick laughed softly, then started stroking Nella over her head and along her back.

Jason smiled approvingly for a moment, then uncrossed his arms and spoke. 'There we go, I think she approves of you Mick! Let's get your paperwork, assuming you'll take her?'

Mick looked over at Jason, his eyes glazed with tears, and managed to choke out a few croaky words.

'Yep, she'll do.'

* * *

As Mick drove home, Nella sat shaking in the passenger seat footwell. She wasn't cold, nor was she excited. She was terrified. She had never left the comfort of her home before, let alone been inside a car. The strange noises and vibration, the different smells and the movement of the car were all so foreign. She looked across at the strange man driving her, wanting to climb onto him for safety, but was too afraid to move. When Mick reached over to stroke her at the lights, she felt comforted. Nella licked his hand and tried to jump up, but was pushed back down into her spot.

'You stay there Nella, we're almost home,' he said to her.

Just as Nella was growing weary from worry, and starting to feel like she was falling asleep, the car stopped, and the vibration of the engine suddenly ended. She looked up to see Mick reaching over to pick her up. She didn't have the energy to struggle. As she was carried out of the car and along the pathway to her new home, she twisted her head around to see what was happening. When Mick quietly knocked at the front door, it quickly opened with Olivia bursting through to see the new arrival. Her face was lit up with a grin as she let out a soft greeting.

'Oh my, you're even sweeter than in the photos!'

'Where's Tess?' asked Mick.

'On the couch watching TV. I got this blanket to put over Nella so we can surprise her.'

Nella felt the soft blanket being draped over her head and body, and tucked under her legs. It was dark and she couldn't see, but the comfort of the new stranger who was holding her helped to settle the nerves. She felt herself being carried through the house, and then laid onto the couch next to Tessa.

Tessa looked at the oddly shaped blanket next to her. It was almost as large as she was, and appeared to be moving.

'What's that?' she asked in a high-pitched tone.

Olivia was beaming as she answered. 'We got you a present Tess! Take the blanket off and look what's underneath.'

Tessa pulled back the blanket and gazed wide-eyed at Nella, her mouth open in surprise. After a few moments, she looked up at Olivia and muttered 'You got me a puppy?'

As Nella sat looking back at Tessa, she hardly moved; she was exhausted yet equally surprised to see a strange child in front of her. Tessa's surprise started to fade as realisation of what was happening came over her. Her shocked look melted away, replaced by a scrunched-up expression as she started to cry. She moved forwards and wrapped her arms around Nella, sobbing as she was overwhelmed with emotion. She looked up at Mick, tears streaming down her face and whined at him.

'I love her sooo much…'

And then she turned back to bury her face into Nella's side. Nella sniffed at Tessa, and recognised her as the smell of the child she had already become familiar with on Mick's clothing. She liked her smell, and started licking at Tessa's face. The taste of her salty tears was nice, and she set to work to clean them all up. Tessa started laughing through her sobs and pulled her face away to get a better look at Nella.

'Are we keeping her?' she asked.

Mick smiled with a tear in his eye as he responded.

'Yes, and we're going to need you to help us look after her, can you do that?'

Tessa nodded her scrunched up face, and started stroking Nella's ears, gazing at her in wonder.

'She's a girl Tess, did you want to call her Nella?' he asked.

Tessa nodded again.

Breeding Dogs

In this chapter, we can see how difficult it can be for people to know where to source their dog from. In some cases, adopting an adult dog will be the right decision. However, the topic of animal shelters is huge, (and will have to wait for another book). When thinking about finding the right puppy, there is a lot that can be said. The story of Mick meeting the strange lady peddling puppies to unsuspecting victims is based on a true story that I experienced. Even if the customer realises that something is wrong in a situation like this, they are left with a moral dilemma. Seeing the cute little puppy in front of them, it's hard to hand it back to a person that you know isn't looking after them well. I have had many clients tell me that they took their dog because they felt sorry for it, and didn't know what would happen if they left it behind. Unfortunately, the large profits that can be made by unethically breeding dogs on a shoestring budget can motivate all the wrong types of people to get into dog breeding. Apart from puppy farms, even registered and esteemed dog breeders can be partly motivated by the dollar signs.

We know very well from existing research, that animals bred in stressful conditions are more likely to be affected by mental and physical health problems.[1] This is made even worse by the inappropriate decisions made about which dogs to breed, and the consequences of heritable diseases being transmitted to the next generation. Some people breed dogs with health conditions unknowingly, but in other cases people do it *on purpose.* For example, dogs with short noses (brachycephalic) are considered to be cute by many people, and so we have bred them for this trait. This has led to the development of the brachycephalic obstructive airway syndrome (BOAS), an entirely human-bred condition. Dogs with this condition often struggle to breathe for their entire lives, and they often require drastic corrective surgery. So, what does this all have to do with behaviour?

How breeding can affect behaviour

As humans, we have bred our domestic dogs for a variety of reasons. Apart from companionship, many ancestral lines of dogs have been selected to have other behavioural traits. Studies have found that you can breed a dog to be extremely anxious.[2] While you might assume that nobody would want to do this—it is not the case. As anxiety helps promote alertness and activity when experienced at the right level, it may be a useful trait for dogs to have. Some working dogs appear to lose their 'drive to work' when they don't have enough of an anxious temperament.[3] So, if we can breed a dog for their anxiety, then, surely, we can just pick the breed that is the least anxious and buy that one? Unfortunately, it isn't this simple. For example, it is well known that people have bred some dog breeds to display behaviours like barking or biting, for specific uses. Despite years of breeding in the past, dogs with these backgrounds do not appear to be more likely to bite or be dangerous than dogs of other breeds when kept as pets.[4] Biting, threatening behaviours and anxiety are present in *all* breeds. Within each breed, there is a huge variation in the temperaments of individuals. The real take-away from this, is that no matter what breed of dog you pick, there will be individuals who are more or less anxious, fearful or combative. Unfortunately, we don't do a very good job at selecting against these traits for pet dogs. Just like we have bred dogs with genetic causes of heart disease or short noses, we have also bred dogs who are predisposed to being anxious or biting from fear. In all of these examples, the welfare impact on the dogs themselves can be severe as a result of their genetics.

The behaviour of a puppy is not only affected by the genetics of its parents; it can also be affected by the *experiences* of the parents. Scientists believe that prenatal stress in animals can cause the behaviour of the offspring to be more anxious.[1] From an evolutionary perspective this makes sense. If an animal is highly stressed, then it's likely they're trying to survive in a dangerous or inhospitable environment. Any offspring born into this environment might be more likely to survive if they remain hypervigilant and are more proficient at detecting threats. When they are born, these offspring are wired to expect a dangerous world. It is not surprising then, that research has found that puppies sourced from inhumane puppy farms are much more likely to have behavioural issues as adults.[5]

What to look for in a puppy

In this book, Nella doesn't rush up to Mick like the other puppies from her litter. She is a bit more fearful and reserved. However, this doesn't actually say too much about how she will behave as an adult. A lot can change as a dog grows up. The most accurate way to predict what sort of a puppy you are buying is to not look at the puppies at all. Rather, if you focus on the parents of the puppies, you are much more likely to see an accurate picture of what they will be like.[6] Obviously, this could be quite difficult if one parent is missing or both parents behave very differently. Siblings from previous litters can also give you a great picture of how the current litter might develop. From a behavioural perspective, the most ideal situation would be for both parents to be well adjusted and calm dogs that are easy to manage in a variety of situations. Another ideal situation is that the mother has not been too stressed during pregnancy or while raising the puppies. This means that having the mother dog stay in its loving family home is the best situation, if possible. The puppies also need to stay with their mother to experience maternal care. The process of having the mother dog nuzzle and lick and clean the puppies almost certainly has beneficial effects on their development.[7]

Understandably, many people want to bring home their new puppy as soon as possible. Some people even collect them as early as five weeks old! If the puppy was living in a safe environment with a caring mother, then they are missing out on many weeks of beneficial maternal care. Puppies can also experience excellent socialisation in their litter—once removed they are deprived of this. It has been suggested that waiting until a puppy is eight weeks old before removing them from their mother would be much better for the puppy.[8] However, if the home the puppy is being raised in is of high quality, then it may be better to wait even longer. Most people want to have their puppy at home with them during the cutest weeks of their life. However, it is best to resist the urge to take the puppy home too soon.

CHAPTER THREE

A Trip To The Vet

Allen looked through the window at the trees streaming past. He didn't like this feeling; it was all so strange and unfamiliar. His stomach lurched again as Nathan turned a final time, stopping the car in a parking lot. The rumbling vibrations halted abruptly, and Allen heard a clicking sound as Nathan pulled up the handbrake.

'Come on little Allen, we have to go into the vet now,' chirped Petra, as she scooped him up in his blanket and opened the car door.

As they walked through the entrance to the clinic, Allen looked around while trembling in his blanket. Petra and Nathan had been in thousands of different buildings during their lives, and so didn't think much of walking into another one. This was not the case for Allen. The first building that Allen knew was where he was born. He couldn't recall much about it, other than the noises of all the dogs barking and the smells of fear and excrement. He only stayed in his second building for one sleepless night, before being picked up by Nathan the next day. The third was now his home. This building was only the fourth he had ever been inside.

Allen's nose was overwhelmed with unfamiliar smells. He could identify dogs, food, people and something else strange that he hadn't yet figured out. Something about the strange smell seemed important, and it worried him too. When he poked his little nose over the edge of the blanket, he saw a large female tan-coloured dog standing only a few steps away. She was so big that it made Allen's heartbeat go from fast to racing, and his eyes widen in fear. He had never seen such a huge dog before, and she was looking straight at him. He struggled to break free and escape. It didn't feel safe being trapped in this blanket. Feeling him squirming in her arms, Petra tightened her grip and laughed in surprise.

'Hey Nath, look how excited he is to play with the other dog!'

At that moment, Allen recognised the strange smell. The smell that had been worrying him since they first entered the building. It was the fear smell, the one he always smelt on himself when he was fearful. Except this time, it wasn't caused by him. It was from others, and it was present with every inhalation he took. As this realisation swept over him, Allen started to panic. Feeling cornered and defenceless, his mind became overwhelmed. This was a serious danger he could not escape. Staying very still to avoid trouble was the only option left. His instincts overtook his body, and he felt his muscles hold; he was perfectly motionless.

'Cute dog',' commented the owner. 'Do you think he wants to meet Toffee?'

'Sure, he seems to have calmed down now,' replied Petra.

As Petra and Nathan sat down on the chairs, the large tan dog walked towards them. Without hesitating, she pushed her large head into the blankets and sniffed at Allen. Allen didn't move an inch.

'Oh, he's so cute,' complemented the owner. 'Is he sick?'

'No, just here for his puppy shots,' said Petra.

Once the large tan dog and her owner had left, they waited around for a few more minutes in the empty reception. With nothing to scare him back into the blankets, Allen poked his head out and started to look around the room.

'Is Allen here?' a man's voice called out.

Petra and Nathan looked up to see the veterinarian leaning out of his consulting room door. He was a short man with grey hair and glasses, smiling at them expectantly.

'Yep, this is Allen' said Nathan, as they rose from their seats.

'Come on in,' said the vet.

Allen felt himself being carried through the doorway, where he was taken from his blanket and placed on the floor. Allen looked around the room, and in front of him he saw the ankle of the strange man standing a few steps away. With his body high above, the vet stepped towards Allen. He watched the black leather shoe, nearly as long as himself, plant itself in front of his nose. As was his usual reaction to new people, Allen felt very small and helpless next to the towering giant. He had grown to love Nathan and Petra, but this person was different. Would he be so gentle?

Allen stretched out his neck and sniffed towards the vet, only to be overwhelmed with the strongest stench of fear he had ever inhaled! The most petrified patients seen over the last few days had released a range of smells that now permeated the room and everything in it. He could hear his people and the vet talking, oblivious to the smell, as he cowered down with his tail tucked between his legs. Just as he was turning around to find an escape, the vet reached down over his head. Allen watched in trepidation as two enormous hands moved slowly towards him. When they scooped him up into the air and the ground fell away below, his heart began racing faster than ever.

Allen was trembling violently by the time he was placed onto the cold metal table in the centre of the room. Facing away from the vet, he sat there frozen, feeling shocked and numb. Looking up at the ceiling far above him, then down at the floor far below, he felt like how a child might feel at the pool, standing at the edge of a diving board. Except Allen hadn't chosen this situation for fun; he had been forced. The whole strangeness and unfamiliarity of the environment overwhelmed him. His heart was still beating at double its normal rate. In a situation like this, many people might break out into a nervous sweat, but dogs don't sweat to lose heat, they pant. Like so many dogs do at the vet, Allen broke out into an anxious pant.

Allen turned to look behind him and saw the white coat of the vet standing against the table. One of the vet's hands worked its way under his lips and pried open his mouth. This was a new sensation for Allen, he was only familiar with hands stroking his fur or feeding him food. His head was turned to face the man as he examined Allen's teeth. The vet's large blue eyes stared directly at him in a confronting and uncomfortable gaze. He continued his examination by pulling up Allen's eyelids to examine his eyes, and then flapping his ears back to assess the ear canals. Next, the vet placed a stethoscope on Allen's chest, while he held Allen's mouth closed to quiet the sounds of his panting. Allen squirmed and struggled for a few seconds, until his muzzle was eventually released. He felt a rush of relief as he could finally pull in a deep breath of air and resume his nervous panting.

'Good boy Allen,' encouraged Petra from her seat at the edge of the room. 'When we get home, we can snuggle on the sofa, okay?'

Allen hardly heard her. At this point, the recollections of safety on the sofa at home with his people seemed a very distant memory. Before he could decide what to do next, Allen was held firm once more as the vet inserted a rectal thermometer into his bottom. Allen did not feel embarrassed or defiled; these concepts had never occurred to him before. Yet he needed to escape the strange feeling that was decidedly uncomfortable and unfamiliar. The sensation in his bottom became painful as he moved and struggled to get away, leading him to panic further. Allen soon heard a high-pitched beeping sound, indicating the thermometer had completed its reading. He was released on the table once more as it was removed from his body.

'It's okay, buddy,' said Nathan. 'He's just making sure you aren't sick.'

Allen didn't notice the voice. He was still processing the shock of what had just happened. His fear peaked again as the hands started moving towards him once more. Allen felt his heart pounding and icy ripples shudder down his body. He knew this was not good, that something was very wrong. At this point, he instinctively realised that it was time to act. He needed to communicate to the strange giant that he was not happy with this behaviour. He needed it to stop.

Overcoming his shock, Allen summoned the courage to lift up his lips and show his teeth while letting out a soft growl. This tentative expression of protest went unnoticed by the vet. He continued to move his hands towards Allen, readying himself to proceed with the examination. When one of the hands touched Allen's shoulder, he snapped. Letting out a loud snarl, he spun his head around and sunk his teeth into the flesh. This got the attention of the vet. He looked down at Allen with a surprised expression on his face, and perhaps a hint of fear. Finally, it seemed like Allen had a solution to stopping this horrible assault.

Allen could hear the people start talking again, this time louder and more quickly than before. The vet walked over to the consulting room door and poked his head out to call for a nurse. Allen watched as a woman entered the room holding something black, which he did not realise was a fabric muzzle. Before he had time to react, the strange lady quickly flicked her wrist and slipped the muzzle over his face. His heart jumped again. Allen felt defenceless, he couldn't bark, bite or even pant anymore! He tried lifting his paws to remove the thing from his face, but he was held still once again by unfamiliar hands. He was tensing all the muscles he could in an effort to escape, but the nurse's grip was too strong. Allen felt the sharp stab of a needle in the back of his neck. Struggling, he let out a muffled yelp through the muzzle, trying but unable to bite at his captors. A moment later he was released once more onto the table. His breathing smothered by the muzzle, he struggled to push and pull the air forcefully through his nose. Allen could now feel that his legs were wet and warm, and he could smell urine in the air. There was more talking and exclamation, as he was once more lifted from the table by the vet.

Finally, Allen felt the muzzle slide off his face as he was deposited onto the floor of the room. Allen sat gasping for a moment, his mouth open wide. He felt the refreshing air cool his body as it rushed over his tongue and expanded down into his lungs. As he regained his breath, Allen cringed into the floor and cautiously looked up.

It was happening again. He watched as the strange man reached towards him yet another time. With his head hunched down and his tail tucked under, Allen rotated his eyes up to watch the hand approach. He growled a defiant warning, not registering that the vet was holding a small meaty treat. It wouldn't have mattered, there was no appetite in Allen's fear-riddled stomach. Now would not be a safe time to eat.

'You don't want the treat, Allen?' asked the vet. 'Dachshunds are such fussy dogs...'

'Oh, that's strange, he normally likes treats,' commented Petra.

Thanking the vet, she lent down and scooped up Allen in his blanket once more. Underneath the blanket, Allen's back was twisted at an odd angle as he was lifted up, causing him to feel a brief pinch of pain.

'So sorry he was naughty,' Petra added ashamedly.

'That's alright Petra,' he replied with a sorrowful smile. 'He just needs a bit more training I think.'

Petra forced herself to smile back, but Nathan just looked at Allen and shook his head, clicking his tongue with disapproval. Allen's body trembled violently as he burrowed his head into Petra's arms. He was relieved to be back with his people, but had no idea what was about to come next.

Once they were out of earshot, the nurse turned to speak to the vet. 'What a horrible little thing, so aggressive!'

The vet sighed with resignation. 'Yes, very nasty piece of work unfortunately... That dog needs obedience training. Urgently!'

* * *

Meanwhile, in a different veterinary clinic's waiting room, Nella sat on the cool floor underneath a chair, peeking out from between Olivia's legs. Her ears drooped low as she surveyed the people and animals around her. She was happy to stay in her hiding place, it felt like the safest spot to be. Panting quietly, with a worried furrow on her brow, she wondered what might be about to happen.

As she sat there, Nella gradually became aware of a strange smell in the room. She knew it was coming from a type of animal that she hadn't encountered before. The animal in question was a small, flighty thing that people call a 'cat.' This cat was out of sight, sitting in its carrier next to a bored-looking gentleman, behind a partition in the waiting-room. The partition had a large cartoon drawing of a white cat on it, showing that the area was designated for feline patients only. Nella wanted to learn more about the strange animal she sensed, so she poked her nose out from between Olivia's legs and sniffed curiously at the air. Amongst the mixture of scents in the room, she also detected the faint aroma of fear, and it made her stomach twist. The warm bed she had been raised in, with her mother and littermates, seemed so far away in this moment. Nella pulled her head back under the chair and let out a worried yawn.

In the other corner of the room, there was a senior lady with a white fluffy dog lying on her lap. Being used to going places with his owner, the dog had a calm look on his face and a relaxed posture. As he felt his owner stroking his head, he watched two receptionists going about their work. Busily talking and shuffling around behind their desk, these two ladies were also the focus of Nella. One of the two ladies had her hair up in a bun that looked particularly strange from Nella's perspective. She was still learning to recognise the human form in all its variations, and the lump of hair sitting atop her head gave her face a very confusing shape.

The receptionist put down the phone and looked over at Mick and Olivia. Smiling, she took a handful of treats and stood up from her desk, walking over towards them.

As they looked up, she greeted them. 'Hi, we're sorry the vet's running behind, but she shouldn't be too much longer. We've got a new vet starting here and she's just giving her a quick hand with another patient.'

'Oh, that's fine we're quite comfortable here,' replied Olivia.

The receptionist bent over and looked down at Nella's head, which was peering back at her through Olivia's legs.

'And aren't you just adorable?' she cooed, her smile widening.

Nella lowered her head and retreated a little further under the chair. She wasn't sure what to do, she needed to get away to safety but there was nowhere else to go, she was trapped.

The receptionist reached her hand towards Nella with a treat in her open hand. 'Here you go little one, would you like this treat?'

Nella watched the hand reaching under the chair, frozen in place with her eyes widening as her heart started to race.

Suddenly, the hand retreated out from under the chair and the receptionist stood back up.

'Aww, the little thing is scared' she said, a compassionate look on her face. 'I'll just leave her be for now, let her get used to the place.'

Mick frowned, he didn't want Nella to make a bad impression. 'Yeah, she does this to new people quite a bit... But once she gets to know you, she's a different dog!'

Looking at Nella under the chair, he whispered 'it's okay Nella, nothing to be afraid of.'

One of the consulting room doors opened and a young lady with large blue glasses emerged carrying a cage with two brindle rabbits nestled amongst tufts of hay. As the receptionist left to take payment, Nella felt a sense of relief that she was gone. Shortly after, two female vets emerged from the room, talking just loud enough that Olivia could make out what they were saying.

While inspecting a medical chart, the senior vet started explaining. 'It's not that they don't cooperate when you flip them on their back, in fact it's the best way to hold them if they won't stay still and something important needs doing. The point is that in most cases you can do everything you need to do without flipping them, and it's a lot less stressful.'

'Okay, I can do that,' the younger vet replied, nodding. 'I swear we were never taught this stuff at vet school.'

'They never show you, that's why I did my behaviour course right after graduating,' added the senior vet.

As the lady with the rabbits made her way outside, the receptionist turned to the senior vet and started speaking. 'Ava, I just have to change over your pheromone diffuser before your next puppy, it's running low.'

'Oh, is that the dog appeasing pheromone that calms them down?' the junior vet asked.

'Yeah, sure is,' replied Ava as they walked towards the back of the clinic. 'It's a synthetic version of the calming smell that mother dogs release for their puppies when nursing.'

A few minutes later, Ava returned to the waiting room with a big smile on her face. 'This must be Nella! Isn't she just so sweet! My name is Ava, I'll be your vet today,' she said excitedly.

After gazing at Nella for a moment, Ava looked up at Mick and Olivia as they introduced themselves.

'Come on in and let's get started,' encouraged Ava, as she turned and walked back into her consulting room.

Mick went ahead and made his way into the room, expecting Olivia to follow with Nella. However, Olivia only made it halfway. She felt tension on Nella's leash and looked back to see her sitting under the chair, not budging. The leash was looped around Nella's neck as they didn't have a collar for her yet. As Olivia pulled on the leash, the loop tightened around her neck like a noose, only adding to her feelings of distress. Realising Nella might be afraid, Olivia attempted to gently coax her out.

'Nella, come on, good girl Nelly...'

Nella looked out from under the chair, feeling the tension of the leash on her collar, and pulled back against it. She felt butterflies in her stomach as she started to slowly slide along the floor out from under the safety of her makeshift den. Olivia kept coaxing her to no avail, so she continued to pull on the leash until Nella had slid halfway across the room.

The man waiting with his cat looked up and chuckled, 'I don't think she likes the vet very much!'

Olivia gave up on pulling and decided to walk back towards Nella to pick her up and carry her in. However, as she walked closer, Nella felt the leash loosen around her neck. Sensing an opportunity, she turned to dash back to safety. Olivia reacted quickly, but Nella was back under the chair before she could catch her. Olivia sighed and slid her arms under the chair, reaching in to drag her out. Nella trusted Olivia, and so she let her slide her hands around the sides of her body. Yet when Olivia pulled, Nella pushed back under the chair with her legs in an attempt to maintain her position. As Olivia finally managed to slide Nella out from under the chair, one of its legs got stuck on the leash. It toppled over, making a loud crash! While no-one had offered to help Olivia before, suddenly everyone was moving. The receptionist stood up and looked over while still on the phone, the man with the cat got up to help, and Ava and Mick both rushed back out from the consulting room.

Olivia looked at Ava with a shocked face. 'I'm so sorry, she didn't want to come and when I picked her up, she knocked the chair over!' she exclaimed.

Nella was now visibly trembling. She hadn't ever heard a noise so loud before, and she felt sick from worry. She had no idea why she was here in this strange place with loud noises, but knew it was not a good place and wished she could be anywhere else.

Ava had a concerned expression as she gazed at Nella dangling from Olivia's arms. 'Oh poor Nella, she's so worried! Carry her in and we'll see what we can do to try and calm her down a bit.'

Mick smiled and started giggling, 'She looks like she's about to wet herself Olivia, watch out!'

Although he was joking, in reality Mick was right. Nella was barely holding on. Olivia walked into the room, with both arms wrapped around Nella, and Ava closed the door behind them. Struggling a little with her weight, Olivia walked to the centre of the room and went to place Nella on the examination table.

'Actually, I'd rather have Nella on the floor please,' suggested Ava. 'Just until she gets a bit more used to the place.'

Olivia took a step back and knelt down, trying to gently place Nella on the floor. As she was carefully lowering Nella down, just as she was about to touch the ground, Nella started twisting violently. She had sensed her chance to hide might be approaching and couldn't wait a moment longer. Olivia quickly lost her grip, causing Nella to fall on her side. Her legs flailing, she slipped on the floor twice in an attempt to stand before she finally stood upright. Unsure of her footing, she stopped, frozen with terror in the middle of the room.

Nella could hear her heartbeat in her ears, and felt her tail tucked so far between her legs it poked into her belly. She held her head down as she cowered, making herself small for safety. Without moving in the slightest, she used her eyes to look around for any imminent danger. As Ava looked down at her, the whites of Nella's eyes made the shape of crescent moons as she stared up and to the side, her nose still pointing at the floor.

Ava had a sorrowful look on her face as she whispered in Nella's direction.

'She's a very fearful little pup, isn't she?'

Olivia sighed before replying, she was feeling a little concerned. 'I think she just takes a while to get used to things, and this is the first time we've taken her out since getting her.'

'Yeah, and she doesn't like loud noises either,' Mick added.

Ava took a handful of treats and slowly crouched down on the floor. Talking in a gentle, quiet tone, she sat down and then lay on her side at the edge of the room.

'Because this is her first trip to the vet,' she said, 'we really want her to have a good experience. She might remember this day for the rest of her life.'

Nella watched as her vet lay down on the ground. She noticed it didn't feel quite so intimidating now that Ava wasn't towering over her.

'I'm going to take a few minutes to try to get her to like me,' continued Ava. 'We haven't had a great start to this visit.'

She tossed a small treat over towards Nella, who sniffed it suspiciously, then turned around and slunk under one of the consult room chairs. Nella liked the smell of the food, but now was no time to eat. As she sat there, with the people around her continuing to talk, she noticed in the back of her mind that there was something familiar about the smell in here. It made her feel like when she was safe and warm sleeping next to her mother only a few days prior. It helped a bit, but her heartbeat, which was still racing, slowed down only slightly.

Over the next few minutes, nothing else bad happened. Nella began to pay attention to the treat sitting in the middle of the room. Feeling a little calmer, she was starting to think about how wonderful it had smelt. Slowly but surely, she crept out from under the chair and made her way over to it, sniffing it briefly before taking it into her mouth and chewing. The people around her responded with soothing tones, and she looked up at Olivia and Mick to see them encouraging her. The soft scuttle of another treat sliding across the floor caught her attention. She sniffed it and then ate it, a little faster this time. Nella was standing up a little taller now, her tail more relaxed; she was starting to feel a bit safer here. Before long, another treat landed halfway between her and Ava. Nella looked at the treat, and then at Ava's sideways face as she lay on the ground.

Nella had met other humans before that were safe and friendly, but this person was new and smelled unfamiliar. Although she still wasn't sure, she summoned the courage to carefully walk over to the treat, without taking her eyes off Ava. As soon as she had taken it into her mouth, Ava tossed another treat, this time closer to her again. Nella took another two steps closer, and carefully stretched forwards to pluck it off the ground, so as to not get too close to Ava. Nella was surprised that Ava just lay there, but it really wasn't very intimidating. She started to feel as though maybe she might be able to trust this person. Soon another treat landed right next to her, and without thinking she quickly snapped that one up too.

That settled it, Nella looked at Ava with a new understanding; this person was a good person. The tip of her tail started to waggle softly as she slowly crept even closer, this time taking a treat directly from Ava's outstretched hand. Nella could hear more gentle voices from the people around her as she started to feel her whole body worming in sync with her tail. Now overcome with curiosity, she walked right up to Ava's legs and sniffed them, then proceeded to start to climb on top of her!

Ava sat up laughing and started giving Nella treat after treat in a row, while guiding her back onto the floor. Nella had now forgotten about her recent feelings of fear and anxiety, this was fun! She vigorously shook off her stress, the skin of her body and ears flapping side to side. Looking up at Ava, Nella now wondered why the treats had stopped. She let out a little yip and lowered her chest to the ground, paws forward, her bottom poking to the sky with tail sweeping side to side. By this stage, Mick and Olivia were openly smiling and laughing.

Mick looked down at Nella and stated the obvious. 'Wow Nella, I think you've made a new friend!'

'Where do you think she'd like me to scratch her, does she have a favourite spot?' asked Ava.

'Oh, she likes on the neck or at the base of the tail' replied Olivia.

Ava slowly reached out to stroke Nella on the neck, who leaned into it appreciatively.

'Okay, now we can start what we came here for!' said Ava.

She proceeded to examine Nella's face and body, all under the guise of some playful petting. When Nella rolled onto her back, Ava took the opportunity to examine her underside. Nella responded by playfully biting at Ava with her tail wagging. Next thing she knew, Nella noticed a small rope toy appear above her. She took it into her mouth and the soft rope felt comforting on her teething gums as she pulled at it. Ava continued with her examination, listening to Nella's heart, and looking over her skin. All the while, Nella was enjoying this new connection with her gentle human friend.

'She's healthy as can be,' commented Ava, 'but now we need to do the not-so-nice things… Can I have a helper please?'

Mick walked over and crouched down as Ava handed him some dog treats.

'Your job is to keep giving her treats, do you think you can do that?' asked Ava.

Mick nodded once, then started feeding the small treats to Nella. As Ava put the thermometer into Nella's bottom, she stopped eating momentarily and looked around for the source of the strange sensation. As she heard more soothing voices and another snack appeared in front of her nose, she forgot about her bottom. She was focused on getting as many of the treats as she could. She heard a beeping noise and some approving words from Ava as the thermometer was removed. Then, as she was biting through a particularly large and crunchy treat, she felt a small pinch on the back of her neck. She stopped and froze, was something bad happening again? Nella felt safe though, and the stinging was quickly gone, so she happily resumed eating.

'And we're all done!' exclaimed Ava, smiling down at Nella.

Nella was released to roam the area and proceeded to start looking for treats while smelling the various strange scents on the floor. As Ava explained the benefits of parasite control, Mick looked down at Nella's tail slowly sweeping from side to side. The tail stopped moving, and her hips lowered as she squatted into the floor. Nella felt relief as she let go, a small puddle of urine forming under her body.

'No, Nella!' exclaimed Mick. 'Oh, so sorry Ava, she did a wee.'

Ava waved her hand across her face and casually replied, 'Who cares, she can't hold on long at this age! We're done now anyway, so let's get out of here. I'll clean it up later.'

As Olivia carried Nella back into the waiting room, Nella remembered the loud noise and feeling of terror she had just overcome. Two young boys, not yet old enough for school, were running in circles squealing and laughing. Noticing that there were other people in here now, strange people, Nella started trembling and panting once more.

'I think I'd better take her outside, in case she needs to go to the toilet again,' said Olivia, as Mick stayed to fix up the account. 'Come on Nelly, we need to go pick up Tessa from play school. I bet you'll be excited to see her, and I'm sure she's missed you too!'

Interpreting Dog Behaviour

As a veterinarian, I regularly see dogs that are in pain, stressed or fearful. I can read them like an open book, it's obvious to me how they are feeling. Unfortunately, most veterinary schools do not teach their students a good foundation in behaviour.[1] As a consequence, I see many vets who are not proficient at reading animal body language. This is not because they are bad vets, it's because reading behaviour is a difficult skill that needs teaching and practice to master. There are so many subject areas that veterinarians need to know, that there just isn't time to cover everything in detail. However, reading behaviour is a very important skill that should be prioritised further. For this reason, many veterinarians enrol in behaviour-themed veterinary courses to further their education after graduating. Understanding behaviour is a fundamental skill needed to maximise the welfare of the patients a vet sees.

In many cases, whether I decide to perform a procedure on a dog showing unsafe or threatening behaviour is *not* determined by whether I think I could be bitten. Rather, I am weighing up what the psychological impact on the patient will be, and whether it can be justified. If I'm going to traumatise a dog by pinning it down to clip its nails or take its temperature with a rectal thermometer, there had better be a very good reason why I need to do that. When a dog is very fearful of handling yet must be examined for their own health and welfare, there are usually only two options at that time: subjecting them to a severely traumatic experience, or using heavy sedatives. This is a sad reality of practicing as a veterinarian, but thankfully most owners understand, once it is clearly explained.

Pain

Dogs will often yelp or cry out in response to sudden sharp pain like being hit or stepped on. After the initial insult, even if they have broken their leg, they won't normally continue vocalising for long. As humans we could imagine someone with a broken leg and no pain relief to be groaning, crying with tears, screaming out, shaking, and complaining vocally to us. This could continue intermittently for a very long time. However, dogs do not cry tears of pain, and they do not complain to us with the intention of letting us know of their suffering. In a pack of wild dogs, there would be no benefit in complaining about their pain to the other dogs for hour after hour, and so they simply don't do it. This doesn't mean dogs in a group would be unaware of each other's pain, as they may be able to sense it in other ways. For this reason, many people struggle to recognise the signs of long-term pain in their dogs. They notice if their dog yelps suddenly or cries out, but that's about it. To cry and complain about a toothache or a painful injury is a very human trait. If their dog isn't doing this, people often assume they are simply okay.

As a veterinarian, we learn to read the body language of a dog in pain. The things we perceive as a vet include trembling, panting while resting, shallow breathing, altered posture, and other changes in behaviour. We can also notice an elevation in their heart rate and a subtle grimace or look when touching a tender region on their body. As a veterinarian, you learn to read all these signs intuitively over time. You are able to glance at an animal walking along the street and instantly tell that they are suffering. While most dog owners are not adept at noticing these signs, this does not make them a bad owner. Over and over, I am impressed by the ability of people to be in tune with their pets on a deeper level which transcends their own understanding. An owner will bring in their dog not knowing the problem, and simply tell us that 'she's just not herself, she's not right.' These most perceptive owners are often unsure of themselves when presenting their pet to the clinic. While it's not always possible to find the problem, most times the cause can be identified.

A very common presentation is as follows. The dog owner has nothing more to say than 'Fluffy is just not herself', and 'A week ago she yelped when I picked her up, but otherwise she just doesn't seem herself, she seems quieter than usual.' In many cases, this could be due to back pain, which can be quickly confirmed on examination. As Allen has experienced in this book, when we pick up a dog the wrong way, we can put too much pressure on their ribs, which can be transmitted to the spine causing pain. While the dog might feel this pain constantly, the owner might just see that their pet is 'off' without knowing why. Most pet owners cannot easily tell when their pet is in chronic pain. Another good example is severe dental disease, which causes severe mouth pain in affected animals. People report that their dog seems fine, yet when we see their mouth, we know this cannot be true. As many people can attest, having a toothache is no laughing matter.

Negative emotions

Just as people struggle to identify pain in their pets, they have similar problems identifying many of the emotions that their dog will experience. This is most pronounced with the negative emotions, like fear and anxiety. These emotions are also very difficult for veterinarians to learn to read well in their patients. I sometimes check an owner's understanding by asking them what they think their dog is feeling in that moment. I can point to their dog who is in the midst of a full-blown panic attack, and they will say something like, 'He's just excited,' or 'He really wants to get outside.' This is not to say that these owners are ignorant. It simply shows that reading dog behaviour is not intuitive—it must be learned. Yet even after learning the body language of fear, people still often struggle to see it in their own dog.[2] It's completely normal for people to feel fear and anxiety from time to time. Similarly, every dog will also experience these emotions. It's normal. If you have lived with your dog for years, and yet never looked at them and thought, 'they're really anxious' or 'they're very fearful', then you aren't reading them properly. As we have seen in this book, this ability to read your dog is particularly important in puppies when they socialise and experience things for the first time. A good first impression really matters.

As was described in this chapter, puppies will experience emotional bursts of fear or anxiety many times, and this is normal. However, very young puppies do not tend to act on their negative emotions as readily as older dogs. This is probably a protective mechanism, as a puppy is vulnerable and does not want to draw attention to itself. In many situations, what seems like a quiet puppy may actually be a puppy that's too terrified to move. This was the case with Allen when the strange dog came up and sniffed him in the waiting room. Unfortunately, this behaviour can lead people to assume that they are giving their puppy a good social experience. In reality, the puppy may be forming traumatic memories that can become the basis of problems later in life.[3]

I am sure you can now appreciate the importance of reading the body language of a dog accurately. However, I am not going to explain how to do this directly. If you pay attention, you will learn to read the body language of dogs by paying attention to the depictions in the story. Throughout this book, the body language of Nella, Allen and the dogs they meet is carefully described in a way that perfectly matches their emotions.

CHAPTER FOUR

Settling In

Allen looked up at Nathan, who was sitting on the couch watching football on the television. Allen often noticed his parents focused on the screen in the corner of the room, always seeming so preoccupied while it was on.

Allen had that feeling again, a fullness in his belly with an urge to release it into the outside world. He circled around the edge of the couch, sniffing the floor, looking for a place to go. Suddenly, Nathan yelled angrily at the screen as a goal was scored by the other team. The loud noise reminded Allen of something. He remembered that many times in the past, he had been the focus of that anger, and it often happened to him while he was relieving himself. Worried about being yelled at again, Allen knew he could not release now, Nathan was too close. Allen circled back around the couch and barked at Nathan, signalling his frustration.

Nathan looked down at Allen. 'Hey buddy, you want to come up?' he asked, leaning over with his hands out.

Allen liked being on the couch, but wasn't a fan of being picked up. Forgetting about his urges, his tail wagging, he walked up to Nathan's open arms. As he got closer, Allen slowed down and crouched, hunched over in anticipation of being lifted. As Nathan pulled him up from under the armpits, Allen felt the familiar discomfort of his spine being pushed up by his ribs. This was made worse by the weight of his unsupported back legs. As Allen was gently deposited on the couch, he relaxed again as the pressure from his spine was released. Nathan produced a cracker from a bowl on the table, and handed it to him.

'Here Allen, want a treat?' offered Nathan.

Allen looked at the cracker in his hand longingly. He had been smelling them nearby for a while now. Salivating, he watched the treat moving towards him, held between Nathan's fingers. He stood very still, desperately hoping that he could eat the cracker. As soon as Nathan's hand came within striking distance, he couldn't help himself. Worried that this might be his last opportunity to eat it, he snapped forwards, lunging at the cracker with his jaws. As he bit down on the cracker, Nathan's fingers happened to be in the way.

'Ouch!' yelled Nathan, pulling his hand back and flicking it side to side.

Allen crunched on his prize and quickly swallowed it, then sat back to watch the cracker bowl expectantly. Nathan shook his head and pulled Allen onto his lap, then turned his focus back to the game. As Allen sat there, he enjoyed the sensation of being stroked. Feeling safe and secure, he laid his head on Nathan's leg and let out a sigh. He really needed to go to the toilet, and despite trying to hold on it was becoming urgent. A few moments later, he started panting as the discomfort became too much to bear. Allen slid out of Nathan's lap and jumped down from the couch. Nathan's eyes were still glued to the game. Allen had to find a spot to go, but it wasn't safe here with Nathan so close. He slowly wandered out of the lounge room and down the corridor to the master bedroom.

In the bedroom, Allen could feel the soft woolly carpet under his feet. He walked around to the far side of the bed where he couldn't see the doorway. This felt safe, he could still hear Nathan watching the screen in the other room, and his fear of being yelled at subsided. Allen could also smell the muffled stench of aged urine that had seeped under the carpet a week earlier, when he had first been forced to go in this location. Petra cleaned the area with a pine-scented liquid, and he could smell this too. The scent of old urine awakened a primal urge in Allen to think of this area as a toilet, reinforcing his current intention. He squatted down into the carpet and released his bladder, feeling a wave of relief as it emptied. The feeling of the carpet under his paws was still a strange sensation for him to notice while urinating, but he was becoming used to it. He would have preferred a patch of grass if there was one available (the usual place his parents took him), but he would have to make do with this spot.

Once finished, Allen trotted out of the bedroom and back down the corridor to the lounge room. Feeling much better, he looked up at Nathan and barked, tail wagging excitedly. Unlike his earlier barks that indicated he needed to pee, this time he really did want to get onto the couch. Nathan ignored him, staring at the screen, so Allen barked again.

'Shoosh Allen!' said Nathan.

Encouraged that Nathan was responding, Allen barked a third time.

'You want up again? You just can't make your mind up Allen!' exclaimed Nathan. He leant down to pick him up, pulling him up from under his armpits once again. Allen held his breath as he was lifted in the air, and then relaxed as his weight landed back on the couch. After making his way to a spot next to Nathan, he snuggled into the cushions and fell asleep.

* * *

Allen awoke to the sound of the doorbell chiming. Excited to find out who might have arrived, he leapt off the couch before thinking. As he landed on the floor, he felt his back twinge where it had been irritated by being picked up earlier. After letting out a little yelp, he paused momentarily before barking as he ran down the hallway to the door.

'Back Allen! Get back!' yelled Petra as she opened the door.

As she stepped through, she used her foot to push him inside, closing the door behind her. Allen frantically barked as he jumped up at her legs with nervous excitement, craving an interaction. It just didn't feel natural for a member of his pack to leave the territory like that, and he was glad she was now home.

'Did you miss me baby?' asked Petra, as she leant down to pick him up.

Allen hunched down as she slid her hands under her chest and started to lift him up. Allen felt his back start to twinge again. Worried it was about to hurt, turned his head around and bit at Petra's hand reflexively.

'Owww!' cried Petra, looking down at Allen with a shocked expression. 'No! Bad dog! No biting!' she yelled.

Nathan muted the television and walked down the hallway. 'What's wrong honey? What did he do?' he called.

'He bit me!' she said with a shocked expression. 'Just as I was about to pick him up!'

Nathan frowned. 'I was picking him up just before and he was fine with me, maybe he was just excited to see you? Was it just a play bite?'

'No, this was a real bite, look, I'm bleeding!' she replied, showing him a small cut on the back of her finger. 'What a little monster... Hopefully he grows out of this puppy biting soon!'

Meanwhile, Allen was cowering down below them, looking up with worried eyes. He was starting to seriously dislike being picked up, not only did it hurt him sometimes, but when it did hurt him, his people yelled at him!

Petra looked down at Allen, hunched up with his tail tucked between his legs and his ears dropped low on the sides of his head. 'Well, at least he knows he did a bad thing. Looks racked with guilt, doesn't he?'

Nathan called out to her as he walked back to the kitchen. 'Maybe he's hungry? It is dinner time after all, do dogs get hangry?'

'Hangry?' replied Petra, smiling as she let out a chuckle. 'Sounds like he takes after you!'

'Allen, dinner time, din-dins Allen!' called Nathan excitedly, grinning at Allen.

Allen quickly forgot his past worry and enthusiastically ran past him and into the kitchen. It had happened again; they had flipped back from angry to friendly. This made him feel very happy. But it was a nervous feeling of happiness, as he wasn't sure how long this current mood would last.

Petra walked into the bedroom to put down her bag, looking suspiciously at a new dark patch on the carpet next to the bedpost.

'Oh sugar!' she grumbled to herself. 'Nath! Allen's gone to the toilet in here again!'

Nathan came running back down to the bedroom. 'When did he do that?! He was on the couch next to me all afternoon! Is it fresh?'

Allen ran back down after Nathan, and into the bedroom to see both his parents looking at him. He noticed their expressions were the ones that they had when they were about to yell at him. He slunk down to the ground and felt a wave of fear wash over him. Feeling sad that things had switched back so quickly, he slowly looked up at them, bracing for them to start yelling.

Petra burst into laughter. 'Oh my gosh he just looks so guilty—how can I stay mad at him?! Did you take him out to the toilet, Nath?'

Nathan shook his head with a smile on his face. 'Yeah, he's pretty cute... I took him out only a few hours ago, but he was more interested in barking at the birds!'

Nathan put his hands around Allen and pushed him towards the soiled carpet. Allen turned his head away, realising what was happening. He had been through this before, and didn't like what was coming.

'No! Bad dog!' scolded Nathan as he tried to push Allen's head towards the mess.

'Oh Allen,' muttered Petra as she shook her head and frowned. 'When will you learn! I do hope you grow out of these puppy habits soon. I can't take it anymore!'

* * *

Nella woke up to the sound of the front door clicking as the bolt unfastened. She jumped out of her bed, and eagerly trotted towards the door. Nella was hoping that this might be her parents. Something had gone wrong earlier; they left the house without her. She had been pacing, whining and fretting ever since, and taken to chewing on the bed to help relieve her tension. Nella was hard-wired to always try and stay with her family, and being left alone was a very unnatural concept to her. She had gained this vital instinct through generations of dogs before her, stretching back to when her ancestors had evolved, tens of thousands of years ago.

As Mick stepped through the front door, Nella was overcome with joy—her whole body waggling, she whined as she stared up at his smiling face.

'Nella! We missed you' said Mick, as Olivia entered the house behind him.

Nella reared up, placing her front paws on Mick's body, striving for contact. Mick stopped and stroked her head, as she panted in-between trying to lick at his face.

'Hi beautiful, how did you go on your own?' asked Olivia. Nella stepped down from Mick and jumped up onto Olivia this time, resting her paws on Olivia's tummy.

'Good girl' she said, stroking Nella's neck before pushing her back down. As Nella was forced back, her paws accidentally scraped down Olivia's leg.

'Ouch' cried Olivia, 'that hurt!'

'What happened?' asked Mick, a look of surprise on his face as he turned back from closing the door.

'She just scratched me! It really hurt,' said Olivia. 'I think we need to get her nails clipped. We must ask Ava about that next time we go to the vet.'

Mick and Olivia made their way into the loungeroom where they sat down on the sofa. Nella had been following them intently, sniffing their shoes and legs as they walked. She could smell fresh cut grass, some bird poop on the bottom of Mick's shoe, and the scent of another dog that Olivia had met on the street. Nella was very excited to see them home, and yet still shaken from them leaving in the first place. As Mick sat down, she started whining again with anxious relief and jumped into his lap.

'No! No jumping up Nella,' snapped Mick. 'You need to learn. You'll be a very big dog one day Nella.'

Nella responded by trying to lick at his face. She loved jumping up onto people, it got her closer to them, and they often stroked her or played with her to reinforce it. After another moment, Mick pushed her back down.

'No,' he said once more, in a soft but firm tone.

Nella was confused. She wasn't sure why he had sounded threatening. She felt very insecure about her place in the house, and desperately wanted to do the right thing. She craved her people's attention, but being told off only made the craving worse. If she wasn't pleasing to her people, then she had to try harder in the future. She would do whatever it took to be accepted. Nella sat down and looked up expectantly at Mick, the tip of her tail wagging rapidly. Ignoring her, Mick pulled out his phone to check a notification. Within seconds, Nella had forgotten the exchange and jumped back onto his lap again. Mick put his hand on her chest and pushed her off, a little more forcefully this time, as Olivia tried to get his attention too.

'Hey Mickey, do you think this plant would look good for the coffee table?' asked Olivia, showing him his phone.

As Mick looked over, Nella jumped back at his lap again. Without looking, Mick pushed her back down. Nella was liking this interaction, it was fun. She jumped back up again. Irritated that she wasn't learning, Mick pushed her back again, even more forcefully this time.

'No,' said Mick in a firm tone.

As she glided back across the floorboards, her paws started to slip. For a moment she was running on the spot as she tried to get back to his lap. Nella loved playing with Mick, even if he was being a bit rougher than usual. It was all good fun. This time as she approached him, she saw him with his hands out and quickly changed tactics. As she closed in on Mick, she dived at his feet and started playfully biting at his shoe.

'Nella, do you want to go outside to the toilet?' asked Mick as he stood up.

Nella stood back and regarded him; her floppy ears pricked a little higher on her head. As he walked over to the back door, Nella continued to jump up and try to get her paws onto his leg, but wasn't able to make any contact. Mick opened the door and they both went outside.

It was a sunny day, with a warm summer breeze and the sound of an aeroplane droning above. Outside, Nella looked up to see what the noise was, worried.

'Nella, go potty,' said Mick. Nella stopped gazing upwards and turned her attention to Mick. Another feeling of joy and love welled up inside her, as she remembered again that she was only just reunited with her family. As Mick bent down, beckoning to her, she bounced towards him. With Mick smiling and Nella panting, they started to gently wrestle together. Nella loved this game, she would try to bite at his hands and arms, while he would try to either get her into a headlock or push her away. After a few minutes, Mick stood up.

'Come on Nelly, go potty,' he encouraged.

Nella jumped back up at Mick, who sighed and pushed her down.

'Well, if you aren't going to go...' he started. Mick opened the door and called her back inside.

Nella ran through and jumped onto her bed, lying down and wagging her tail.

Olivia, still sitting on the couch, looked up and gasped.

'Nella, what have you done to your bed?' she exclaimed.

With the corner chewed into pieces and white stuffing spilling out and onto the floor, it was surprising they hadn't noticed it sooner.

'Oh Nella! You naughty girl!' exclaimed Mick in a surprised tone. 'Don't you know that's for sleeping on? What will you sleep on once that's destroyed?'

Nella looked back at them both, panting with one of her long ears flopped back, relishing the attention. Eager to interact, she got up and started walking over to Olivia, her tail slowly wagging. Nella was starting to feel better now. The playtime with Mick outside had helped her shake off most of the nerves from being left all alone earlier in the day. However, Nella was still wondering where Tessa was, as she hadn't yet returned. She looked up at Olivia and slowly but deliberately jumped up with her front paws onto her lap. Olivia smiled down at Nella and stroked her head.

'It's okay, Nelly,' she said in a soothing tone. 'We aren't angry, but why didn't you chew at the toys we left you?'

Nella leaned into Olivia's hand as she scratched her behind the ear, her eyes squinting with pleasure.

'We have some exciting news for you Nella!' said Olivia. 'Petra just messaged me; we've set up a play date with Allen this afternoon. Do you want to meet another puppy?'

Nella looked back at Olivia, both her ears pricked up with attention.

'We just have to pick up Tessa from her friend's house first,' she continued. 'Is that okay?'

Nella continued to gaze at Olivia, her tail wagging faster from the excitement of being spoken to.

'Oh, it's okay? You approve? What a good girl!' cooed Olivia.

Nella was happy to be entertained in this way as she stood with her paws up on Olivia's lap. It also reinforced in her mind that jumping up onto people was a good thing to do.

* * *

Later that afternoon, Olivia was washing the dishes when she called out to Mick in the loungeroom.

'Mickey, we need to go soon. Can you get Nella's new collar and leash out please?'

'One step ahead of you honey,' he replied. 'I'm already putting it on her now.'

As Mick bent over Nella, she felt the collar slide around her neck, and then heard the clip close shut with a loud click. Mick released her and looked down as Nella took a few steps away from him, unsure what had just happened. Mick pulled out the leash and showed it to her. Nella looked at the leash, and then took it in her mouth, pulling backwards.

'No silly! It's not a toy!' exclaimed Mick, as she turned around and ran off with the leash into the kitchen.

Olivia, having just finished washing up, saw Nella trotting in with a very satisfied look on her face. Wagging her tail, she walked up to Olivia as she bent down and called her over.

'She thinks it's a toy...' Mick said, letting out a chuckle.

Olivia bent over and took the leash from Nella's mouth, praising her warmly. 'Good girl Nelly.'

Once Nella had let go, Olivia opened the clip on the leash and reached towards her collar.

'There we go, ready for your next adventure!' said Olivia once the leash was attached.

At this point, Nella noticed the strange feeling of the collar around her neck wasn't going away. She sat down to scratch at the area with her back leg.

'She's scratching, did you give her the flea stuff?' asked Mick, frowning.

Olivia frowned too. 'Yeah, I think so. Wasn't that in the tablet we gave her last week? Maybe she needs more, we'll have to check with Ava.'

As Mick and Olivia started walking towards the door, Nella pulled back against the leash tugging at her collar, refusing to walk.

Mick bent down and lifted her up into his arms, sighing. 'Might be easier to carry her to the car. I don't think she's used to the leash yet.'

Once in the back seat of the car, Nella remembered her last two car trips. She started to shake. She knew something different was happening, and was feeling nervous in anticipation of what might come next. The vibration of the engine was now becoming more familiar, but it worried her. Strange things often followed trips in the car. After turning down a few streets, they had soon pulled over on the side of the road. Olivia left the car for a few minutes, and when she returned, Tessa also entered the car.

'Hi Nella!' said Tessa excitedly, her face beaming as she sat down next to her.

Nella, who had been trembling on the seat next to her, vigorously waved the tip of her tail as she leant over to sniff her face. Before long, Nella had let out a couple of soft licks on her cheek and Tessa was giggling in delight. As the car took off to visit Allen, Nella sat back in her seat and resumed her anxious panting.

* * *

When they arrived at Petra and Nathan's house, Mick placed Nella on the ground at the front door as Olivia rang the doorbell. Tessa was bouncing on the spot with excitement.

'I can't wait to meet Allen!' she repeated over and over.

Nella frantically looked around, unsure of where she was and trying to get her bearings. Then she heard the sound of a dog barking from behind the front door. She looked at the door intently as the barking sound got louder. Next, she could hear the scuttling sound of Allen's feet on the floorboards, as he ran up to the other side of the door. Nella wagged her tail in nervous excitement. She liked other dogs, and wanted to see who was making all the noise.

'Just a minute…' called Petra from the other side of the door. She scooped up Allen and unlocked the latch. As Petra opened the door, Allen looked through the doorway to see two strange people, a child, and a seemingly large and unfamiliar dog on his doorstep. Allen felt his heart leap into action as adrenaline surged through his body. Having strangers appear in his territory was a very frightening experience.

'Hi guys!' said Petra with a welcoming smile on her face. 'Come inside, Nathan is just in the other room.'

Nella looked up at Petra, worried by the strange human figure in front of her. Her nervous excitement at meeting a dog had quickly changed to a feeling of cautiousness. Seeing Allen quivering in Petra's arms, Nella felt a burst of excitement but was too worried by Petra to get any closer. As Petra started walking down the hallway with Olivia and Tessa behind her, Mick and Nella followed them into the house. Wanting to keep close to Olivia, Nella pulled forward on the leash, her paws slipping beneath her on the polished floorboards.

'Easy there Nella,' said Mick. 'You can play with Allen in a minute!'

Tessa laughed in delight, unable to contain her excitement.

Nathan greeted them as they entered the lounge room, offering them all seats on the couch. Nella stood with her tail tucked beneath her legs and a worried look on her face. This was a strange place, and the two strange people seemed to be talking and laughing very loudly.

'Okay, shall we let them introduce themselves?' asked Petra excitedly, still holding Allen in her arms.

Nathan leaned forward and reached his hand over Nella's head, smiling at her. Seeing the hand of the strange man looming over her, Nella panicked and pulled back on the leash with all her might, slipping the collar off her head in doing so. Free at last, she ran back to the corner of the room and stood there, panting heavily from her feelings of stress and anxiety. She kept a particularly close eye on Nathan, as the shock of him reaching towards her still ran through her head. She just wasn't sure she could trust these people, they were very strange, and the whole house smelled so unfamiliar.

Allen was also feeling uneasy, he squirmed in Petra's arms to look over at Nella, his pupils wide.

'Nella, what's wrong?' queried Tessa.

'I think she just hates the leash,' replied Olivia. 'She's still not used to it!'

'Also, she's a bit funny with new people sometimes,' added Mick.

'Okay then, I'm going to put Allen down so he can go say hi,' said Petra excitedly, as she lowered him onto the ground.

Allen, feeling himself being released on the ground, moved in behind Petra's legs to hide.

'Go on Allen, go play with Nella,' encouraged Nathan.

Nathan got up off the couch, and started walking over to Nella. As Allen watched him moving away, Nathan turned to him encouragingly.

'Come on Allen, over here! Come say hi to Nella,' he said.

Nathan squatted down next to Nella. She was sitting in the corner, still as a statue, her eyes wide with fear at being cornered. She was not staring at Nathan directly, but was standing frozen with her face turned away to the side as she watched him cautiously.

'It's not like Nella to be so quiet,' said Olivia. 'She is normally full of energy. Maybe she's feeling a bit shy…'

When Allen saw Nathan crouching next to Nella, he started to venture out from the protection of Petra's legs. Having intruders on his territory was not safe, but Nathan seemed to be calm, so Allen felt reassured by that. He was intrigued by the strange dog. It certainly stayed still and didn't move much, which he felt was a good sign. He slowly made his way towards Nella. When Allen was only a few meters from Nella, Nathan tried to speed up the process.

'Good boy Allen!' he encouraged. 'Come on, come say hi.'

Nella looked at Allen, feeling conflicted. She really wanted to play with this new dog, and to sniff his smells. It wasn't safe here though, especially with Nathan so close to her.

Watching Allen walk over to him, Nathan absentmindedly reached out to pat Nella on the head. Nella, fearful and cornered, saw Nathan's hand moving towards her once again and panicked. She had no other option, she was cornered. Lifting her lips, she let out a soft growl and then quickly snapped at his hand. Nathan was blocking the view of Nella from the others on the couch, and so they did not see this happen.

'Ouch!' yelled Nathan in pain. He turned to face Nella and see what had happened.

Allen, on the other hand, had seen the whole thing. Hearing Nathan scream out, and already distrusting Nella, he reacted instantly. Allen had to protect his territory and his family! This strange dog had just proved to him that it was a serious threat. Allen ran up to Nella and snarled and snapped at her face, landing a bite on her lip. Nella yelped and ran along the wall towards the other corner of the room. Allen ran behind her, barking and snapping at her heels.

By this stage, everyone on the couch had stood up.

Nathan ran after Allen, quickly picking him up. 'No! Allen, you naughty boy!' he yelled.

'What happened with Nella?' asked Olivia, concerned.

'Nella bit me!' exclaimed Nathan. 'It's not bleeding, she has sharp teeth though, it really hurt.'

Mick laughed sympathetically. 'Yeah sorry, she was probably playing, she bites me all the time.'

'Allen, you really need to be more welcoming to our guests' scolded Petra, looking at him sternly.

Allen, shaking in Nathan's arms, didn't even register the words. He was too worried about Nella.

As the shock of what had just happened wore off, Tessa burst out into tears.

'Oh dear,' said Olivia, as she leant over to give her a hug. 'It's alright Tess, Nella is fine, everything's going to be okay. Allen is just trying to be the boss dog.'

'Not off to the best start though,' commented Nathan. He looked down at Allen in his arms with a worried frown on his face. 'I think we need to do some more training with you Allen, you're becoming far too dominant.'

'I have an idea,' said Olivia excitedly, looking at Nathan. 'We've just booked Nella in at our vet clinic's puppy school. You should book in for the same class!'

'Oh shoot,' replied Petra. 'We should have thought of this before! We already paid for Allen's puppy school classes. He's starting next week at Bark Stoppers. It has really good reviews!'

Canine Anxiety

As you are probably starting to notice, Allen and Nella tend to get anxious about things pretty easily. We see Nella experiencing anxiety at Allen's house, because she couldn't predict what was going to happen, and was worried it might be something bad. Nella was also feeling a similar anxiety at home, particularly when she was left on her own. However, even once her family returned, she still couldn't calm down. Not all dogs have this problem, so it was bad luck that both Allen and Nella are affected.

Anxiety is an uncomfortable (negative) emotion that all mammals can feel, and for good reason. It's designed to protect us. Anxiety is the brain's way of trying to ensure that the future versions of ourselves avoid danger and feel happy and content. This can be done by acting to minimise the bad outcomes and maximising the good outcomes. As you may have noticed, when you're worried about something, it's always related to something *uncertain* that might happen in the future. This is different to fear, which we feel in response to something that's *actually present* at that moment. However, these two emotions are often felt together. Because anxiety is a feeling of worry about what might happen in the future, it's often triggered by unfamiliar situations. Conversely, stable and predictable situations help to ease anxiety.

Coping with anxiety

Anxiety isn't a comfortable feeling, and it leads to many unwanted behaviours in our dogs. When speaking to clients, I like to ask them about what goes on at home when they're having a quiet day hanging out with the family. In many cases, they describe their dog doing a range of behaviours that they do not realise are influenced by anxiety. These might be behaviours that clearly show the dog is stressed out, and can include things like destructive behaviour, barking or escaping. However, in many cases the dog will use 'normal' behaviours as an anxiety coping mechanism. By actively doing something, the dog's mind is distracted from their uncomfortable feelings of worry. In fact, this is similar to how people can use mindfulness techniques or activities (like watching television) to help manage their own anxiety. The anxiety-coping behaviours we see in dogs are often happening more frequently or intensely than would be expected if the dog was relaxed. These behaviours are also difficult to stop, as there is a strong emotional motivation behind them. Doing nothing is not an option when you are in a frantic state of mind.

One way that Nella deals with her anxiety is by interacting with her people. This is an enjoyable activity that keeps her mind busy, preventing her from focusing on things that might worry her. While her interactions with family help Nella feel better, the way in which they respond unfortunately makes things worse. Because they're so inconsistent with the way they react to her demands for interaction, she can't predict the outcome. This lack of consistency is a recipe for anxiety. For example, when she jumps up on them, she doesn't know if she will be petted or scolded. However, Nella continues to jump up because sometimes she is rewarded. The positive outcomes of jumping up outweigh the negative outcomes.

When people see a dog panting and jumping up at people, they often tell me that the dog is 'excited'—maybe because it likes people. As we see with Nella, there is indeed some truth to this, but it is only half the story. As explained earlier, different emotions can be occurring at the same time. So, in this case Nella is both excited and anxious. Most people are familiar with this feeling. It's often described as a nervous excitement. The kind of feeling you might get before a first date or a holiday overseas. Some dogs that have serious anxiety issues are misunderstood by their owners, who believe they are not anxious, but 'excited all the time'. However, this would be a very strange phenomenon. Could you imagine the feeling of winning the lottery every day? You might be very excited the first few days, but soon enough you'd get used to it. These dogs that *appear* to be constantly over-excited never actually get over their excitement. This is a clear sign that there is more to the picture—anxiety is to blame.

The positive side of dog anxiety (for us)

While canine anxiety sounds like a horrible affliction, this isn't always the case from our point of view as owners. For example, an anxious dog is more likely to notice a stranger approaching the house, which is useful if you want them to guard your property. Although Nathan and Petra do not appreciate Allen doing this, some people really value a dog that guards their house. In dogs with excessive anxiety, it can become a major part of their personality. When I talk to clients with dogs that have anxiety problems, they often love them just as much as everyone else loves their dogs, if not more. Some of their anxiety-driven behaviours can be very well received. They are seen as a part of their personality. Like when a dog follows their owner around more than usual, or snuggles into them for cuddles all the time, or constantly wants to play. Some people really like dogs that have an anxious need to be constantly tended to. Unfortunately, this can create a conflict of interest for the owner. If their dog becomes less anxious, it might become more independent and less playful and needy. Some people really don't like seeing this, even though their dog is feeling happier.

The role of unpredictability in anxiety

By this stage in the book, we can see that Nella spends a lot of time feeling anxious. You might also have noticed that she interacts with the people or animals in the world around her, she has unpredictable and inconsistent experiences. Sometimes good things happen, and sometimes bad things happen, and she can't figure out how to predict what the outcome will be. Fixing this problem is harder than it sounds, because dogs don't think like we do. People naturally tell each other what's going to happen, and this can help a lot with our anxiety. We can also read signs, we study scenarios, and have control over our own life to set things up so we know what will happen. Dogs obviously can't do any of this. One of the main ways that a dog learns what's going to happen to them is by experience. If every day is the same, they can predict what's going to happen next.

Imagine a day in the life of a dog. They wake up at sunrise, then they go for a walk, then they get fed, then they stay at home alone while you work, then you return before sundown, then they play with you for a while, then you feed them, then they sit on the couch with you until bedtime. If this sequence of events happens in the same order and at the same times each day, it gets very predictable. This consistent daily routine is easy to understand, but many dogs have to cope with a routine that is random and chaotic. If they are used to a regular routine, and then that routine is suddenly changed, they can also have a lot of difficulty coping. For example, if you only occasionally go out in the evenings and leave your dog alone, it can be quite difficult for them to deal with. Not only are things out of routine, but they could also be mourning the loss of a night spent on the couch next to you.

Other than routines, dogs also experience unpredictability in social experiences. This can obviously happen when they meet different dogs at the park which behave in different ways, but also when they interact with people too. When Nella was jumping up at her people in this chapter, she really struggled to make sense of the large variety of responses she received. When a person responds to a dog in different ways with little consistency, it can be very confusing. This is particularly true when a dog initiates the interaction with a person; they seem to really struggle if the reaction they get is hard for them to predict. Understanding one person can be tricky for a dog, but when they have to interact with lots of different people it can be even harder. Dogs don't understand human behaviour very well to begin with, so if we all behave differently to them and change our behaviours depending on our moods it can be impossible for them to keep up with!

CHAPTER FIVE

First Day Of School

Nathan and Petra looked at each other with worried expressions. It was Allen's first day at puppy school and things were not off to a good start. When Petra was carrying Allen into the class, he growled at one of the other owners when they tried to pat him. Everyone was sitting on white plastic chairs that had been arranged in a large circle around the room. Allen was sitting in Petra's lap, trembling with terror as he watched the activity around him. Strange people and dogs were sitting everywhere he looked, and they represented a plethora of likely threats.

One particular dog on the opposite side of the circle required extra close monitoring. She was a tan-coloured mastiff puppy, with oversized legs and a boisterous nature. She was tugging at her leash to get to the other dogs and people, barking in frustration at being restrained. As the instructor was making her final preparations, the puppy looked over at Allen with her large brown droopy eyes. After pausing briefly, she suddenly jumped in his direction, only to be pulled back by the leash once more.

Frightened by the sudden movement, Allen let out two sharp barks as a warning. A tall woman with blonde hair had been sitting next to Petra, and the sudden noise caused her to look closer at Allen.

'Your one sure has a loud bark for its size!' she said to Petra as she tilted her head to the side.

Petra looked over, smiling. 'Yeah, I think he has small dog syndrome!'

Before the woman could reply, the class instructor raised her voice and started the session.

'Okay folks, welcome to week 1 of puppy school! My name is Donna, and I will be your instructor today. We will get to introductions in a moment, but firstly, does anyone know why puppy school is so important?'

Donna looked around the room expectantly at her audience, but no-one said a thing. Now pacing back and forth as she spoke, Donna continued.

'The reason puppy school is so important, is that puppies need socialisation! They need to meet as many other dogs and people as they can. Does anyone know why?'

The woman sitting next to Petra put up her hand.

'Is it so they don't become aggressive?' she asked.

Donna smiled encouragingly. 'Correct! Puppies that aren't socialised become aggressive, so it's a good thing you all came here today.

'Now, before we start our first socialisation session, how about we go around and introduce everyone... Let's start with you, what's your name and who do you have there?'

Donna was looking at an elderly man sitting to the right of Nathan, with a scruffy brown dog sitting calmly next to his feet.

'Joseph's the name, and this little furball is called Reggie,' he replied in a raspy voice.

As Donna bent down, Reggie looked up at her as he slowly walked forwards. His tail frantically shook from side to side as a sign of his willingness to interact.

'What a beautiful puppy, and may I ask what breed he is?' she asked.

Joseph chuckled. 'We're not too sure,' he answered. 'The vet thinks he might be a terrier crossed with something.'

As Donna put her hand out and started stroking Reggie on the head, Allen watched intently. Reggie leant into Donna's hand and sat down, enjoying the feeling of her acrylic fingernails scratching along his back.

Then Donna turned her attention to Petra and Nathan. Standing up and walking towards Allen, she had her head tilted to the side and a wide grin on her face.

'And who do we have here?' she asked.

'This is Allen, that's Nathan, and I'm Petra' said Petra, smiling.

She was hiding it well, but Petra was almost as anxious as little Allen at this point. Worried that Donna might be about to reach in and possibly be bitten, she didn't know what to do. The scent of Petra's anxiety was palpable from Allen's perspective, and his heart was racing as he quivered in her arms. With his person being this anxious, Allen felt that his own feelings of anxiety must be well founded.

Donna reached in, oblivious to Allen's feelings and his subtle body language of fear. She stroked him on the head and down the side of his body as he turned his head away to look for a way to escape. Trapped in Petra's arms and feeling completely overwhelmed, Allen was too frightened to respond to Donna's incursion.

Relieved, Nathan smiled. 'Wow, he seems to really like you. He's not normally too fond of strangers!'

Petra's mood brightened too, she was glad to see Allen responding so well to Donna, due to his lack of aggression.

Donna chuckled knowingly.

'I've been doing this for 10 years now,' she commented. 'I've learnt a thing or two about how to approach a dog... Also, dachshunds are one of my favourites.'

As Donna moved on to the next puppy, Nathan and Petra exchanged approving looks with each other. As Donna continued, she introduced the room to Bambi, an apricot-coloured toy poodle owned by the lady to the left of Petra. This was followed by Chipper, a blue Staffordshire bull terrier owned by two well-dressed men. Then finally Pippy was introduced, the large tan mastiff puppy who was attending with two teenage boys and their mother.

Once the introductions were complete, Donna moved back to her section at the head of the circle.

'Okay, so I think it's about time we let these puppies start their socialisation! When you are ready, just take your puppy off its leash and put them on the floor.'

Joseph bent down and unclipped Reggie's leash from his collar. Reggie stood up and turned his head to look back up at him. Being new to the leash, he was completely unaware that he was now able to roam around the room should he wish, so he just stood there.

Petra slowly lowered Allen onto the floor, who immediately turned around and tried to jump back into her arms. Bambi was also placed on the floor next to him, but she was similarly inclined to find a way back into the safe lap of her owner too. When Chipper was unclipped from his leash, he immediately ran across the room to investigate Reggie.

As Pippy was released from her leash, she watched Chipper running past her and immediately chased after him. Her large legs and paws were too long for her body, giving her a clumsy-looking gait as she ran. Pippy was very excited to finally be able to play with some other dogs, but it was a nervous and frustrated excitement. This was the first time she had seen another dog in weeks. As Chipper stopped to sniff at Reggie, Pippy caught up to them. She pushed her nose between the two dogs, knocking them both back as she couldn't decide who to sniff first.

When Reggie was gently knocked backwards, he realised there was no longer a leash holding him in place. Curious to find the source of an interesting scent he could detect, Reggie put his nose to the ground and started to move along under the circle of chairs.

Chipper put his front paw up onto Pippy's back, testing her to see if they could start playing. Pippy rolled onto her back and started mischievously biting at his paws, while Chipper circled around her and tried to nip at her ears in return. They both enjoyed the playful tussle, and soon became the centre of attention in the room.

'There we go, that's what we like to see!' said Donna, smiling as she watched them play.

Allen was now sitting under Petra's chair, watching the exchange between Pippy and Chipper with wide-eyed disdain. From his point of view, he saw their playful behaviour as that of two dogs fighting for their life. He couldn't grasp the concept of playing with a dog that caused so many fearful emotions.

Meanwhile, Reggie had continued to make his way under the seats towards Allen, and was beneath Nathan's chair before Allen even spotted him. When Allen finally noticed Reggie, he was already staring back at Allen with his shaggy brown tail wagging furiously. Allen's heart jumped as a wave of fear swept over him. Allen moved a little backwards, his head down, looking at Reggie with an angled gaze. Reggie was naturally gifted at reading the body language of other dogs, and he immediately noticed that Allen wasn't displaying welcoming behaviour. Reggie responded by staying put and not approaching any closer. Wagging his tail slowly, Reggie lowered his gaze in appeasement and carefully backed away. As Allen realised that this dog wasn't going to invade his space, he calmed down a little. A few moments later, he was becoming curious about the brown dog. If it wasn't for everything else going on in the room, he might have considered taking a step closer.

On the other side of the circle, Pippy had moved on from her game with Chipper as she sought to explore the rest of the room. After spotting Allen and Reggie watching each other under the chairs, Pippy started running in their direction. Before Allen had time to react, Pippy had slid under the chair and was pushing her nose under his chest in a blundering attempt at a play bite. Allen was overcome with shock at the situation he now found himself in. Reacting on instinct, he snarled as he bit hard at Pippy, who yelped out in pain. Before Pippy could respond, Allen scuttled out into the centre of the room with his tail tucked under his bottom. Pippy, undeterred by the overly forceful bite, thought that chasing Allen seemed like a great game to play. She regained her footing and chased after him into the centre of the room. Allen waited, frozen as he cowered down on the spot. Pippy bowled Allen over and started trying to playfully bite at him again. Allen was so scared he lost control of his bladder as he bit at Pippy repeatedly in defence. Pippy cried out again and took a few steps back, this wasn't like the game she was expecting.

'Is this okay Donna?' asked Nathan, looking up at her. 'He seems a bit serious...'

'Oh, it's fine!' Donna interjected. 'They just need to sort it out, it's all part of socialisation.'

Allen, seeing Pippy had backed off a little, slowly slunk back towards Petra's chair. Pippy wasn't so interested in playing with Allen now, given the rather painful bites she had received, and soon her attention shifted to Bambi.

Bambi had been watching in shock as she saw Allen defending himself against Pippy, and was ready when Pippy approached her. She dodged Pippy's playful lunge and started running under the chairs, tail tucked between her legs. Pippy continued to chase her around a range of obstacles, trying to catch up to her, but Bambi was too agile to catch.

Under Petra's chair, Allen sat panting and quivering as Pippy continued to chase Bambi around the room. Petra put her hand down to stroke him.

'Good boy Allen, did you sort it out?' she asked gently.

Allen tried to jump up onto her lap again, but Petra didn't respond to his request. Being denied safety by Petra, he felt vulnerable. He was alone against these threats. His people were not his guardians, they would not protect him. It was up to him to defend himself.

A few minutes later, Donna called an end to the play session and started discussing obedience.

'So, I want everyone to hold the treat over their head and slowly move it backwards. Once your dog sits down you need to say "Yesssss," and give the treat straight away.'

Petra was excited by this task. She had already trained Allen to sit, and was eager to show off how accomplished he was. Nathan and Petra stood in front of Allen and held out the treat to him. However, Allen wasn't interested. Given the ordeal he had just been through, he was much more preoccupied with monitoring the other people and dogs. His stomach was knotted with anxiety and food was the last thing on his mind.

Nathan put the treat right in front of Allen's nose. 'Allen, sit!'

Allen didn't even sniff at the food. A part of him did register that the treat was there, but his appetite was non-existent.

Frustrated that Allen seemed to be ignoring him, Nathan tried a firmer tone.

'Sit down, sit Allen!'

As Donna walked over to see how they were going, Petra felt herself flushing with embarrassment. She glanced at Donna sheepishly.

'He's normally great at home, sits for everything, but he just won't do it here.'

Donna took a treat out of her pouch.

'Okay, let's see if I can try' she said confidently. Putting the treat towards Allen and saying 'sit', Donna watched as Allen stared at her wide-eyed, and moved a step away from her.

'I think he doesn't like these treats; they aren't high enough in value. Maybe next time you should bring some treats from home that you know he likes?' suggested Donna.

Petra smiled, relieved. 'Oh, that makes sense, we don't use these ones at home. We'll bring his favourite treats next time.'

Shortly after, Donna addressed the class.

'Okay everyone, back to your seats. Now we are going to talk about some common issues you might be facing with your new puppy!'

Petra picked up Allen to put him back on her lap, but did so awkwardly, straining his spine. With all the adrenaline circulating through his veins, Allen didn't even notice the discomfort. Relieved that he was now in the relative safety of his person's lap, he did a body shake. His ears flapped side to side as he felt himself calm down ever so slightly.

Donna started with advice on toilet training, however Petra and Nathan were too embarrassed to confess their problems. Given the recent failure at demonstrating his ability to sit, they didn't want to seem like bad owners. The toilet training advice was followed by a discussion on biting.

'You need to teach them that it's naughty, or else how will they know not to do it?' said Donna. 'If your puppy bites you, you should say "Ouch" in a high-pitched voice, because this is how dogs communicate in the wild. If they don't respond to that, then you should give them a little tap on the nose just to let them know they've been badly behaved.'

Nathan couldn't hold back his curiosity any longer. Sitting up straight, he interjected with a question.

'But what about barking? Allen sometimes barks at us, or at other dogs.'

Donna sighed knowingly. 'Yes, a very common problem, but the principles are the same! You need to let them know they are behaving badly, so you should say "Uh uh uhh" to Allen in a firm voice.'

Nathan nodded again. 'Yeah, makes sense, I think we need to do that more consistently.'

Donna continued. 'There will be lots of behaviours like this we need to correct. Another common one is jumping up at your legs. This behaviour might be cute when they are a puppy, but once they are older it can be a real problem, especially for larger dogs, like you Pippy.'

Donna smiled at Pippy who was pulling at her leash to get towards Chipper. Donna sat back down on her seat and explained.

'So, if Pippy was jumping up at me now, I would say "Uh uh uh" and push her back down, that way she knows she shouldn't be doing that. If this didn't work, I would also raise my knee up to knock her back as she jumps into me. This way she'll soon learn not to bother trying…'

Donna watched approvingly as Pippy was pushed back down off her owner's lap as they scolded her. Pippy looked back up at them confused, but didn't try to jump up again.

'Good,' she commented. 'So now it's time for our second puppy play session of the night! Don't worry though, it's not the last one. There will be one more at the end as well.'

* * *

Olivia, Mick and Tessa were sitting down in the waiting room of their vet clinic. It was after-hours, the reception door was locked, and it was dark outside. Nella was sitting by Mick's feet. There were four other puppies in the room, with their owners sitting down in wooden chairs arranged in a wide circle. Nella was feeling nervous, despite her fond memories of this place. She remembered meeting Ava, and getting lots of yummy treats. When Nella sniffed at the air, she could tell that Ava had been here recently. However, this time she was nowhere to be seen. Instead, there were lots of strange people sitting around her that she wasn't ready to trust yet. One person had tried to touch her while they were waiting, and she had been forced to go under the chair to escape them.

A young-looking lady with short brown hair made her way to the front of the circle and began talking to the room.

'Okay everyone, let's get started! Welcome to your first day of puppy school, my name is Sarah. I am one of the vet nurses here, but for the last few years I've also been running the puppy school.

'So, today we will be talking about any problems you might be having with your puppies at home. These problems might include toilet training, biting, jumping up, and other things like that...'

Sarah looked around the room as people were nodding along, and continued. 'But first, we need to have some introductions to all of your puppies!'

Going around the circle, Sarah chatted with each of the owners as she introduced them. There was Benny the golden retriever, Tiffany the miniature schnauzer, a pug called Boston, and a small white fluffy dog named Cookie. Tessa couldn't stop smiling. She was very excited to be surrounded by so many puppies, and struggled to stay still while Sarah was talking. Mick was soon forced to hold Tessa on his lap, as she kept climbing off her chair to get closer to the other dogs. Meanwhile, Nella sat under the chair, softly panting and leaning into Mick's legs.

While introducing them, Sarah squatted down in front of Nella as she was talking. She put her hand out towards Nella, but she shied away. Sarah smiled as she pulled her hand back away, and proceeded to explain the reaction.

'So, Nella is telling me that she doesn't want me to touch her right now. But that's okay! Puppies need time and space to adapt to new things. They should never be forced into it.'

'Yeah, she's like that with new people. She's a different dog at home!' replied Olivia in agreement.

Tessa held up her hand. 'At home she always loves pats and hugs too,' she added.

Sarah giggled, before replying. 'Good! She sounds like a wonderful puppy.'

Nella watched Sarah as she moved onto the next puppy, feeling conflicted. She was relieved that Sarah had moved on, but at the same time liked the way she smelled. Nella's tail wagged ever so slightly, as she felt the urge to interact in some way. Then she noticed the golden retriever puppy that Sarah was now talking to. Feeling the urge to try and play with it, she stood up and pulled forward, only to feel the leash pull back against her neck.

Once the introductions were over, Sarah sat back down at the head of the circle and addressed the group.

'So, now that we know everyone, we're going to try letting some of the puppies interact for a little bit...'

Tessa jumped back down off Mick's lap and bounced up and down, smiling at Sarah.

'I know the dogs might be itching to play,' continued Sarah. 'But it's important that everyone understands a few things first. To start us off, does anyone know what socialisation is?'

She looked around the room, waiting until one of the two ladies with the pug spoke up.

'It's when dogs play with each other,' she said with a smile on her face.

'Good!' said Sarah, 'but it's actually even more than that! It's not just learning to play with other dogs. Socialisation is also about learning to interact with people too, and all the sounds and objects in their world around them.

'However, not all socialisation is good! Most people don't think about this, but it's really important. Just providing socialisation is not much use if it's no fun for the dog!

'Just imagine if you were a kid at school and everyone you met was a bully and you never made friends. You might be socialised at school, but you could end up being very antisocial!'

There were a few confused looks around the room, so Sarah continued.

'So, from the puppy's perspective, what if they have a fearful and stressful experience interacting with a new person or dog? Do you think that would help them to be comfortable with that experience in the future?

'You would need lots of other positive happy experiences to outweigh that one bad impression, don't you think?'

Mick and Olivia nodded as they glanced at each other, both having traded stories of being bullied at school.

'Great!' continued Sarah. 'So, keeping that in mind, we'll be trying to get the puppies to interact, as long as they're enjoying it.

'However, if your puppy learns to play roughly with every dog it meets on the street, that's a sure way for them to end up getting bitten!

'So, if it looks like they're playing a bit too rough, I'll be breaking them up. We only want each puppy to get the level of interaction that they're comfortable with.'

Sarah looked around the room and started pointing at the dogs one by one.

'See Nella is sitting down leaning into Mick's legs?' said Sarah, pointing at Nella. 'Well, she might want to take a bit of time to start exploring today. Compare that to Benny who's pulling at his leash and can't wait to meet everyone.'

Benny was panting with nervous excitement as he watched the other dogs, his golden tail swishing slowly from side to side.

'Now look at Boston, hiding under the chair and peeking out,' said Sarah, pointing at Boston. 'He could get quite frightened if another dog ran under there to try and play with him. So, we can't just let them all play in a free-for-all. I'll be picking specific puppies to play with each other. To start with, can we please have Nella and Benny let off their leashes now?'

Tessa squealed with excitement as Olivia unclipped Nella's leash and pushed her away from them into the centre of the room. Once Benny was unclipped, he ignored Nella and immediately ran over to Sarah, wagging his tail and jumping up at her.

'Don't you want to play with the other dogs, Benny?' asked Sarah, as she bent down to give him a chest rub.

As Nella saw Benny running, she stood up. Forgetting about all the strange people in the room, she started walking over to Benny. While he was sniffing at Sarah's feet, Nella gently put one of her large paws on his back. Benny turned around to see Nella nearly on top of him, and immediately started trying to sniff at her bottom. Nella lay down and rolled on to her back as she gently bit at Benny's back legs. Benny, unconcerned, continued sniffing at her bottom for a few more moments before reacting. Then, with an exaggerated exuberance, he quickly turned back around and stood over the top of her. As he was gently biting at her chest, Nella rolled over and then stood back up. This caused Benny to fall on his back, where he stayed as Nella took her turn being on top.

'Wonderful play!' exclaimed Sarah. 'See how they are both taking turns lying down? They're both taking turns giving each other an advantage in the game. That's a sign they're really enjoying it!'

Everyone in the room was watching the interaction intently, smiling or laughing as the two puppies tussled.

'Okay, it's obviously lovely to watch them have fun,' said Sarah. 'But remember that most dogs aren't comfortable doing this kind of play with other dogs they have just met. Would you like it if you were walking along the street and someone you didn't know tackled you for fun? They might think they're playing, but you might end up screaming at them!'

There were various nods from the people around the room.

'Okay,' said Sarah. 'We will split these two up now and let some other puppies take a turn. Benny and Nella can go back on leash, and let's try Boston and Cookie next!'

Boston and Cookie didn't pay each other much attention. They spent most of their time sniffing at the floor and trying to interact with all the people sitting on chairs. Nella sat watching excitedly, hoping one of them would come over so she could play with it. When Boston the pug did come within distance, Nella tried a playful nip at his foot. Boston jumped backwards and moved on to the next person, leaving Nella quite frustrated. She barked and pulled on the leash.

'Now Nella, you have to understand he doesn't want to play right now,' said Sarah in a firm but friendly voice. 'Could you try distracting her with a treat, Olivia?'

Olivia grabbed a treat from her bag and held it near Nella's head, but she wasn't paying it any attention.

'Just move the treat so it's right in front of her nose Olivia, she hasn't noticed it,' said Sarah.

As Olivia moved the treat closer to Nella's nose, she finally paid it attention. She took the food into her mouth and quickly swallowed it without thinking. The treat tasted great, some kind of meat flavour. Nella turned her attention away from Boston and onto Olivia, hoping for a second helping. Nella was starting to feel a little better now, she had been in this room for half an hour by this stage, and nothing horrible had happened. Even better, she had enjoyed playing with Benny and now she was getting treats!

Soon the puppy playtime had finished, and everyone was listening to Sarah speak again.

'So, I noticed that a few of the puppies today have been jumping up at people's laps.'

Sarah was looking at Nella as she spoke, who was at that time standing with her front paws on Olivia's lap while trying to lick at Tessa's face as she stroked her.

'Is anyone having a problem with their puppy jumping up too much?' asked Sarah.

'Yes!' screamed Tessa, as a few of the other owners chimed in as well, adding their own concerns.

'It is very cute,' said Sarah as she laughed. 'But it hurts when they accidentally scratch you, they might knock you over, and it's not a good behaviour for them to show to everyone they meet.' Sarah looked back at Nella again. 'It's extra important for big dogs too, as when they are older, they could do some serious accidental damage!'

Olivia and Mick exchanged concerned looks, nodding at one another.

'Listen to this bit Tess, it's important' whispered Mick in Tessa's ear.

Sarah continued. 'So, the best way to stop a dog from jumping up when you don't want them to, is to stop rewarding the behaviour! The reason they are doing it is because they're getting the things they want by jumping up. Every time they get rewarded, they learn to do it more. Does anyone know how a dog might get rewarded for jumping up?'

'Giving them a pat?' said Tessa as she raised her hand.

'Yes, very good!' encouraged Sarah. 'And other things might include treats, getting on your lap, asking to go outside or on a walk. Even just having you give them attention and talking to them can be rewarding.'

At this point, Nella put her front legs back up onto Mick's lap and pawed at his arm, while panting with nervous excitement. She was seeking direction, unsure of what was happening. It was very strange to Nella that all these unknown dogs were kept apart from her, she really needed to meet them all. She needed to do something, sitting still was not a good way to deal with her nervous energy.

'There are lots of good reasons why a dog might need to jump up at a person,' continued Sarah as she glanced back at Nella. 'Your dog should be allowed to get your attention to ask for things, they need to be able to communicate with us. But the only problem is that they shouldn't be jumping up to do this! It's much better if you teach them to sit or drop as the way to ask for things.'

There was more agreement from the group.

'So, how might you stop reinforcing this behaviour of jumping up then?' she asked.

'I normally just say "No" in a firm voice. Seems to work pretty well,' said the young man holding Benny's leash.

Sarah paused, looking at Benny sitting quietly while enjoying a scratch behind his ear.

'Okay, I guess it might work for Benny, but he seems like a pretty calm dog,' responded Sarah. 'I don't think that would work for *every* dog, especially if they really desperately need the thing they are jumping up for!'

Mick sheepishly put up his hand and interjected. 'I have to say, we have been trying the whole saying "No" thing, and it's not really working.'

'It's okay,' said Sarah, smiling. 'There are better ways to communicate with our dogs than saying the "n" word! There are other ways that work well for every dog, and we don't have to tell them off either!

'Everyone needs to ignore their dog while they are jumping up, turn away, pretend they are invisible. Then, whenever they have all four paws on the floor again, give them what they want.

'You might pat them, pick them up, play with them. I like to call this game "fore-paws on the floor".

'Soon they learn that good things only happen when they are sitting or standing, and that nothing good appears when they jump up!'

Mick frowned, thinking to himself before saying, 'But how come when I push her back down, she doesn't learn she's not supposed to do it?'

'She probably thinks it's a game,' responded Sarah. 'Also, it's still giving her attention and interaction, so she is still getting what she wants, so better just to ignore her until she gets down.'

'Okay,' agreed Mick, as he started to understand. 'But what about when she's biting at Tessa's ankles? We can't really ignore that!'

'Yeah, when I'm running, she bites my ankles—it hurts,' added Tessa with a frown on her face.

'Tessa,' said Sarah, sighing. 'I'm sorry she's doing that to you, it's not nice at all. But she isn't trying to be naughty, she probably just wants to play.

'Puppies have to play and bite at everything around them, it's just how they are made. The trick is to redirect that behaviour onto something more appropriate than your shoes. So next time she does that, you need to stop running, okay?'

Tessa nodded her head slowly, with a very serious look on her face.

'Then you might like to get a toy for her,' continued Sarah. 'And move it around to make it look exciting. Hopefully she will grab onto it. Mum and dad also need to be around to help supervise this too. Do you think you can do that?'

Tessa nodded again, now smiling with a hopeful look on her face.

'Olivia, if you are both too busy to supervise their play at that moment, best to keep Tessa and Nella separated if it's happening too much, okay?' added Sarah.

'Yeah, we can do that,' responded Olivia confidently. 'They aren't alone together much anyway.'

The Good Dog Stereotype

When someone decides to get a puppy, they normally have an idea about the kind of dog they would like. This includes how it will look, what its needs might be, and how it will behave. Different people look for different things in their dogs, which seems pretty obvious. Not everyone is the same; we all have our own preferences. However, when people think about dogs, they often don't consider that they might also have their own preferences.

Many people have the idea of what I like to call the 'stereotypical dog'. This imaginary dog loves affection from people, and enjoys playing with other dogs. People also believe that the stereotypical dog 'needs' to have affection from people and to play with other dogs for it to be happy. These preferences are reinforced in the stories, videos and media that we see. There isn't much thought given to the possibility that not all dogs will enjoy these things. The idea that a dog wouldn't want to roll around, wrestling with another dog in a lush field of grass seems impossible. Similarly, the thought that being stroked by a person might feel uncomfortable for some dogs isn't normally considered. People seem to have a very hard time letting go of these stereotypes.

As we saw in this chapter, everyone loves to see puppies chasing or play-wrestling with each other. Many people are willing to go to extreme lengths to try and socialise their puppy in a way that will get them to behave this way with other dogs. I also believe that this is the reason that so many people stand around in groups at dog parks waiting for their dogs to play. However, just as not all people love socialising at parties with strangers, many dogs don't like socialising with unfamiliar dogs. In some cases, the 'unfriendly' dog had a bad social experience that explains their behaviour. In other cases, a lack of socialisation is blamed. Sometimes no cause can be found. But does that really matter? Think of anything that you aren't too fond of: the chances are that you had a few bad experiences too. These societal expectations of what a dog 'likes' are responsible for a lot of uncomfortable situations for many dogs.

So how do we know then if a dog likes something? The easiest way is to ask them. For example, when Nella was in her puppy class and Boston the pug came up to her, she clearly wanted to play. However, Boston walked away and ignored her because he wasn't interested. Holding one dog still and allowing the other to choose whether to play is a simple way of testing consent from the dog that isn't being held.

Habitual rituals

Now that we have dispensed with the notion that a 'good' dog has to enjoy certain activities, we can talk about how to get a dog to have good manners. No matter what a dog likes or dislikes, we need them to behave a certain way if they are to fit in comfortably with the human social structure. The list of manners includes toileting in the appropriate location, only chewing appropriate objects, refraining from jumping up, and to not bite people when playing, to name a few. The amount of advice, tips and tricks available to teach owners how to train these manners is endless. As discussed in the first chapter, some people incorrectly believe that the dog needs to behave this way through a moral understanding of doing good. Thankfully, the most common advice you will find focuses on rewarding your dog for performing the correct behaviours. Unfortunately, as Allen has experienced, this is not always the case.

There is a fundamental principle that often gets ignored when teaching a dog to have good manners. This is the idea of focusing on forming habits. If a dog (or a person for that matter) is in a habit of doing things in a certain way, they tend to continue behaving that way in the future. This behavioural inertia happens because changing the way you have always done something requires a lot of conscious thought and effort. Obviously, you still need to shape the dog's behaviour in the first place to form these habits. However, the benefit of thinking this way is that you realise your techniques don't have to be feasible in the long term. If you can somehow trick your dog into behaving the *right* way, and they don't have a negative experience, and you keep up the ruse, eventually it will stick. They will behave that way just because it's how they always did it. This is why dogs that never learned to jump up at people as a puppy tend to never have this problem as an adult.

Having an obedient dog

When most people think about what an 'obedient' dog is, they imagine a dog that will quickly respond to commands without so much as a treat for reward. I often hear of owners complaining that their dog will only ever sit when they have a treat, and never come when called. They are frustrated by their lack of control over their dog's behaviour. In Petra's case, she felt embarrassment at Allen's lack of obedience. On the other hand, owners that do have obedient dogs get a lot of satisfaction out of seeing their dog respond to their every command. It's almost as though the dog has a remote control, they have become half-dog, half-robot. When I ask people why a dog should do as we say, I get a lot of different answers, but it often comes back to the idea of a dog being 'good' or 'well behaved'.

Personally, I find this confusing; I don't know why people expect their dogs to do things when there is nothing in it for them. Perhaps they hope that their dog loves them so much that the idea of instantly responding to a command makes them happy for pleasing their 'master'?

Personally, I think the idea of having an 'obedient dog' is another example of where society's expectations of dogs are unfair. If you think your dog owes you a debt for looking after them, you're kidding yourself—they aren't smart enough to understand that. They just don't think that way. If people love their dogs so much and they are a 'part of the family,' then why are they so keen on having them do things when there isn't anything in it for them? If someone complains that their dog doesn't listen to their commands, I respond by saying, 'But why should they? What do they get out of it?' If you aren't giving them a treat, or something else they want, then it makes perfect sense to me why they couldn't be bothered. Unfortunately, many people respond to their dog's 'disobedience' by raising their voice. What I find even more crazy, is that in many cases they do this only seconds after they issued their first 'command.' The dog isn't even given five seconds to consider what they want to do!

When I train a dog, I don't command them to do anything. I offer them a trade. If I want the dog to sit, I hold out a treat and ask them, 'Would you like to sit?' If they understand what I am saying, but they still don't sit, that's okay by me. Obviously, the treat wasn't worth them sitting for! If you asked me to get up off my seat for one peanut, I would probably say 'No' as well. What often frustrates owners when they see me do this, is that I just wait patiently as their dog stands there staring at me blankly. They often feel bad for having a 'disobedient' dog. After about 15 seconds, at the stage where most owners would have repeated the 'Sit' multiple times loudly, something magical often happens. The dog sits. They just needed a bit more time to decide if it was worth it. As soon as the dog sits, I give them the treat immediately. Most owners are so focused on having an obedient dog that instantly obeys their commands that they didn't even realise their dog could remember the word 'Sit' for more than three seconds. The dog doesn't always sit though, and that's okay. Obviously, what I'm offering in return just isn't worth it for them. I don't bother asking them more than a couple of times. The problem is that I don't have the right motivation for the dog—not that they are disobedient. In some cases, figuring out why we can't entice a dog to sit can be tricky, but one common example is that they are too anxious and have lost their appetite. This was the case with Allen at puppy school, however the people around him couldn't see it.

Once people abandon the idea of wanting their dog to be 'obedient,' they stop trying to force the dog to do things it doesn't want to do. Rather, they learn to motivate the dog to want the same things they want. This leads to much calmer and more relaxed training sessions, with much less frustration on both sides. One consequence of training a dog like this is that they will quickly learn that when you ask them to do something, it's almost always in their best interests. This means that they will start to do things for free, but it won't last forever if you don't keep rewarding them. Personally, if my dog does something I asked that I know they *didn't* want to do, I feel really bad if I don't *pay* them for it. It doesn't matter if they would do it for free, I feel like they deserve a reward anyway.

CHAPTER SIX

Venturing Out

Now that she was four months old, Nella was starting to look for jobs to do. She still hadn't figured out what her role in the house was. Sure, she liked how things were going, but it felt like something was lacking. Nella was sitting down on the rug, wagging her tail and looking up at Mick. It had taken a while to get her head around it, but jumping up just didn't work any more like it used to. People no longer played with her or stroked her when she jumped up onto them. However, if she sat down and looked at a person, they seemed to notice her more than before. Soon after sitting and looking at someone, they would talk to her and touch her, play with her or take her out to the toilet. She still got plenty of attention at other times too, but when Nella was asking for something, there was only one way. It was quite simple really—she had to sit down; that was how good things came to her.

'Good girl, Nella, that's some good sitting,' said Mick, giving her a quick scratch under her chin.

As she sat there watching him, Nella noticed Mick start to tie his shoelaces. Her heart sank, this wasn't a good sign. Nella knew he was getting ready to leave her. She had seen this routine before, he tied his shoelaces, got his keys from the table, then left out the front door. When she saw him get the keys from the table, Nella started to quietly pant from distress. Her mouth was just barely open, and she was breathing faster than normal, but no-one noticed. Mick turned off the lights and the television.

This was it; Nella was now sure he was going to leave. She started pacing and breathing heavier, her panting getting louder as she watched him. There was no chance of any food or games while her people were gone. The whole house looked different too, it was depressing, quiet. As far as Nella could tell, her role as the dog in her family hinged on being with them, all the time. She needed to be there for her people, to be around them.

As Mick walked down the hallway, there was a clicking noise as the room instantly changed from bright to dim. The only light remaining was from the morning sun peeking through the closed blinds. Nella was used to this effect now; as the humans in her house moved into and out of rooms, there was often a sudden change in light. As people entered rooms, lights would appear, and as they left, they disappeared; each time with a click.

With Olivia and Tessa already in the car, Mick walked out the front door and closed it behind him. Nella listened to Mick walk along the path away from the house, then ran into the next room to peek through the crack in the blinds. She watched Mick enter the car, which promptly drove away. Feeling her heart sink even lower, Nella raised her head into the air and howled in mourning. For a while, Nella paced around the house whining, looking at all the familiar toys and furniture. They had left her with a rope to chew on, and a piece of fresh rawhide. But she didn't have the appetite to eat the rawhide, nor the happiness to play with the toy. The house was so dark and quiet. She needed to chew something to relieve her anxiety, not to mention her gums were aching too.

When Nella wandered into Tessa's room, she saw her white puffy down-filled jacket on the floor. Nella walked up to the jacket curiously, and then took it into her mouth and dragged it into Tessa's bed. She relished the familiar smell of Tessa and the soft feeling of the jacket on her lips. The jacket felt intimate, almost like Tessa was there hugging her. Nella started to lick at the jacket, creating a wet patch in the fabric. Then she proceeded to bite into it and pull, feeling a satisfying vibration as the cloth ripped open. A small cloud of feathers puffed into the air, much to Nella's satisfaction. As she set to work pulling out the filling and tossing it onto the floor, it relieved her frustration at being separated from Tessa. Now she had a job to do, a task to keep her anxious mind occupied. Nella set to work, it was entertaining, enjoyable, satisfying and fulfilling all at once. Most importantly, she wasn't having those unpleasant feelings of being left alone. Before long, the job was done. Nella lay down in a pile of fluff, sighing as she closed her eyes and started to drift off into a snooze. It was not a restful sleep though, as she was still feeling very alone. She needed to keep alert for any sounds that might be a sign of her family returning.

* * *

Later that morning, Nella heard the front gate open. As she leapt down from Tessa's bed, another plume of feathers blew into the air. Nella sprinted down the stairs two at a time. When she saw her people coming in through the front door, her heart leapt. She whined and panted as she paced up and down the hallway with anxious excitement. Nella was very relieved. She needed to let her people know how much she had missed them. She had to show them how much she liked being around them. She needed to remind them how playful and friendly she could be.

'She's so happy to see us!' said Tessa, giggling.

Nella stood panting and whining as Tessa gave her a big hug around her body.

'Yes, she is!' agreed Mick. 'Want to go for a walk Nella? You're all up to date with your shots now so it's safe!'

'I don't think she even knows what a walk *is* yet,' commented Olivia as she beamed lovingly at Nella. 'I hope she likes it!'

No one noticed the feather that had managed to stick itself onto the side of Nella's face. As Olivia attached the leash, Nella's mind started racing. It was a lot for her to process. She knew the leash meant that something different was happening. Perhaps they were going into the car again? Nella did feel excited, but she was mostly nervous at what might be coming next. One thing she knew for sure was that wherever her people were going, she needed to be with them. As everyone walked back down the hallway, Nella followed them. When Mick opened the front door to the outside world, she gazed out in wonder, her heart racing.

After a brief pause, Nella ran forward to explore the garden. She knew her back yard well, but rarely got to visit the yard at the front of the house. However, Nella had become familiar with the layout from looking out the front window. The first thing that caught her attention was the smell of an animal. Her nose to the ground, she tracked it to its source—at the base of a small bush. It appeared to be from a cat as far as she could tell, and one she hadn't smelled before. It felt wonderful, inspecting the intricacies of the scent in all its dimensions. This cat was definitely a girl, and very receptive to mating. It had recently eaten something with fish and chicken. However, this animal smelled stressed, it was fighting some kind of battle or sickness.

After examining the smell for a few moments, Nella pulled ahead on the leash and rushed out the gate after Tessa. She was eager to explore the world. Her instincts were directing her to search the area around them and detect any food or animals she could find. However, she was being impeded by her collar that kept pulling back on her neck. She wanted to scout a large area around her but could only make it as far as the end of the leash. This was frustrating, and the only thing she could do was to pull ahead to gain as much distance as possible.

As Olivia was dragged along the path, past Mick and Tessa, the warm sun crept out from behind the clouds. Nella pulled into another smell—this time at the base of a rugged looking tree growing close to the road. The scent of urine swept through her nose, and she focused in to inspect the details. This was from a dog, a female, but not in season, and she was well fed and happy. Nella looked around and wondered where this other dog might be. Then she stepped forward and added a spot of her own urine on top of the other dog's scent. This behaviour was only natural for Nella, as she needed to mark out her territory.

Nella's understanding of her home territory was based on her instincts as a dog. A territory should be large, at least as far as you can see, she had no reason to think otherwise. Her house was a small place in the very centre of her territory, only the walls and fences prevented her from going any further. Now that she was on a walk, she could finally explore further. She trusted her people, they wouldn't take her off their own territory, that would be very dangerous. As she sniffed the scent of yet another dog on the pavement, Nella felt it was strange to be living in the same territory as these other dogs she could smell, even though she had never met them.

Nella pulled ahead once more to try and scout ahead, only to feel the collar lurch back on her neck yet again. She leant her whole body into the collar, straining down the street until she caught the scent of another interesting smell. This time it seemed to be hidden somewhere in a large patch of grass. She put her nose to the ground and tried to locate the source. Nella wound her nose back and forward, noticing the scent slowly grow stronger as they meandered along. Once she found it, Nella sniffed in confusion. She struggled to understand all the smells at the base of the tuft of grass under her nose. This was certainly dog urine, but from many different dogs! There were boys, girls, adults, puppies, some scents fresh, others stale—a whole community in one spot. It was hard to tell which parts of the smell belonged to which dog. Someone had been eating chicken recently, she knew that smell from home, and some other foods too that smelled delicious, but she couldn't identify them. Nella wondered where all these dogs could be that she couldn't see. Instinctively, she leant forward to add a few drops of her own scent to the mix. This was her territory too, after all.

Mick, Olivia and Tessa were besotted by Nella. Just watching her do the little things in life tugged on their heartstrings in a way that had brought them to tears on more than one occasion. As she sniffed at the various things on her walk, they were fixated on her, smiling and talking as they tried to imagine what she must be thinking or what she might like. When she veered too close to the road, Mick attempted to lure her back onto the path.

'Nella! Good dog, come here, come on girl,' said Mick in an encouraging voice.

Mick was now a familiar sight and smell for Nella, and she had learned to associate him with feelings of comfort, safety, excitement and companionship. These emotions usually led Nella to follow him whenever she could. As Mick called, her focus shifted from the invigorating scent of rabbit poo, and firmly onto him. She couldn't contain her eagerness to interact, and her whole body waggled from side to side as she ran clumsily towards him. The discomfort of her collar that had been nagging at her was now forgotten.

Together, the family ran two houses further along the street to where a small local park appeared. As they turned a corner to enter the park, Nella stopped to look around. She saw an open field of grass lined with tall eucalyptus trees, but the movement of another animal quickly caught her eye. A shaggy brown shape twice her size was walking away from her along the park trail. Nella was shocked at first, feeling unsure of how to proceed. As her people continued to walk forward, Nella's curiosity overcame her. She hurled herself towards the shape, eager to see what it was. As she ran towards it, Nella felt something suddenly pull her back by her neck. To her surprise, she flipped around and ended up facing back towards Olivia who was still holding her leash. Confused, Nella turned back around to look at the brown shaggy beast.

Olivia's arm had been tugged hard by Nella pulling on the leash, and she was still smiling from the surprise of it.

'Now, now Nella, calm down, you will hurt your neck doing that!' she said.

A few metres ahead, a young woman in her morning activewear was walking her brown shaggy dog on the end of his leash. She turned at the sound of Olivia's voice, and immediately noticed Nella with her oversized paws staring back at her. Mick looked up and locked eyes with her, smiling a greeting.

'Good morning there, I think our dog wants to say hello,' he said.

The lady smiled and crouched down, encouraging Nella to come towards her.

'Wow, what a cute puppy! How old is she?' asked the lady.

Nella ignored her and excitedly ran up towards the brown dog and launched towards him. He was a scruffy looking labradoodle who was well accustomed to the exuberant way of puppies. As Nella jumped into him again and again, he turned his head to avoid the potentially painful bites of her puppy teeth while slowly wagging his tail. Nella was in another world, enjoying the excitement of playing with this giant animal that she now knew was another dog. Every time she landed a bite into its fur, she felt the adrenaline of the game building inside her.

'Whoa there Nella, go easy!' said Mick.

Tessa laughed in delight and asked, 'What's his name?'

'Oh no it's fine,' replied the lady. 'Toby is great with puppies, he just loves them, he's always playing with them.'

Toby wasn't worried or fearful but would have preferred not to be bitten quite so much. A few moments later, the lady smiled and waved goodbye to Mick. Toby was happy to be moving once more.

After trying to follow Toby and lurching against the leash one more time, Nella turned and followed her family deeper into the park. Shortly after, she spotted another dog approaching behind them. It was a very spotty dalmatian being walked by a boy who looked young for his tall stature. Nella felt excitement overflowing inside her as she pulled towards the dog.

'A spotty dog, look mum!' screamed Tessa. Olivia stopped and turned to see.

'Should we let them play? Mine's friendly,' said the boy, smiling at Nella.

'Sure, she'd like that!' replied Mick.

Nella and the dalmatian immediately started to wrestle, gently mouthing at one another. They were even taking turns being on top and lying on their back. Their leads promptly became tangled together in all the boisterous movement. Nella was really enjoying herself. Being a similar size to the other dog, she could appreciate the challenge of the play without feeling outmatched. The dalmatian was also having fun as he loved to play roughly. However, he didn't trust Nella yet as he had only just met her, and she was too relentless for his liking. She wasn't taking his more subtle hints that she was being too rough. As a sign to get her to back off, he bit into her leg more forcefully than was appropriate. Nella yelped and stood up, shocked for a moment that she had been bitten so hard. She ran back a few steps before forgetting about the pain, deciding to jump back into the fray.

Olivia, concerned with the noise Nella had just made, untangled the leash and pulled her back from the dalmatian.

'It's okay, she's just playing,' said the boy, smiling.

'Yeah, she's okay, didn't stop her for long,' replied Mick as he chuckled.

'Anyway, we'd better go now, nice to meet you,' said the boy as he pulled his dog away.

'Bye-bye spotty dog!' said Tessa, waving as they went their separate ways.

Nella's mind was racing with a frantic excitement. This was such a great place. She felt so happy to be meeting all these other friendly dogs she shared her territory with. As her family continued to walk along the path once more, they found themselves smiling or laughing at Nella's exuberant manner. She was enthusiastically pulling towards every little thing that caught her attention.

Up ahead they could see a park bench next to the pathway, with an older lady sitting down admiring the view. She had a frail-looking golden retriever with a greying face, standing at the end of a long pink leash. Nella noticed the dog and started pulling towards it.

Soon the golden retriever noticed them too. She looked over at Nella bouncing on the end of her leash and froze. She held her ears back and stood completely still. Her head was still facing across the path at an angle to Nella, but her eyes were swivelled to the side and watching her.

'Mum, can she play with this dog too?' asked Tessa.

'I don't see why not—she needs the socialisation' replied Olivia. She smiled at the lady, who looked up at them and smiled back. 'Your dog's beautiful, what's her name?' asked Olivia.

'Mandy,' responded the lady.

Nella felt her nervous excitement rise again as she looked forward to meeting yet another dog. She pulled into the leash and dragged Olivia right up to Mandy, who was standing as still as a statue. Mandy, however, was not looking forward to meeting Nella. She was an old dog, and not as playful as she used to be. Her hips and shoulders had taken a toll over the years, and they were becoming quite painful if moved the wrong way.

Nella launched at Mandy, ready to wrestle once more. She pushed into Mandy's shoulder, trying to jump on top of her.

Mandy felt a stab of pain in her shoulder, as Nella pushed into the painful joint. As she was pushed to the side, she moved further back to try to get out of the way. Nella jumped forwards once more. Mandy's mind was suddenly overcome with the fear of more pain coming her way. She had no choice; she bared her teeth and bit forcefully at the side of Nella's face.

Nella squealed in pain, shocked at the response from this dog. She tucked her tail back under her body and cringed away from Mandy.

Mandy's owner yanked back on her leash, saying 'NO' in a gruff voice. Mandy whimpered softly again as the force of the leash pulled her stiff neck sideways suddenly.

'I don't know what's gotten into her! She doesn't normally bite,' said the lady, clearly shocked by the encounter.

Mick looked down at Nella to see a spot of blood on the concrete path.

'Oh no, she's bleeding!' exclaimed Mick. 'It's okay, she seems alright, but I think we'd better get this looked at.'

Tessa, seeing the blood, felt tears welling up in her eyes as she stood watching, shocked and numb.

Nella was feeling similarly numb. She didn't understand why this dog had bitten her so badly, and her lip was throbbing painfully. Her heart racing, she cringed down and moved towards Olivia for protection.

Tessa started crying aloud now, and Mick picked her up to comfort her.

'Okay let's go honey, it's okay, Nella will be fine, it's just a scratch.'

As they walked away, Nella staying close to their side now, the lady called out to them, a sorrowful look on her face.

'I'm terribly sorry, I hope your dog's okay, she's never done that before.'

On their way back home, Nella noticed yet another dog. But she didn't pull towards it this time. This dog was a small, white shaggy-looking thing, and after noticing Nella it let out a series of loud warning barks. After her last encounter, Nella realised that these barks might not be friendly, something about them felt confrontational. She wasn't sure what to think about other dogs now. She didn't realise they could hurt or threaten her like this, and for no reason at all. Her whole view of what other dogs meant to her had changed so suddenly.

Once back at home, with the family surrounding her, Nella felt safe once more. Olivia inspected her lip and saw there was a tear in the flesh, which had mostly stopped bleeding but looked very painful.

'We had better call the vet, Mickey,' she said, frowning.

'Already on it,' replied Mick, as he quickly pulled out his phone.

* * *

As Petra walked along the footpath, Allen was trying to walk alongside her, but the pace was awkward. With his short little legs, the speed she was walking at was halfway between a walk and a trot. He found himself constantly having to switch back and forward, either pulling ahead or lagging at the rear. Determined not to be left behind, he decided on a trot and pulled ahead once more. He felt himself come to the end of the leash and pulled into it. Then it happened again, he felt himself being choked as the chain tightened around his neck.

'No Allen, stop pulling!' said Petra firmly, as she pulled back on the leash.

Allen felt the chain tighten further as he was lurched backwards. He would have paid more attention to the fact he was being choked had he not been so stimulated by everything else around him. There were hints of so many smells that he could sense on the tip of his nose. Despite wanting to explore them all at once, he chose *one* to focus on. It was a sweet, fermented odour, located somewhere on the grass next to the pavement. Allen pulled towards the smell to get closer. As he located the source, he realised it was something he wanted to eat.

Petra looked down too late, as Allen was already licking the mess in the grass.

'Ewww, gross Allen!' wailed Petra in disgust, yanking him back again by his leash.

As they continued down the street, another dog came into view in the distance. The dog was a chocolate-coloured Labrador, and it was being walked by a young man. He had a scruffy face, brown hair and was dressed casually in a hoodie jumper and sneakers.

As they came closer, Allen started paying them more attention. His first instinct was to try to avoid this person and his dog. They looked pretty huge, and probably weren't friendly. Allen fell back behind Petra on his leash, trailing at her feet for a few steps. Then it dawned on Allen, he was actually trapped! He couldn't leave Petra's side and escape if things got bad, he was tethered to her by the leash. His heart racing, Allen continued to walk beside Petra, ready to attack if the strangers made a move in their direction.

The man smiled at Petra as he walked onto the grass, giving her and Allen some space.

Petra smiled back, and the man and his dog continued on past them.

Allen was thankful for the near miss. He looked back at them walking away to make sure they didn't turn around. As their shapes got smaller in the distance, Allen felt his racing heart slow back down to a more normal rhythm.

Petra thought to herself that the man walking his dog had a kind, friendly-looking face. With his large green eyes and a warm smile, she wouldn't have any reason to think otherwise.

As the man walked away, however, a tear rolled down his cheek. He had chronic depression, which he had been battling since his wife passed away three years ago. He found it hard to enjoy much of anything. He didn't particularly enjoy walking his dog either, and yet still went every day, sunshine or rain. He felt a strong sense of duty and responsibility to his dog, and despite feeling sad the entire walk, he appreciated the beauty of the world around him.

Petra often walked past people in crowded streets that were similarly sad or unhappy. She hardly ever noticed though, because people are good at hiding their emotions.

As she turned a corner and walked into the park, the fenced-in off-leash dog play area came into view. There were over a dozen dogs inside the fence, and most of them were just standing around like their owners.

Just as Petra had not understood the true feelings of the man she had passed in the street, she also did not understand what the dogs in the park were feeling.

'Look Allen—there are so many dogs having fun playing, and you get to join them!' said Petra, smiling as she looked down at Allen.

Petra wasn't alone though, none of the other people in the park understood how the dogs were feeling either.

Three of the dogs were actually having fun. There were two dogs playing together and one that had just got there and still hadn't smelled everything yet. The other twelve dogs were either anxious, worried, frustrated, or just waiting patiently. These other dogs mostly stood around just like their owners. Some of them would occasionally sniff at something out of interest or move out of the way of the more boisterous dog. The owners smiled as they watched the two dogs playing together. This was what they came here for, everyone wanted their dogs to play like this.

Petra opened the gate and tried to walk Allen into the play area, but he pulled back on the leash. Allen remembered he had been here before, and it wasn't a good experience.

'Come on Allen, time to play!' said Petra, rolling her eyes at him as she dragged him through the gate. Once inside, Petra closed the gate and unclipped Allen from his leash. As she started to walk towards the large group of people and dogs, Allen reluctantly followed behind her. He didn't like this place, and it felt safest to stick close to his person.

One of the other ladies standing around looked over at Petra and smiled.

'Nice day for a dog walk, isn't it,' she commented as she stood there, not walking at all.

'Yes, it's lovely,' replied Petra. 'And Allen needs more socialisation, so I figured this would be a pretty good way to get some.'

The lady talking to Petra had a German shorthaired pointer standing next to her. He was a large dog, with his shoulders as high as his owner's hips. He stood around in this enclosure almost every day, and he enjoyed being outside with his person. However, the walk to and from the enclosure were his favourite parts of the daily excursion. Sure, the enclosure had a few smells to check out and spots to mark, but he didn't feel it deserved the amount of time spent here. For the first five minutes after he arrived each day, he did enjoy exploring things. But then he just stood around and looked forward to leaving. He had currently been ready to leave for the last 20 minutes. Once he left, he knew he could enjoy exploring the pathways with his person until he got back home.

Petra looked down at Allen, and then over at the two dogs playing. All the other people were also watching the playing dogs, enjoying the spectacle and wishing their own dog would do the same.

Allen was panting and visibly trembling. He looked up at Petra hoping she could take him away.

'Allen, oh my gosh, you're literally shaking with excitement,' commented Petra. 'Go on then baby, go have a play with them.'

A golden cocker spaniel noticed Allen's arrival, and not recognising him, walked over to have a sniff.

Allen watched the strange dog coming for him. Without taking his eyes off it, he moved his body behind Petra's legs for protection.

The spaniel continued to walk right up to them. It proceeded to poke its head around Petra's legs to sniff at Allen's bottom, curious to know what he smelled like.

As the spaniel leaned in, Allen felt cornered. It wasn't safe for him to move away from Petra, that was simply not an option. So now that this strange dog had entered his space, he was trapped. Allen felt seriously threatened by this dog, it saturated his blood with adrenaline. The only thing that he could do was to try and communicate his feelings.

Allen growled and lunged at the strange dog, telling it to back off.

The spaniel immediately shied away and pulled backwards, not interested in a fight.

Encouraged by the effectiveness of his communication, Allen let out a series of loud barks to scare it off further.

The dog quickly trotted back to his owner.

Allen felt a sense of relief that his tactic had worked. He realised he now had some control over whether other dogs came up to him. If he barked and lunged at them, they might go away like this dog had.

Petra apologised to the dog on Allen's behalf, then turned to the lady standing next to her.

'See, I told you he needs more socialisation!' said Petra.

'Well, you came to the right place, that's for sure,' replied the lady. 'The dogs just love it here.'

They both stopped talking and went back to watching the two dogs that were still playing together.

Allen noticed yet another dog start to walk towards him. This time it was a rather fat-looking beagle. He decided to step in before things got worse.

Allen started barking at the beagle, warning it to stay away. But the beagle just ignored him and kept walking closer.

'Oh dear Allen, what's wrong with you!' cried Petra, as she picked him up and started to walk back to the gate. 'How can I socialise you when you're behaving so rudely to all the other dogs?'

As they started walking home, Petra got out her phone to call Nathan.

'Hi, so I think we need to take Allen to the dog park more often,' blurted Petra, as soon as Nathan answered. 'He's really unsocialised and I think he's becoming reactive.'

'Reactive? Is he playing with the other dogs yet though?' asked Nathan.

'Even worse, Nath,' whispered Petra, barely holding back tears. 'He tried to attack a dog that came up to him today. I just don't know what to do. Why is he so naughty?'

Nathan paused before responding.

'Maybe we just have to take him there every chance we get, so he can learn to be more social. We can take him every day after work this week, I'm sure that'll work. Did he have fun today though?'

'Yeah, he loved it in there,' replied Petra, managing a small smile. 'He was so excited he was shaking at one point, and he was so well behaved with his leash off too. He didn't even run away, Nath. He just stayed by my side. It was so cute.'

'Well, that all sounds pretty good,' said Nathan hopefully.

'Yeah, but I just don't get why he is so well behaved sometimes and then completely disobeys me five seconds later!'

As they walked down the path to their home, no other dogs were in view. Allen was enjoying his walk once more, and felt himself relaxing. He stopped often to inspect an interesting smell here or there, but each time Petra kept walking ahead. He would be only halfway through the smell when he was forced to move on, as the collar pulled him forwards.

Unfamiliar Territory

When I try to imagine what a dog is thinking, there are some cognitive dimensions where I feel completely inadequate. This is because as a human, my brain is different to that of a dog, and I am lacking some modifications that they possess. Dogs surely have similar problems when trying to understand humans. What does a dog think when we bare our teeth, and make the high-pitched repetitive sound that we call laughter? How could an animal without a sense of humour (as far as we know) understand why we laugh? Does a dog know *why* we wear clothes on our body? Why we spend so long looking at screens? I suspect dogs don't even ask themselves these questions, let alone know the answers.

Just as a dog cannot imagine what it would be like to speak English or play a game of chess, I cannot imagine what goes on inside *their* heads when they smell another dog's bottom. I am in unfamiliar territory, the same as if I try to imagine how a bat would experience the sense of echolocation (using sound to see the world). We do know that the dog brain has a region named the olfactory bulb, which is dedicated to processing the sense of smell. This region takes up a much larger proportion of the dog brain than does the human olfactory bulb, which is very small.[1] Due to our underdeveloped olfactory bulb, we cannot imagine the complexity of thought that they might derive from their sense of smell. We obviously know that they are very good at smelling, that they enjoy smelling things and can detect scents with far more accuracy than we can. But *knowing* these things is not the same as *experiencing* them.

One interesting consequence of having an advanced sense of smell is that animals can smell how other animals are feeling, to some degree.[2] You will notice many examples of Allen and Nella smelling emotions in this book. We know that dogs and many other species of animals can detect stress-related smells that are secreted. For example, dogs have two glands in their bottom called anal glands, which can release a smelly substance when they are frightened, much like a skunk. We also know that dogs can smell disease, cancer, drugs and all manner of things undetectable to us. While dogs may or may not always know what it means, they would certainly be able to detect many of the emotion-related molecules that animals release from their body. Dogs are also likely to have a very good memory for smells, given they have so much of their brain devoted to it. This means that they can make associations between certain smells and the behaviour of other dogs. When two dogs meet and sniff each other, they may be able to smell the signature of stress or anxiety in the other dog. If they remember that other dogs with this smell had growled or snapped at them in the past, they might treat the smell of stress as a sign that the other dog cannot be trusted. This could even account for why some dogs seem to be attacked by other dogs more frequently at dog parks; although there have been no studies to look into this yet. The idea of sensing emotions through smell will be further explored throughout this book.

Just as humans struggle to imagine living in a world of detailed olfaction, other concepts are also foreign. Linked to their understanding of smell is their concept of a territory. We know these two things are linked, as dogs mark out their territory with urine and even faeces. This is a common behaviour in many species—they use smells to signal to other animals that a particular area is part of their range. This is an extremely foreign concept to most people. Could you imagine if instead of using fences, we painted urine around the boundaries of properties? We know that most dogs love going on walks, and one of the main things they like to do on those walks is to sniff things and urine mark. Are they trying to mark out a territory? It's a difficult question to answer for sure, but it seems likely to me.

In the wild, dogs will spend most of their lives within their own territory.[3] They don't regularly venture into the territory of other dogs, and if they do there is a very good reason for it— and it's a very big deal. They also naturally defend their territories against incursions from unknown dogs. If this is the natural way that dogs think about the world, our human way of thinking must be very foreign to them. We have shared public amenities such as roads, footpaths and parks, which are not considered to be a part of our own property. I suspect that dogs don't understand this concept of a communal territory, and find it very confusing, as is the case with Allen and Nella.

At home, Allen often barks at the front window in an attempt to defend his territory from strangers. Not only is territorialism a normal way of thinking for many animals, it's also pivotal for their survival. As is well known by now, the devastating habitat loss we are presiding over on this planet leads to the extinction of *entire* species. A habitat, or territory, is an absolute requirement for survival. Without this, they die. Despite how important the territorial drive must be for dogs, I don't think humans can imagine what this feels like, just as we struggle to understand their world of smell. What we *do* know however, is that the territorial arrangements of most pet dogs are very different to how they would have been in the past. The natural size of a dog's territory is far larger than the average suburban house and yard.[4] The size of any animal's territory needs to be large enough that they can gather the resources required for survival. This is a matter of life or death. For a predatory species like the wolf or dingo, this would be a very large area.

Although our pet dogs have been domesticated since their wild ancestors, they still show many signs of having strong territorial instincts. If a dog has plenty of resources and feels safe and secure, a well defended territory might not be needed. However, if a dog feels unsafe, threatened or worried, their territory could be a large source of worry. Territorial barking is clearly one symptom of this worry, but there could be many other ways it influences their behaviour that humans haven't yet identified. In this book, I have tried to imagine how the territorial instincts of dogs might influence their behaviour, and especially for dogs with anxiety.

CHAPTER SEVEN

Problems At Home

Nathan was sitting on the couch, with Petra and Allen snuggling into him under the blanket.

'When you got home today, I brought up dinner plans and you seemed pretty snappy at me,' said Petra softly.

'Oh yeah, sorry about that, wasn't a great day at work,' said Nathan, looking down at Allen while stroking him.

'So, what happened at work?'

'Well, the new computer system was driving everyone crazy again…' complained Nathan, shaking his head.

'I don't get why your work did that,' said Petra. 'It seems so much worse than the old system.'

'It is supposed to be way *better,* but things just take so much longer. We have deadlines to meet and it's making us miss them! Mick couldn't even sleep last night from all the stress it's caused.'

'Well, you aren't sleeping great either, honey,' said Petra, a concerned look on her face.

'Yeah, but that's the thing, my part of the computer system is fine, it's the bits everyone else is using that's causing the issues.

'Honestly, the new system doesn't stress me out at all in my own work. I think it's just being around everyone else who's on edge. It changes the atmosphere, and I think it's rubbing off on me. Like in a bad way.'

Nathan gazed down at Allen, who was fast asleep on his lap.

'This little guy helps calm me down though, just look at that face,' said Nathan, smiling warmly.

As Nathan stood up to get to the bathroom, Allen stirred. Jostled from his slumber, his consciousness slowly grew more alert. He noticed the feeling of the couch through his fur, and the breeze caused by the blanket falling back down. Allen rolled over to his side and stretched forwards, yawning widely. As he inhaled, Allen registered the various scents around him. Some of these odours had been released by Nathan, evaporating off his skin. Amongst them, was a smell caused by a molecule that was released due to stress. Nathan had no idea this happened when he was stressed out, but Allen could clearly smell the evidence.

Allen subconsciously knew what a stressed mammal smelled like. He had noticed this scent getting stronger and stronger over the last week. It was mostly on Nathan, but you could detect it through the whole house. Allen couldn't understand exactly why this alarming smell was around his people, but he knew it was a sign of danger. It put him on edge. If his people weren't at ease, how could he be? Just as Nathan was affected by the contagiousness of the stress at his work, so too was Allen affected at home.

As Nathan returned to the couch, Allen noticed that the stressful stench was particularly strong on him at the moment. This worried Allen, it made him feel insecure. Allen decided to try and get Nathan's attention, to help soothe himself. He stood up with his front paws on Nathan's chest. Tail wagging, Allen tried to lick him in the face.

Nathan laughed, rubbing Allen's fur along the sides of his body before pushing him back down.

Allen felt comforted by this interaction, easing some of his own worry.

'Dogs just seem to know when you need them, don't they?' said Nathan, looking down at Allen.

Allen was gazing back into his eyes, tail still wagging.

'Yep, they sure do,' replied Petra. 'They're like our little guardian angels looking out for us.'

Petra smiled sorrowfully as she watched Allen roll onto his back, tail still wagging as he looked up at her. She couldn't resist the offer. Petra reached in and stroked him over his chest and down his belly.

Allen loved being touched this way. His heart rate dropped as he squinted his eyes, groaning softly.

As Petra ran her hand over Allen's underside, it brushed over his desexing scar. Since being castrated a few months ago, when he was six months old, the wound had now faded and was hardly visible.

Allen's relaxed stupor was soon interrupted by the sound of a child laughing. It was coming from outside the front of their house, and it made the fur on the back of his neck stand up on end.

Before thinking, Allen jumped down from the couch. He didn't like hearing noises like this, it meant there was a stranger on his territory, and that meant danger. Things had been going pretty good in the house, and he intended on making sure it stayed that way.

Allen ran down the hallway barking, and then raced up to the window next to the front door. He looked out to see a family walking along the street next to the front fence.

The child had a stick, and was dragging it along the fence, making a loud clicking sound as she walked.

Allen's heart bounded in his chest as he barked through the window. It was very concerning that there were strange noises and an ominous family passing by the house. Feeling stressed, Allen started panting between barks.

The sound of Allen's bark was very unpleasant. It was grating at Nathan's own anxiety, causing it to spike as a result. As was natural for someone in such a situation, Nathan tried to stop it. He used the same technique he always did when Allen barked.

'No! Allen, get back here, stop that barking!' yelled Nathan.

Nathan's outburst helped ease his own frustration a little, but it didn't work very well on Allen.

Allen hardly heard him, and although he did pause barking for a few seconds, it didn't last long. He continued to bark at the family as they paused to point at the birds in the trees.

Petra decided to stop the noise by grabbing Allen and taking him back to the couch. As he stood there barking, she approached him from behind and reached down to pick him up. As Petra put her hands around his chest, Allen felt a sudden twinge of fear. He was already scared by the things over the fence, but now the memory of his painful back shot through him. He didn't want to be moved from his position, and he didn't want his back to get hurt.

Allen snarled and bit at Petra's hand, forcing her to let him go. There was no 'decision' made to do this, it was just his knee-jerk reaction.

Petra screamed and cursed.

'He bit me!' she yelled, walking away and shaking her hand.

Allen immediately looked back out the window and resumed barking. He felt himself relaxing slightly as the people slowly moved away from the fence and out of view. From Allen's perspective, the barking had worked! He had managed to ward off the intruders this time.

Once the strangers had been out of sight for a minute, Allen finally let his guard down. Relieved that it was over, he shook his body side to side, ears flapping against his face. At the end of his shake, his tail vibrated for a moment as he started trotting back towards the couch.

Nathan was helping Petra bandage her hand on the coffee table. They both glared up at him as he approached.

'You made me bleed Allen, that's not cool!' said Petra in a stern tone, frowning.

'BAD dog Allen, BAD dog!' added Nathan, pointing and staring at him.

Allen crouched down and looked up at Nathan.

It had happened again—his parents were yelling at him. He *hated* it when this happened. However, he was getting used to it, and so performed his normal response. Allen rolled over, his tail tucked into his bottom, and exposed his belly. He didn't want to fight with his parents, and needed to let them know that he wasn't a threat.

'See, he knows he did wrong, I just don't understand why he doesn't learn though!' exclaimed Nathan.

Petra stared at Allen as he lay on his back, but through her anger she felt herself forgive him.

'I think we need a dog trainer,' she said. 'Maybe they can give us some tips?'

Nathan mumbled in agreement. He got out his phone to start searching.

A few minutes later, Nathan and Petra had agreed on a listing.

'She seems pretty good,' said Nathan, 'she's a dog behaviour specialist. And she has 20 years' experience working with reactive dogs...'

'Member of the National Dog Training Club too,' added Petra. 'I'll give her a call.'

Petra dialled the number on Nathan's phone and put it on speaker so they could both hear.

'Hello, this is Bite Breaker's Dog Training, Brooke speaking,' said the voice.

'Hi Brooke, my name is Petra, how are you?'

'Great thanks Petra! How are you going?'

'Honestly, not great,' replied Petra. 'I just got bitten by my dog. I think he's reactive or maybe dominant too.'

'Crikey, is it bad? How large is your dog?' asked Brooke in a concerned tone.

'Oh, he's small, just a little sausage dog, but it's bleeding...'

'Well, I hope you're okay. And rest assured you've called the right person. So, what situations seem to flare-up his reactivity?'

'Where do I start! He is sort of reactive with everything, like around people, other dogs, the garbage truck, you name it! And it's happening on walks, at home, in the car, pretty much everywhere,' explained Petra.

'Right-o then, sounds like the full package!' replied Brooke. 'I'd recommend our Reactive Dog Special; it comprises three training sessions and equipment included. That's normally enough to educate them on what's unacceptable behaviour, and to teach them to follow you as their leader.

'Would you like to book in? I've got a spot this Sunday at noon if you're home?'

Nathan and Petra looked at each other, signalling their agreement.

'Yes, I think we need to, but do you have expertise in the dachshund breed? And what sort of accreditation do you have?' questioned Petra.

'Well, since you asked, I am part of the National Dog Trainers Elite Alliance. We use balanced techniques, so you will have the power of all four quadrants of training at your disposal. And I have fixed a lot of dachshunds in my time, don't you worry about that.'

Petra glanced at Nathan, looking hopeful. 'Okay wonderful, let's book in for Sunday then.'

As Petra booked the appointment, Allen picked up his toy mouse and climbed up onto the couch, wagging his tail as he stood watching her.

* * *

Nella's family was fast asleep. It was dark outside, the wind chimes on the back porch were gently tinkling in the breeze. A white van slowly pulled up in front of the house. Two men exited the car, softly closing their doors behind them.

'Are you sure this is the one?' whispered one of them.

'Yeah, you can see the big TV through the window, it's against the right wall,' the other replied.

Nella was dreaming of running through a field of grass when she heard the faint tinkle of a window breaking downstairs. She jolted upright from her mat, which was lying on the floor next to Tessa's bed. Her ears pricked up in worry as she focused on listening. She didn't know what the sound was, but she hadn't heard it before. It sounded like it was in the house, Nella was worried. On high alert, she started silently creeping towards the bedroom door. As she was slowly poking her head out of the room, she heard the sound of a foot crunching on broken glass. Nella froze, a shiver running down her spine and into her tail. She realised the noise was indeed *inside* her house, somewhere downstairs.

Nella's hackles bristled and her heart raced as she bounded down the stairs while barking. It was the loud, booming bark of a nine-month-old, 40kg Irish Wolfhound. Her deep chest added a low pitch to the warning that shook the whole house. At the bottom of the stairs, she turned and bounded down the hallway towards the door. Nella could see shapes moving in the front room and instinctively let out another loud bark, followed by a growl as she closed in.

Mick was up out of bed by this stage and walking towards the stairs to see what the noise was all about.

The two men stared, frozen in shock as Nella appeared only meters away from them. She came to a halt just outside the front room, standing in the hallway as she sized them up, growling.

One of the men let out a curse and started slowly reaching towards a lamp on the table next to him. Nella was a large dog, and these men were not dog people. Once the man had grasped the lamp in his hand, he quickly threw it towards Nella. It was firmly attached by a cord to the wall, which caused it to crash onto the floor with a loud noise as it shattered on the floorboards. The two men both turned as one and scrambled to climb out the window.

Hearing the lamp smashing downstairs, Mick now realised that there were intruders in his house. Adrenaline coursed through his veins as he sped down the stairs to confront them.

'Get out of my house!' he yelled, as loud as he could.

Tessa was also frightened from all the noise, and had crawled under her bed, trembling.

Olivia was pacing back and forth in her room; she had closed the door and was trying to find her phone. She had panicked and fumbled it, causing it to slide under the bedroom dresser.

As the two men climbed back out the window, one of them slipped and fell on the front lawn.

Mick ran into the front room and saw the broken window and smashed lamp. Without hesitation, he ran past Nella and jumped through the window. As the fallen man scrambled to get up, Mick chased them both into the van. They climbed in and slammed the doors behind them, just before Mick caught up. In nothing but his underwear, he started banging on the van door as they started the engine. The tires screeched as they sped off down the street, leaving Mick standing alone on the road.

As he walked back to the house, Mick realised his feet felt wet. When he looked down to inspect them, he realised they were bleeding. Worried about his family, Mick climbed back through the window. He was more careful this time to avoid any glass he could see, but only had the dim light from outside to help him.

Hearing Mick climbing back inside, Nella let out another round of booming barks, this time from upstairs.

'It's okay, they've gone,' yelled Mick.

He started turning on lights as he made his way upstairs, now limping.

Nella was standing in the doorway to Tessa's room, hackles up, barking and growling with wide eyes.

Olivia opened her bedroom door and rushed up to Mick.

'What happened! Are you okay? Who were those people?' she cried.

'Robbers I guess,' replied Mick, as he walked towards Tessa's room. 'Where's Tessa?'

As they walked past her and into Tessa's room, Nella stayed put in the doorway. The sound of the wind chimes in the breeze set her off again with another round of barks.

'It's okay Tess,' said Mick gently, as he looked under her bed. Tessa was there, out of Mick's reach, huddled up against the back wall.

'You can come out now honey, we're all safe.'

'Is Nella okay?' asked Tessa as she crawled out from under the bed.

Olivia picked her up and held her, squeezing her tight.

Mick wrapped his arms around the both of them before replying. 'Nella is fine, she scared them off then came up here to protect you. I ran after them too, but I think they were more scared of her than me!'

'That was silly Mick,' said Olivia. 'They could have hurt you, why did you run after them?'

Mick looked down at his bleeding feet. 'Yeah, I dunno. I wasn't thinking… I was just so scared and went into defence mode, all I could think about was protecting you both, and the house.'

'I hide when I'm scared' said Tessa, looking up at him with a confused expression.

Mick frowned, surprised by the comment. 'I guess different people react in different ways Tess. Nella was probably scared too but her instinct was to come back up here and guard you!'

All of a sudden, Olivia burst out into laughter. 'Well, I found out that I'm next to useless in an emergency. I was trying to call the police, but I dropped my phone and accidentally kicked it under the bed… I still haven't even found it!'

'Never mind' said Mick, comforting her. 'I suppose we can call the cops in the morning, now that they're gone.'

* * *

The next morning, Mick was sitting on the couch with his feet bandaged up when the doorbell rang. Unable to get up and answer it, he watched as Nella leapt out of her bed next to him. She started barking loudly as she ran towards the door.

'No Nella! Shoosh! It's just the police, Nella!' yelled Olivia as she ran down the hallway after her.

'Just give us a minute,' Mick called out in the direction of the door.

Olivia grabbed onto Nella's collar and walked her into the study. Nella was happy to follow her, but kept turning her head to look down the hallway. She hadn't slept well since the break-in, and was now worried that the person at the door could be another intruder.

Once Olivia had closed Nella into the study, she was finally able to answer the door.

When Olivia invited the two police officers inside to show them the crime scene, Nella continued to bark loudly. Olivia pointed to the smashed lamp and explained how one of the men tried to throw it at Nella.

'Well, from the judge of Nella's bark,' said the female police officer, 'he was probably pretty scared! But you need to be careful in situations like that. In my experience, people are most dangerous when they feel threatened.'

Locked behind the door, Nella was feeling frantic. She panted heavily, worried that these strange people in the house might be like the people who broke in the night before. Seeing the way Mick had reacted last night had strengthened Nella's suspicion that strangers entering the house were not a good thing. Seeing him yelling so loudly, and smelling his fearful stench afterwards had left a mark on her that wouldn't be easily forgotten. After a while, she stopped barking and began to whine and pace next to the door, feeling both frustrated and anxious. Finally, after what felt like a very long time, Olivia opened the door again. Nella rushed out of the study and ran straight to the front door. She immediately set to sniffing the ground and letting out the occasional bark. Looking out the window to the side of the door, she saw the police van drive off. Alarmed at the sight, Nella let out another series of barks for good measure.

With the house cleared of intruders and safe once more, Nella let out a big sigh of relief. She shook off her worry before trotting over to where Mick and Tessa were sitting on the couch. Just as she had done as a puppy, Nella jumped up onto the couch. However, from Nella's perspective the couch was a lot smaller than it used to be. She now took up almost half the size of it. She plonked her bottom down onto Tessa's lap, and looked over at Olivia standing in the kitchen.

'Nella, I'm stuck!' whined Tessa, laughing as she squirmed to get out from under her.

Nella hardly noticed Tessa moving, she was busy watching Olivia slice up some fruit on the bench.

As Tessa pulled Nella's foot out of the way to wriggle out from under her, she accidentally moved the leg in an awkward direction. Nella let out a yelp in pain, and turned around to look at Tessa. Tessa's mouth was open, her eyes wide. Then, as the shock wore off, her expression quickly changed to one of sorrow.

'Sorry Nella, I didn't mean to hurt you,' she said in a sad, whining voice.

Nella had been surprised by the pain, but hearing the friendly tone in Tessa's voice, she felt happy that she wasn't being threatened. She trusted Tessa completely, and was very closely bonded to her. This little bit of pain didn't change that relationship, she was just a bit confused. A few seconds later, as Nella's confusion wore off, she felt a wave of relief. Realising that everything was okay, she started wagging her tail and licking at Tessa's face eagerly.

Tessa squealed and laughed, pushing Nella's face away as best she could.

Mick, having seen the entire thing, started laughing too. 'Liv, I don't think we need to worry about Nella attacking Tessa, she doesn't have it in her!'

Olivia smiled smugly as she watched them together on the couch. 'Tessa is safe, it's strangers I worry about now! After the way she acted with those robbers last night, I think she's earned her keep!'

'Yeah, I know right?' agreed Mick. 'She's the perfect dog.'

Olivia furrowed her brow and looked straight at Mick. 'Well, she's the perfect dog when she's at home and it's just us around. If only she wasn't so excited and difficult around other dogs though…'

Mick frowned, watching Nella on the couch. 'I tell her off when she barks at other dogs, she just doesn't listen though! Treats don't work either…

'Ever since she got bitten in the park as a puppy, she just hasn't been the same. It's so strange how she is such a good dog the rest of the time except for those circumstances.'

'And visitors in the house too,' added Olivia. 'She was pretty bad with the police today. I'm worried that she'll always be like that now, because of the break-in.'

'I've actually been thinking we should get a dog trainer,' said Mick, sighing. 'To help stop her barking so much, I think she's scaring people on walks now.'

Olivia looked down at her shoes and agreed. 'Yeah, that's not a bad idea. Where do you think we would find a good trainer though?'

Mick paused and thought for a moment, before replying, 'I think we should ask her vet. Ava was really good with her when she was a puppy, maybe she knows someone?'

'Of course!' exclaimed Olivia excitedly. 'I remember seeing a sign for a training business in their waiting room. It said they are 'force free', which means they don't use punishment, just treats.'

'Alright, we can call and get their number from the vet,' said Mick, sighing as he pulled out his phone. 'Hopefully they'll have an opening this weekend.'

Emotional Learning

With Allen and Nella both being booked in for training, their owners are hoping to solve all their problems. When people think of how a trainer teaches a dog to behave, they are normally imagining something called 'operant' learning (also called operant conditioning). This is when you reward or punish a voluntary behaviour, to try and make it happen more or less frequently. Most of the behaviours that people imagine are voluntary. We decide to go somewhere or say something, eat something or go to bed. A voluntary behaviour can be trained, because you can decide to do it. People can easily learn to perform a voluntary behaviour in exchange for a reward (like food or money). Dogs also make decisions and perform voluntary behaviours. A dog can decide to sniff a tree or run to a toy, sit down on the spot or bark at nothing. All these behaviours can be operantly trained in exchange for some food. This is the kind of learning that we are all familiar with. However, as we can see in this chapter, the problems that Allen and Nella are having are emotional. They are not *deciding* to do the wrong behaviour, they are reacting to their emotions on instinct. What they actually need is for their *emotional* reaction to change, which is more complicated than it might seem. An emotional reaction is not a voluntary behaviour you can decide to do, which means operant learning doesn't apply.

To change the emotions of an animal, we need to be able to recognise their emotions first. The brains of humans and dogs both experience emotions, which often motivate their behaviours. Making the distinction between a behaviour (e.g., panting) and an emotion (e.g. happy, excited or anxious) is difficult for many of the clients I see. There is a distinct difference between a behaviour and the emotion that causes it. You can *do* a behaviour and you can *feel* an emotion, but the reverse isn't true. The problem is that many people automatically jump to the emotional motivation of their dog (often incorrectly), without noticing the actual body language. For example, many people who see a panting dog don't even notice the body language, they just see a dog that is happy or excited. Their brain will jump straight to a conclusion, and this is often all they see. Once a person has learnt to read the emotions that their dog is experiencing, they can then work on trying to change them. The process where a dog learns to have a different emotional reaction to something is called 'classical' learning (also called classical conditioning), which you may have heard of in relation to 'Pavlov's dog'.

Classical learning

Classical learning is a type of learning where an animal associates or disassociates an emotion with something in the world around them. It is essentially 'emotional' learning. One example from this book was when Nella learnt to associate fear with unfamiliar dogs. She learnt to have this emotional reaction after she was bitten by Mandy in the park. To understand how this type of learning works, we will go on a journey into your mind. Have you ever wondered why your friend is able to scare you by jumping out from behind a tree? Even if you see them jump out and recognise them, you can still be frightened. Why do you have a different reaction than when you see them walk up to you normally? Even if you know your friend won't hurt you, it feels like they could, when they surprise you like this.

The reason is that there's another layer of your mind, deep under the surface of your consciousness. This primitive layer of your mind doesn't have any conscious ideas or thoughts. It sees the world as a blurred and muffled realm which is scoured under its watchful eye. Although its senses are handicapped, it makes up for it with exceptional speed. This inner mind sees, hears and feels a blurred version of the things around you, a fraction of a second before it enters your consciousness. It acts like an early warning threat detection system. When your friend tries to surprise you, this inner version of you sees a large object unexpectedly appear from behind the tree. With blurry vision, this inner layer of your mind has no way of knowing what the object could be. Before your conscious mind can recognise your friend, your subconscious sounds the alarm. Fear and adrenaline rush through your body, you might even scream or jump. A fraction of a second later, the image of your friend enters your consciousness. You can perceive them normally, and now know there was no threat, but you were too slow to realise it. However, if your friend tries to surprise you too often, the trick will no longer work. This is because the inner layer of your mind has learned through the process of classical learning.

Without us noticing, classical learning happens continuously in our brain. Every animal has this type of learning, regardless of how smart they are. Classical learning is responsible for all emotional learning. It is how people develop a fear of flying, spiders, cars or clowns. This type of learning doesn't only happen naturally, we can also learn to control it. This is how we train an emotion. Training an emotion is very different to operant (voluntary) learning that most people are familiar with, as was discussed above. Concepts like rewarding or punishing are useless for training emotions. If rewarding and punishing worked on emotions, then the world would be a very strange place indeed. You would be able to make someone stop feeling sad by hitting them, as it would punish the emotion so that it occurred less! Similarly, if you rewarded a sad person with some chocolate, it would make them feel sad more often as they try to get more chocolate by feeling sad! This crazy example is actually how a lot of people think about dog training. If a dog is barking from fear, they would never want to give the dog a treat, because that would just reward the barking. This is like being afraid to give someone who is crying a piece of chocolate, because you might just reinforce their crying. Sounds pretty crazy when you put it that way, doesn't it? However, this is a very common way in which people try to train their dog. In one of the many examples in this book, we see Nathan trying to teach Allen to stop barking at the front window. He yells at Allen to punish the barking behaviour, but we can see how it does nothing for his fear of intruders. So, if we can't punish and reward emotions, can we train them in other ways?

Training emotions in general

Emotions can be trained to be more (or less) intense by the process of classical learning. This method of learning happens via simple association. To train an emotion we only need two things! The first thing we need is something that already triggers an emotion. For some people, we could pick 'seeing a spider' (fear trigger) or 'seeing chocolate' (hunger trigger) as our emotional trigger. The second thing we need is something we want to attach the emotion to. For this example, let's use a red box. That's it, you don't need anything else to train an emotion!

Let's start by imagining how we could train you to feel hungry when you see a red box. Every day just before lunch time, someone walks up to you with a red box and opens it in front of you. There is chocolate inside, and every day for a month you take some chocolate and enjoy eating it. At the end of the month, when you see that red box, you will start to feel hungry. You might even start salivating before you see the chocolate. We have now trained you to feel hunger in response to a red box by simply using association.

Now imagine that for the next month the box contains spiders (or something else you fear). Every day this person walks up to you and tries to open the box in your face. By the end of the month, you will be fearful of the red box. You have now been trained to feel fear in response to a red box, using simple association. The more times we pair the emotion with the red box, the stronger the association will become.

As most people don't understand classical learning, they intuitively explain emotional associations like this in other ways. For example, when you have learned to fear the red box, you might say to other people that you fear it because you *know* there are spiders inside. However, this is just what we tell ourselves because classical learning isn't intuitive. We often explain our emotions with logic, but it isn't that simple. If you question a person with a fear of spiders about why they feel that way, they might say something like 'because they are poisonous and can bite you'. But then, if you try to show them a spider that is proven to be non-poisonous and not dangerous, they still have the same reaction. We actually learn to fear things at a deeper level than we can explain. This is why people often struggle to give a rational explanation for their feelings.

To illustrate this point, imagine that next I show you a green ball, and tell you that there are spiders inside it. Imagine you completely believe me. Then later that day you are walking through a doorway when you notice the green ball on a desk. You stop and look at it for a second before you remember that it might have spiders inside, so you move back and maybe feel a little worried. However, if we did the same experiment with the red box from before, it would happen like this. You walk through the doorway and see the red box sitting on the desk. Your inner mind recognises the red box before you consciously process it, it remembers all those times you saw the red box and got frightened. Before consciously processing what you see, you would be likely to feel a jolt of fear as you step back. This shows that you didn't just fear the red box because you consciously know it has spiders in it. You fear the red box itself, on a subconscious level.

Training the emotions of dogs

Emotional training can be a powerful tool that we can use to help our dogs, and would certainly be helpful for Allen and Nella. So many of the behaviours that we dislike in our dogs (like biting, barking, being destructive) are a direct result of negative emotions like fear or anxiety. Once you understand how emotional training works, you can understand why you should give your dog a treat when they bark or growl at strangers from fear. The layperson who sees you do this will think that you are rewarding the behaviour, causing it to get worse. They might think that you should be telling your dog 'No', so that they learn to bark and growl less. However, we have seen how unsuccessful this is for Allen, which describes a very normal reaction to this technique. Yelling at your dog will not make the fear go away, and might even make it worse. However, by giving your fearful dog a treat every time they see an unfamiliar person, an association will form between the enjoyment of eating food and the presence of unfamiliar people. This is how you train an emotion. Over time, the positive happy emotions associated with the enjoyment of food will become associated with the unfamiliar people. These happy emotions will help your dog to overcome the fear. You will never need to teach your dog that barking and growling is 'wrong' (even if that was possible), because why would they bother doing it unless they were scared? These behaviours (barking and growling) tell us that our dog has an emotional problem (fear). Then, once we train the emotions of the dog to fix the problem (remove the fear), the barking and growling will disappear. We never need to bother teaching the dog not to bark or growl! This is the same way we treat a crying baby: we don't need to teach them not to cry, we just need to make them happy!

Professional dog behaviour clinicians can use the knowledge of emotional training to reduce the fear or anxiety in a whole range of dog issues, including fearful or dangerous behaviours, separation anxiety and thunderstorm phobias. However, emotional learning is also responsible for the *development* of most dog behaviour issues. At some point, the dog must learn to feel panic when hearing a thunderstorm or to be anxious when left alone. We saw an example of this earlier in the book, when Nella was bitten by Mandy, the old golden retriever. This experience pairs the fear and pain of being bitten, with the presence of an unfamiliar dog. In the future, when Nella sees another dog, she has learned to feel fearful.

Emotions are learned by association, so every time a dog experiences an anxious or fearful event, the association becomes even stronger. It's like a self-reinforcing feedback loop. Problems like separation anxiety or fear of other dogs are often experienced many times per week. Each time, the emotional association is further consolidated. This means we need to try and avoid the situation before we can start to see improvement. This can be understandably difficult in many situations, and is the most common reason for treatment failure. Only once we stop consolidating the emotional memory can we start to teach the dog to 'forget', or 'unlearn' these damaging emotional associations. This will be explained in a later chapter. However, it is important not to have a false sense of confidence when attempting emotional learning techniques in dogs. They can be highly difficult, and many different issues can crop up. A competent dog trainer should always be employed for difficult cases.

CHAPTER EIGHT

Shocking Revelations

Nathan heard Allen barking in the front room of the house and winced. He took a deep breath and yelled out from his seat in the dining room.

'Allen, shut up!'

The barking stopped, and Nathan turned back to Petra. As he went to take another bite of his toast, they heard the barking resume.

'Allen, come here now!' he yelled again.

Allen could hear his people yelling from the other room, but there were more pressing issues that he needed to worry about.

'Maybe we need to send him to the pound,' muttered Nathan under his breath.

'Don't even joke about that Nathan, it's not funny' snapped Petra, scowling at him.

'Well, you train him to stop then,' retorted Nathan.

Petra paused and with raised eyebrows she rolled her eyes dramatically. 'He doesn't listen to you, and you're much louder than me, so why would he hear me any better?'

'I really hope this dog trainer can fix the barking,' said Nathan, sighing. 'It makes my head feel like it's splitting open.'

Allen was sitting at the front window, intently focused on the street outside the house, visible through the wide-spaced pickets of their garden fence.

It was a difficult world he inhabited, where you could never be sure what would occur next. Allen felt he had little control over how or when things happened, and it was hard to cope with. His humans would leave the house at all hours, only to return later as though nothing had happened. He wanted to follow them, but was always blocked by the door just as they left. They normally left him in the mornings, and returned home in the evenings. However, some days they didn't leave at all, and other days they left a second time or stayed home, and then didn't leave until the evening. It was all very confusing.

Feeding times were also unpredictable. Sometime every morning and every night, his people would make the food appear. There would be a popping noise, followed by a grinding sound, and then they would shovel the food from a shiny tin into his feeding container. The food appearances seemed to happen whether he wanted them or not, and without routine. Some days the food appeared before his people had their breakfast, other days afterwards. Most days the second feeding came when it was still bright outside, but other days it was dark. Allen would sometimes bark in an attempt to get them to make the food appear, but this seemed to work only half the time. Often his people would respond by yelling back at him, forcing him to slink away.

This lack of control in his life was difficult for Allen; it made him generally worried. He had been trying to compensate, by gaining influence over what little things he could. Every day when Allen was out in the yard, he would carefully select the best spots to pee. He tried to go in a different spot each time, to space out his pee around the fence and garden. This helped make the property smell like he owned it, and would help defend it from the others. Allen had an instinctive understanding that maintaining a safe home territory was important for surviving in this crazy and unpredictable world. When you can't be sure of the way things work, it's really important to protect what resources you have; it's a matter of survival.

Allen stared through the front window of the house, waiting to see if more intruders would arrive. He felt that guarding the property was his purpose. He would spend many hours every day working at this job, he didn't have much else to do. As Allen sat at his post, the afternoon sun was directly on his head. A drowsy warmth was beginning to wrap itself around him. His eyes closed sleepily, then opened again to see a shape move behind the fence. He jolted upright, eyes wide and ears pricked up, fur on the back of his neck standing on end. His heart skipped a beat, and then raced into action. Allen was in a simultaneous state of fear and anxiety. Scared of what he could see, and worried about what it might be.

Without knowing the identity of the shape, Allen let out a loud double bark. As the shape continued to move, Allen quickly identified it as a human walking along the sidewalk. He felt the ownership of his territory being questioned by this presence. He desperately needed to prove his belonging. If he sounded like he was dangerous and ready to attack, he knew he could get them to leave. It almost always worked. If an intruder was walking along the fence line, he would bark at them, and they would eventually disappear at the other end of the path.

However, this time was different. The figure opened the latch on the gate and started walking down the path towards the house. Allen started panting as his anxiety surged, he let out another series of barks. His breath started fogging the window in front of his nose, blurring his vision of the stranger.

'Allen, come here now!' shouted Nathan, just as the doorbell rang.

Allen continued to bark; this was not a drill.

As Nathan reached towards the door handle, he tried one more time to quiet Allen. 'No Allen, shoosh!'

Petra lifted him up into her arms as he continued to bark, and then Nathan opened the door. As the door opened a crack, they could see a lady in a Bite Breakers uniform standing outside. She smiled at them all and raised her voice to be heard through the noise.

'Hi, I'm Brooke from Bite Breakers. I see we have a lot of work to do, this must be Allen!'

As they all moved inside, Allen stopped barking and settled into a pattern of low grumbles and growls. As Brooke stood there talking to his people, he watched her intently, unable to take his eyes off her. His heart was galloping with fear. It was not safe having this stranger in the house. He needed to do something about it, but he felt helpless in Petra's arms. While talking, Brooke casually turned to look at Allen, making eye contact with him. Seeing her looking directly at him, Allen felt acutely threatened. It caused him to shudder in fear. Without thinking he let out another round of barks, baring his teeth at her in warning.

'So, I think the best thing we can do now is all go for a walk together,' continued Brooke. 'That way I can see his behaviour for myself.'

As they all began to leave the house, Petra attached the leash to Allen and placed him back on the ground. Allen was surprised that they were going on a walk while an intruder was over. This wasn't how things normally went. As they moved out of the front gate, Allen's urge to bark at the stranger reduced. Now being used to her presence, he understood that she was quite resistant to his efforts, she wouldn't leave so easily. Furthermore, they were now moving away from the core of his territory and towards its outer edges. Her intrusion into this area, while unacceptable, was not as frightening as it had been in the house.

Allen pulled forward on the leash in front of them, choking himself on his collar as he tried to scout the area ahead. He didn't bother sniffing at anything, there wasn't time for that now. As Allen walked down the street, he went straight past smell after smell that any calm dog would have found fascinating—being on edge, he hardly noticed them. A few houses later, he had spotted something to focus his worry on. There was movement on the other side of the road. From what he could tell, it seemed like a dog or animal of sorts. Allen's hackles went up and he started barking in its direction, causing Brooke to laugh loudly.

'He's barking at that plastic bag caught in the bush over there. Gosh, he sure is reactive!' she said gleefully.

A little further along the walk, a dog came into view. It was an Italian greyhound, prancing alongside a mother and her pram. As they walked past the other dog, Allen pulled on the leash to get closer to it, barking and snarling ferociously. The other dog pulled back behind the pram, eyes wide and trembling from nose to tail. Satisfied with the response to his defensive behaviour, Allen felt empowered. Keeping other dogs away was not fun, but the effectiveness of his tactics did give him some comfort.

'See, he's pretty bad isn't he' commented Petra, as they continued down the street. 'Just so dominant and excited!'

'Yep, he sure is,' agreed Brooke, a resigned expression on her face. 'I hate to say it, but it's worse than I thought. He's in the red zone. He doesn't understand that it's bad to be reactive when he's excited, which means he can't spend any time socialising!'

As they turned the corner, the dog park came into view.

'If I hardly spent any time around other dogs or people,' explained Brooke, 'I reckon I'd also be a bit too excited when I finally saw them.'

'Yeah, that makes sense,' agreed Nathan. 'We didn't socialise him much as a puppy... Just a bit eager aren't you, Allen?'

Allen was panting heavily from anxiety and the effort of pulling on the leash. As his heart continued to thump hurriedly in his chest, he had the feeling of butterflies in his stomach.

'I think it's time I took over for a bit, to see what he's capable of,' said Brooke. She opened her bag and pulled out a leash with a metal chain loop at the end. 'This is a check chain.'

'Oh, we already tried one of those, it doesn't work on him,' said Petra, frowning.

'Well, you probably weren't using it right,' countered Brooke confidently. 'If you could just put this around his neck, I can show you how we do it properly.'

As they entered the dog park, Allen was confused and scared. His leash was now connected to the strange lady. As he pulled to get back towards his parents, he felt the chain tighten around his neck like a noose. He choked for a moment, struggling to breathe. High on adrenaline, he automatically tensed the muscles in his neck. This held back the chain from his throat and allowed his airways to stay open. However, this led to the effect of blood pooling in his head as the veins in his neck were constricted. The abnormally high blood pressure in his head felt very disconcerting. Despite this, his head looked normal to those around him.

'Now Allen, it's time you learned to behave yourself,' said Brooke as she gently pulled him back towards her.

Once he was next to her, she released the tension in the leash. As Allen started to rush away again, she sharply tugged upwards. Allen felt a sharp pain in his neck and let out a small yelp. He stopped in his tracks and turned to look up at Brooke, fear in his eyes.

'See that?' she said, smiling, 'that's called a correction, just to get his attention, I think that surprised him a bit! Don't worry, it doesn't hurt. We just need to remind him we're here.'

'Makes sense,' said Nathan, unfolding his arms.

Allen decided to try escaping in a different direction, off to the side of the path this time. Brooke sharply snapped the choker chain up again, causing Allen to stop in his tracks once more. The way in which she pulled up on the chain exposed the most sensitive part of his neck, a spot right at the top, just under his jaw. Allen froze, panting on the spot, unsure of what to do and afraid to move.

'Yesssss. Good boy Allen,' encouraged Brooke. Her hand whipped into a pouch at her side and she pulled out a dog treat.

She tossed it down at Allen who ignored it, hyperventilating from anxiety.

'As you can see, I always use positive reinforcement. But because Allen is a picky dog, it looks like he'll take a while to respond to that. Never mind, let's start walking.'

Allen looked up at Brooke and reluctantly followed. When he started to move ahead again, Brooke immediately snapped on the chain, a little softer this time. Allen got the picture though, he understood threats. The memory of the pain of the chain jerking upwards wouldn't be forgotten quickly. He stopped pulling ahead and carefully walked to the side of Brooke, too afraid to look her in the eye.

'Wow, that's amazing!' exclaimed Petra. 'I can't believe you got him to walk beside you so calmly like that!'

'They don't call me a dog behaviour specialist for nothing' replied Brooke, a satisfied smile on her face. 'He just needed a bit of direction, to help explain to him the way he should be acting. He didn't know you see.'

Shortly after, Allen was walking next to Brooke when he spotted another dog coming towards him. This dog was small, white, off leash, and running in their direction. Allen let out a flurry of barks and started to run towards it. It was a pre-emptive attack, he needed to keep it away. As he moved away from Brooke, she yanked up firmly on the chain. Allen registered the feeling of a sharp constriction in his neck as he saw the other dog running towards him. He didn't respond at first, as his heightened adrenaline had dulled his sense of pain. He barked again and started pulling forward. This time, Brooke yanked up again in a motion that turned Allen around to face her. Allen responded this time, he stopped focusing on the dog he was so fearful of. Now he was more fearful of the chain around his neck, and he was starting to learn what it wanted. Subconsciously, Allen's brain had linked the pain with the other dog. He had been focusing on the threatening dog while the sharp pain constricted around his neck. This pain had the effect of heightening the fear he was already feeling, and his brain linked it with the dog he was thinking about at the time. Through the process of emotional learning, these events strengthened his feeling that other dogs are to be feared.

'Gypsy!' called out a person in the distance.

The white dog swiftly turned to run back the way it had come.

Fearing the pain from the leash more than the dog that was now running away, Allen stopped defending himself and settled back into his nervous pant.

'There we go, that's better Allen' said Brooke, 'just needed to teach you the right way to act.'

Petra scrunched up her face as she glanced from Allen up to Brooke. 'I do worry though, that he won't act that way with us because he knows he can get away with more.'

'There's no harm trying Petra,' replied Nathan. 'She can teach us what to do.'

Brooked smiled encouragingly and offered the leash to Petra. 'Go on, you can walk him all the way home, I'll show you how.'

When Petra reluctantly took the leash, they turned around to start heading home.

Allen wasn't thinking clearly with everything going on, and quickly forgot about the consequences of pulling ahead. He was too stressed to learn properly; he was reacting rather than thinking. Before long, Allen had moved forwards once more and pulled into the choker chain, feeling it constrict around his neck.

'Petra, you need to do the correction before he gets to that point, darling,' instructed Brooke. 'Pull him back next to you, then try again.'

The next time Allen pulled forward, he felt the sharp pain around his neck. He winced and stopped in his tracks, then waited for Petra before continuing on. In an attempt to avoid the pain, he didn't try again.

'Much better,' complimented Brooke. 'But make sure you do it really fast in a quick snapping motion like I was doing, that way it just gets his attention, but doesn't hurt.'

They passed two different dogs and then a family on their way back home. Each time, Allen tried to bark at them. Under Brooke's instruction, he was stopped short within the first few barks, using her correction technique. By the end of the walk, Allen was finally starting to learn how to avoid the pain. He had realised it wasn't safe to bark at other dogs, at least while this chain was around his neck. Allen was feeling even more fearful now, and increasingly defenceless. He was more stressed than he'd ever been before. He was also panting like he'd just run a marathon. As they arrived home and walked through the gate, Nathan smiled happily.

'I've never seen him this calm, hardly barked all the way home, it's amazing!'

Petra smiled too, tilting her head as she looked down at him. 'I knew he was a good boy, well done Allen!'

Allen looked up at her, huffing and puffing with his mouth wide and the muscles on the side of his face bunched up from stress.

'I think he's even smiling at us!' added Brooke.

Once inside the house, they all sat down at the table. As Petra got up to fix drinks for everyone, Allen was left free to roam the house. Too afraid of Brooke to bark at her, Allen kept his distance, watching her from under one of the chairs.

'So, his barking is driving us crazy,' complained Nathan. 'Like when you first arrived, but all day—every five minutes.'

'That's the problem with reactive dogs,' said Brooke knowingly. 'They just don't understand any better, so it's all they do. But I will need to watch how he reacts from inside the house, so that way I can decide how best to address the issue. Hopefully he starts barking again soon.'

'It won't take long, five minutes tops,' said Nathan, laughing.

Petra made everyone a hot drink, but by the time they had all finished, Allen had still not barked. He was staying under the table, sitting behind Nathan's feet, too afraid to leave.

'It's amazing isn't it,' said Nathan. 'When we don't want him to bark, he won't stop, but now that we need to see it, he won't do it!'

Brooke nodded with understanding, before explaining. 'He might be reacting to my presence in the house, I have been showing a lot of leadership today, and most dogs respect that.'

As Brooke stood up to use the bathroom, Allen heard the sound of a car door closing on the street outside. Despite the stranger in the house, he summoned the courage to run into the front room and see what the noise might be. When Allen looked out the window, he saw a man walking away from his car down the street. Without pause, he let out a round of barks through the window.

'Ah yes, I see,' said Brooke knowingly. 'Very reactive to the noises on the street. He even ran from the other side of the house to bark at it...'

'Yeah, it doesn't matter what he's doing,' added Petra. 'Even when he's eating or playing on the other side of the house, if he hears a noise, he drops everything to bark at it. It doesn't matter if we tell him off, he still does it.'

Brooke paused and closed her eyes, thinking. 'I think I know the best solution for this, it will cost a little more, but it has the best chance of working. I think we need to use an anti-barking collar.'

Nathan frowned. 'Like a citronella collar?'

'No, they are good but won't be enough here, I can tell,' explained Brooke, gently. 'It's called a static collar—it gives them a little jolt just to remind them of the right way to act.

'Mind you, I don't recommend this for all my dogs, as I always use the least intrusive, minimally aversive method.

'However, in a case like this, I know the other methods just won't cut it. He doesn't know who the leader of the pack is at the moment, and that's half the problem. This will help him understand your role as his leader.

'If he feels as though he has good leadership in the house, he won't feel the need to protect you all the time, will he?'

'Okay,' said Petra, sighing. 'I suppose that makes sense. If it works as well as the check chain did, it should be worth the money. Don't you think, Nath?'

'Yeah,' agreed Nathan, nodding eagerly. 'Definitely worth a shot, help show him who's boss around here!'

Brooked nodded back slowly, in an exaggerated manner. 'Glad you understand. And the bonus is that you can also use it for other things. Like to teach him not to bite when you're picking him up, like what happened to you the other day.'

'Oh, that would be great!' replied Petra eagerly.

'Well, I happen to have one in my bag that I packed just in case, we can try it out on him if you like?' suggested Brooke.

After attaching the collar, Petra released Allen from her arms. He quickly ran back under the table and hid. He crouched there, frozen, feeling a weight around his neck. The two metal electrodes gently pressed through his fur and sat touching his skin. The strangeness of the new collar led him to try and scratch at it. He sat down and used his back leg, which could only just reach. Unable to remove it this way, he tried standing up and doing a body shake. Realising that the collar was not coming off easily, he gave up trying for the moment.

Allen turned back to look up at Petra, feeling a jolt of worry when doing so. This surprised him, he didn't normally feel this way. Since returning from the walk, he felt there was something different in his relationship with her. She didn't make Allen feel as secure as she used to. He retreated further back under the table, where he felt more protected. It seemed safer under the table; it was a more sheltered space than the rest of the room with its high ceiling. Allen was also starting to feel exhausted, the stress seemed to be never-ending, and it was draining him fast.

Moments later, a dog walking past the house started barking, and everyone in the room could hear it. Allen felt a jolt of adrenaline surge through him, as was usual for sounds such as these. He bolted into action, running down the hallway and letting out the first loud bark of many that were intended.

However, as soon as the bark had left his mouth, he felt a sharp jolt of electricity zap along his neck. Allen was mentally stunned; he felt an overwhelming surprise at this unexpected sensation. He stopped running and stood still, frozen in fear. The pain had been significant, but it was gone almost as soon as he noticed it. Feeling shocked and very confused, he forgot all about the sound of the dog barking.

'Wow, that was incredible!' said Nathan, grinning. 'So do you have to press the button when he barks?'

'Nope, this mode is bark-activated,' said Brooke, shaking her head. She leant over to show him the black remote. 'See here how the dial is pointing that way? And the number five here means the static level is half of the maximum.'

'Ahh, I see now, very clever!' said Nathan, nodding with a satisfied smirk. 'I can't believe it's so easy to fix all his problems!'

Allen, still standing in the hallway, was feeling overwhelmed. His tongue lolled out of his mouth as he started panting quietly. Craving the feeling of safety, he walked into the lounge room and jumped up onto the couch. He made his way to his usual sleeping spot and sat down, trembling slightly. Allen was unsure why he'd felt a shock of pain in his neck before, but would soon figure it out.

'So, I think that'll do for today,' said Brooke. 'We can leave the biting problem for next time, just keep your hands away from his mouth until then! Also, don't forget to leave me a review online, we need other people to know that my method of training works, there are a lot of incompetent dog trainers out there!'

Petra smiled and winked. 'Yes of course! I can post a review—we'll do it online tonight.'

As Brooke stood up to leave, Allen felt another jolt of fear. The stranger was suddenly moving once more in his house. He had been used to seeing her stationary, but to have her move around again was very unsettling. He stood up on the couch and let out another bark of warning in her direction.

It happened again. Allen's world rocked as he felt pain jolting through his neck. He was now terrified. Without thinking, he reacted to the pain by letting out another bark. Predictably, mechanically, the collar responded. Allen shuddered as he was shocked again. This time, he made the connection; the realisation that the barking might cause the pain. With that thought in his mind, he was too afraid to release a third bark. The fear of the pain was now greater than the fear that caused him to bark. His heart thumping in his chest, he stood frozen on the couch, panting and too afraid to move. As Brooke left the house, he didn't bark again. In fact, he didn't bark again for the rest of that night.

Punishment Works

One of the saddest things about the use of force to make a dog behave, is that the people inflicting the abuse in most cases love the very dogs they are abusing. Allen is loved by his people, but he is not *understood*. The reason that some trainers recommend these methods to control a dog's behaviour, is that they appear to *work*. Dog trainers using these methods surely wouldn't turn to them if they weren't sometimes effective. Once people see the behaviour improving, this reinforces their belief that they are doing what is *right*, and they feel good about finding a solution. However, just because punishment *can* control the behaviour of a dog, it doesn't mean we should use it.

When Allen barks, it's normally due to fear, and he often turns to this behaviour without thinking. However, barking isn't always due to fear. Dogs often bark for all sorts of reasons. They can bark for attention, to alert their family of something, to ask for something, or for play. However, in relaxed dogs, owners almost never have a problem with these kinds of barks. They aren't annoying, they are easy to stop when ignored, and don't go on for long. These kinds of barks are voluntary, the dog decides to do them because they want to, it isn't an instinctive reaction. When a dog barks due to fear or anxiety, it isn't so much a decision as it is a reaction. This is why it's so hard for them to stop the behaviour.

Barking in dogs is very much like screaming in people. Sure, people *can* scream voluntarily, but other times they can't help it.

When someone feels a strong emotion like fear or pain, screaming can be an automatic reaction. How easy would it be to hold back a scream if you stubbed your toe, or a spider landed on your face? Not very easy for most people, but it can be controlled somewhat. Some people might be able to hold back their scream if they were in a crowded room, but it would be difficult. The reason they might do this, is that the fear of embarrassment outweighs the benefits of screaming. Most people wouldn't bother stifling their screams if they were at home.

Similarly, dogs too can learn to stop barking at things they fear. However, they need a good reason to do so. An electric shock is a pretty good reason. Essentially, the dog learns that the negative consequences of barking are so painful that they can overcome their instinctive reaction, and enter a state of learned helplessness. This is what happens to Allen when he is fitted with the shock collar. However, an electric shock is not the only aversive consequence that can teach a dog to inhibit an emotionally driven behaviour. People have been very inventive in this field, they also use spray bottles, yelling, smacking, prong collars, citronella spray, ultrasonic tones and more.

The severity of the aversive punishment that is required to stop a dog from barking is not the same for all dogs. Personally, I know that my ability to suppress a scream of pain is directly related to how much pain I am feeling. In some situations, a dog will be so fearful that even the highest (most painful) setting on a shock collar will fail to stop their barking. In other situations, if a dog is barking *without* any fear, a stern word from the owner will be enough to silence them. The level of punishment required to stop the behaviour is proportional to the strength of the emotion driving that behaviour. Sadly, due to Allen's extreme level of fear, only a very painful punishment is effective at stopping his barking.

Just as punishment can be used to control emotionally driven behaviours in dogs, so too can rewards. As discussed earlier in this book, punishment and reinforcement (reward) are both operant learning techniques, which can teach a dog to change their behaviour. Punishments teach an animal to do a behaviour less, and rewards teach them to do it more. However, reward-based training has the same limitation as punishment training: the reward required to convince a dog to suppress a fear-motivated bark is proportional to the intensity of the fear the dog is feeling. This means that when Allen is very fearful, he would need a very *powerful* reward to convince him to overcome the urge to bark. As we have seen so far, the food treats he is offered are not nearly rewarding enough to overcome his fear. Unfortunately, it is much easier to create a very strong punishment than to create a very strong reward. Imagine how you could be rewarded yourself. If money and assets didn't exist (dogs don't understand these things), can you think of anything that would be rewarding enough to out-compete the pain of having your neck choked or shocked? Fear and pain are strong motivators of behaviour, because ignoring them can result in death. This is why there is no positive reward that can compete with them. This is why training with punishment is easier than training with rewards; you can get strong motivation relatively easily. This is also the reason you can get much faster training results by shocking a dog than giving it a treat. However, as explained above, this has tragic consequences on the welfare of the animal.

In a world of ever-expanding technology, instant gratification is becoming more common. Online shopping is a perfect example, with companies delivering more things to your door faster than ever before, at the click of a button. We are becoming used to simple solutions for all our problems. It is logical and reasonable for people to expect an easy fix for dog behaviour issues, based on a simple and intuitive explanation. This is the poisoned apple that is so attractive to the carers of troubled dogs. As Nathan and Petra experienced, they found a dog trainer that promised a fast and easy solution. They see quick 'results', and this convinces them that they have chosen the best approach.

When owners or dog trainers turn to the dark side, and use punishment to control a dog, they sometimes achieve these fast results. However, as explained above, this is because pain and fear are much stronger motivators of behaviour than treats and praise. This can create a real conflict of interest for trainers that use punishment. As we see with Brooke in this chapter, 'balanced' trainers justify their use of pain to control a dog's behaviour in various ways. They tend to overlook or misread the emotional reaction to their techniques, and focus on the results. The ends justify the means. Trainers that aren't force-free also justify the use of punishment by only using it when 'necessary'. They have codes of practice that describe how punishment should only be used when other techniques don't work.[1] They also believe that when punishment is used as a last resort, only the minimum effective amount of punishment should be used. In this way, these trainers see themselves as being forced into using these techniques by necessity. However, as explained above, we know that the amount of punishment required is proportional to the amount of emotion driving the behaviour. This means that according to such trainers, the only cases where severe punishment is 'necessary' are the dogs like Allen who are already suffering the most.

CHAPTER NINE

Another Path Taken

Nella hated the feeling of being all alone at home with no people to sit next to. Everything was so different when they were gone. Even the television, normally a constant source of background noise, was silent as it waited for their return. At times she was able to distract herself, she could nearly forget she was alone. At other times, she would get worn out from all the worry. As she lay down on the mat at the front door, she was forced to endure the constant sinking feeling in the pit of her stomach. Unable to take it any longer, Nella got up to explore the house. She was looking for some kind of distraction to settle her nerves. Doing nothing wasn't an option. She climbed the stairs to check the bedrooms on the first floor, but the doors were all closed. Nella could remember from a long time ago that the doors used to be open when she was alone. Those were good times. She would lie on Tessa's bed, and she felt safer there than anywhere in the house. There were also lots of things to chew on in the rooms, which helped to soothe her anxiety.

Wanting desperately to get into Tessa's room, Nella stood up on her hind legs and scratched at the door. As she did this, her right paw got stuck over the handle. Then, as she gave up scratching and pulled her paws back down, she pulled the handle with it. Much to her surprise, the door swung open. Nella just stood there, staring in disbelief at the open bedroom in front of her. She had walked past this door countless times while alone, and not once had it opened for her. Nella soon recovered her senses and happily entered the bedroom. She immediately felt a little calmer, comforted to be in a central sleeping area of the house. This was the safest place to wait for her people. To further ease her worry, she selected one of Tessa's shoes from the floor, and picked it up in her mouth. Then she stepped onto the bed and lay down, shoe between her paws. It smelled like Tessa, and the soft white sides of the shoe felt good on her teeth as she gnawed into it. Eventually, once the shoe was destroyed, Nella had finally calmed down. Feeling tired from her stressful day, she drifted off to sleep.

* * *

Sometime later, Nella was awoken by the sound of the front door opening. She leapt up off the bed and hurried down the stairs. To her relief, she saw her family coming down the hallway. Nella started whining with anxious excitement, she was very happy to be reunited. Tessa grinned as she ran up to Nella and wrapped her arms around her neck.

'We missed you,' she whispered into her ear.

Nella leaned into Tessa, groaning softly as she panted, her wagging tail knocking into the wall. Mick and Olivia were happy to see her too. As they walked past, they both gave her a gentle pat on the head.

'Mick, did you remember to close Tessa's door before we left?' called out Olivia from the lounge room. She was looking up the stairs, and could see the door ajar.

'I'm certain we closed it, I made sure of it," said Mick in disbelief.

'Well, in that case she might have learned how to open doors!' exclaimed Olivia, as she climbed the stairs to investigate.

As Tessa and Mick followed Olivia into the room, they saw the dismembered shoe lying on the bed. Mick turned to Nella, who had followed them up the stairs, and spoke to her in his angry voice:

'Nella! You naughty girl, bad dog! No eating shoes!'

He picked up the remains of the shoe and tried to show it to Nella. Her heart sank, she hated it when her people spoke like this. She had faced this situation many times before. They would yell at her while showing her something she had chewed. Although she was familiar with the circumstance, Nella didn't understand why she was being yelled at. She just felt unwanted, and like she had failed them somehow. Trembling, she dropped her ears down, lowered her head, and looked up at him in appeasement. Mick pushed the shoe closer in front of her face, trying to press it into her mouth as he continued to scold her. Nella didn't need to chew the shoe now that everyone was home, and wasn't about to take it off Mick while he was yelling like that. She shied her head away, now looking at the ground.

'It's okay Nella, I forgive you,' said Tessa, leaning over to stroke Nella's neck.

This prompted Olivia to laugh, but she quickly covered her mouth and then looked guiltily at Mick. Mick responded by throwing his hands up in the air and stomping out of the room.

'I give up!' he said. 'When that trainer comes over later, they'd better have some good advice!'

As the family were finishing their lunch at the dining room table, Olivia heard a scuffling of paws behind her. She turned around to see Nella, standing in the doorway, holding a pair of socks in her mouth. She was wagging her tail and had a sparkle in her eye.

'Nella!' yelled Olivia, getting up from the table. 'Put those socks down now!'

As Olivia walked towards her, Nella turned and ran down the hallway. Nella loved the attention she got when she had human clothes in her mouth. As she ran down the hallway, away from Olivia, her heart raced with joy and excitement. Olivia groaned and chased her up the stairs and into her bedroom. She saw a basket of folded washing sitting next to the bed.

'So that's where you found it!' exclaimed Olivia. 'Nothing is safe with you around!'

Nella, now cornered, moved back to the other side of the room. As Olivia approached her, she lowered her head and moved it into the wall, preventing her from taking back the socks. Olivia reached over and took hold of them, pulling the socks back towards her. Nella wagged her tail; she liked playing tug of war! She was hopeful they could start the game now. Olivia, frustrated that Nella wasn't letting go, yanked hard on the socks and barked a command.

'Drop!'

Sensing that Olivia was angry, Nella submitted and released the socks. It was just a game after all, there was no sense in starting a fight. Nella lay down on the floor and rolled onto her back, tail wagging. With Nella looking up at her, Olivia frowned and stomped her foot.

'Great, so now you are acting all cute. How am I supposed to stay mad with you?'

Olivia ushered Nella out of the bedroom and closed the door behind her. Nella bounded down the stairs, found her rope toy under the table and then ran up to Tessa. Hoping to play with her, Nella pushed the toy into Tessa's lap.

'I'm gonna play with Nella now, Dad,' said Tessa as she slid off her chair while holding the rope.

Nella slowly pulled Tessa along from the other end of the rope, shaking it gently from side to side. Tessa pulled back, and Nella moved with her. Tessa suddenly dropped the rope and ran into the front room of the house. Nella followed, bringing the toy after her. They played there together for a while, taking turns with the rope, until they were suddenly interrupted.

The sound of a barking dog echoed through the front window. Nella quickly dropped the toy and pricked up her ears. She sensed that the bark was an alarm call, so she rushed to the front window to check out the street. Nella was on edge, she knew that other dogs were dangerous, as were strange people. She worried that some of them might be coming close to her territory.

'Nella, why did you stop playing? Here—get the rope' said Tessa, as she shook the toy at her.

Nella didn't pay any attention to it, as she had just spotted some movement outside. A lady was walking a shaggy white spaniel with brown splotched fur on the footpath outside the house. This was serious, Nella had to act now. She let out a booming bark through the window. Her bark was so loud that the lady got startled, despite being all the way out on the street. She jumped to the side, looked at the house briefly, then kept walking. Nella, standing with her hackles up, watched them walk away. Feeling relieved that her bark had worked, she started to calm down for a moment. It didn't last long though, as a car pulled up out the front of the house. She had seen this happen before; Nella knew that people often climbed out of cars. As expected, a person soon emerged. She was a tall lady wearing jeans and a collared shirt. Worried by the stranger, Nella let out another loud bark.

'Nella, too loud!' cried Tessa, her hands over her ears.

The lady opened the front gate and started walking towards their house through the yard. Nella barked again—with more fear this time.

'Nella quiet!' called Mick, as he came to see what all the noise was about.

'There is a lady here Dad,' said Tessa, just before the doorbell rang.

As Nella continued to bark, Mick pulled her back into the study. Olivia answered the door.

'Hello, are you the dog trainer?' asked Olivia as she opened the door.

'Yes, greetings! My name is Lily, and that must be Nella I can hear inside!'

Olivia rolled her eyes in exasperation, nodding as she beckoned Lily inside. Once they had all introduced each other, their attention turned to the loud noises coming from the study.

'Would it be safe to let Nella out of the room if she was on a leash?' asked Lily as she sat down at the table.

Mick and Olivia looked at each other and nodded in agreement.

'She's a big sook really,' said Mick. 'All bark and no bite. I don't think we need the leash, but it wouldn't hurt just to be safe.'

A few minutes later, Mick opened the study door with Nella on the end of a leather rope. Seeing the stranger sitting at the table, she let out three frantic barks before settling into a low rumbling growl. Nella was fearful of the stranger in her house, and felt unsure of what to do. She just stood there in the doorway, watching Lily, with her front left foot held off the ground. She was ready to move at a moment's notice, but wasn't sure if she would be going forwards or backwards. Being unsure, she stayed very still with her head a little lowered, and her tail tucked slightly between her legs.

Lily didn't move either, she kept very still and in a calm voice began to explain. 'Okay, she's obviously worried about me being here, which is fair enough, I am an intruder after all!

'I'm just going to try ignoring her for a few minutes. Olivia, do you think you could try feeding her some treats in the meantime?'

As Olivia went to fetch the treats, Nella stayed still, silently watching Lily. Nella wondered why she was just sitting there, not reacting to her barking or even looking in her direction. People always reacted when Nella barked, this was quite disconcerting! On the other hand, seeing Lily doing nothing and just sitting still wasn't very threatening. Nella found it much more intimidating when the things she was worried about actually moved. Stationary threats seemed safer.

Lily felt herself sliding off the edge of her seat and readjusted herself without thinking.

Nella's heart jumped in her chest. The stranger had moved. Automatically, another round of barks erupted from her chest.

'Nella! Be nice!' hissed Mick, before looking at Lily apologetically. 'I'm so sorry. As you can see it's pretty bad.'

Lily slowly shook her head, smiling. 'It's fine Mick, I'm used to it. All part of the job.'

Olivia approached Nella and held a morsel of chicken in front of her nose. Staring at Lily, Nella sniffed at the chicken once before ignoring it. With a stranger in the house, this was not the time to eat.

'Come on Nelly,' cooed Olivia, offering it to her again. 'Don't you want a little bit of chicken?'

Reluctantly, Nella opened her mouth and took the piece of chicken. This was one of her favourite treats after all. She chewed it once and swallowed, all the while watching Lily from the doorway.

Olivia smiled and stroked her head. 'Good girl Nelly. See? It's okay, she's a nice lady.'

'Wonderful,' encouraged Lily softly. 'Now keep giving her little bits of chicken, don't stop!'

As Olivia continued to give small pieces of meat to Nella, her appetite was reignited. Olivia's hand was soon covered in slobber.

'Perfect, now see if you can encourage her to come a bit closer?' suggested Lily.

Olivia made some clicking noises as she took a few steps back towards Lily, beckoning Nella with another piece of chicken. Nella was torn. She looked at the treat, then back at Lily, then back at the treat again. Slowly, Nella took two tentative steps forwards. Staying as far away as possible, she stretched out her head and took the reward.

'That settles it,' remarked Lily. 'Looking at the way she's behaving, I can't imagine she'll launch at me if I stay still. If I move though, it could be very dangerous.

'Why don't you keep her on the leash, but come sit down at the table with me? I have a few questions to ask about her behaviour.'

'I agree,' said Mick, lifting Tessa onto his lap and seating himself at the table. 'She doesn't seem to want to get close to you at all right now.'

Nella stood back and eyed Lily suspiciously, panting anxiously. As they sat around the table, they discussed her issues at length. Including her barking at dogs on walks, and strangers in the home. Her reaction to loud noises and thunderstorms, and her problems with destroying things when left alone.

'So, is that all her problems then, nothing else you would like to add?' asked Lily.

Olivia paused, then smiled. 'No, that's it. I would think these are quite enough problems for one dog, don't you?'

By this point, Nella had been watching Lily for quite a while. She was starting to feel more familiar with her. While she was talking, Lily had been inconspicuously tossing very small beef-flavoured treats towards her. Initially, Nella had been suspicious of the treats, and ate them only after carefully inspecting each one. Now she was gulping them up as soon as they landed on the ground. She fell into the routine of quickly eating each titbit and then patiently waiting for Lily to drop the next one. Nella didn't consciously realise it, but she was starting to *like* Lily due to the positive association. While this was making her less fearful of Lily, part of her remained very suspicious. When Nella ate a treat that had fallen very close to Lily, she noticed an interesting smell on her shoe. Overcome with curiosity, Nella started sniffing at the shoe, and then up her leg. This lady had the scent of many dogs on her. Nella could smell that Lily was a calm person, not stressed like how Mick smelled. She started to trust her even more. When Lily offered Nella a treat directly from her hand, she slowly wagged her tail and gently took it.

All the while, Lily was continuing to talk to the others.

'I think we should go on a dog walk now, so you can show me her other issues.

'Firstly, I'll just get you to put Nella on the leash in advance and walk her away from me, so she doesn't get frightened as I stand up, okay?'

Mick walked Nella away from Lily and towards the front door. When Lily did stand up, Nella was quite far away and didn't pay her any attention. She had realised they might be going for a walk, and was focused on the door.

As Lily followed Nella and her family down the street, Nella fell back into her usual routine. She needed to look out for dangers. She had become progressively worse in this regard over the last few months, to the point where it was almost all she focused on. While they were walking, Lily continued to give Nella more of the small treats, one after another. This would momentarily disrupt her vigilant state, but each time it only lasted a second.

After passing a few houses, they walked past a tall green bush covered in autumn leaves that had fallen from the tree above. As they came past the far side of the bush, Nella spotted a man on the other side of the road. He was wearing a large floppy hat as he watered his garden with a hose. Nella stopped and stared, but Lily quickly reacted. She offered Nella a particularly large treat to distract her. But Nella ignored it, her stomach was knotted with worry. Food was the last thing she could think about. She tried to pull forwards but was held back by the leash. Needing to vent her fear and frustration, Nella let out a very loud bark. The man across the road was startled, tripping over the hose as he walked. It fell to the ground and started snaking back and forward, wetting him in the process. He quickly started chasing after it, but from Nella's perspective, all this commotion only made things worse. She readied herself for another loud bark.

Sensing things weren't going well, Lily decided to deescalate the situation immediately.

'Okay everyone, let's turn back—look what's over here!' called out Lily in a cheery voice. She quickly started walking back the way they'd come.

Mick, surprised by the sudden change of course, stood stunned for a second, which allowed Nella to continue to bark. Mick trusted Nella, he had always thought that letting her do a bit of what she wanted would be good for her. He would normally have waited in this situation, to try and get Nella used to the thing she was worried about. After all, she was literally pulling to get closer to this person.

Once Nella had been begrudgingly pulled away, they quickly moved back behind the bush. With the man out of sight, Nella found it easier to follow them down the path. Even though she was keen to try and scare off the stranger with her bark, she was relieved to have moved in the other direction. Lily tried offering her another treat, but she wasn't ready yet—things were still too dicey.

'See, I told you she was bad,' said Mick, looking at Lily. 'She started doing that about a month ago, and it seems to be getting worse.'

Lily sighed, looking down at Nella sadly as she panted while scanning the street. 'She isn't a bad dog Mick, she really isn't.'

Tessa looked up at Olivia knowingly. 'I told you Mum...'

'I know she isn't bad around us,' agreed Olivia, glancing from Tessa to Lily. 'But she just misbehaves so much in other situations.'

'I think she's just a bit misunderstood,' Lily continued. 'Nella is showing me today that she has a lot of stress in her life, there are a lot of things that really worry or scare her, and she has to deal with these things on a regular basis. It can't be easy to go through all that.'

'But I don't get it, she has such an *easy* life' said Mick, gazing down at Nella as he shook his head. 'What's she so scared of?'

'Well, she is clearly fearful of people,' replied Lily. 'Like when I arrived at your door, and the man watering his lawn just now.'

Mick frowned, tilting his head to the side. 'But I thought she just didn't like strangers and was a bit protective. If she was scared of them, wouldn't she run away or something? Why would she want to draw attention to herself by barking?'

'It's hard to explain,' said Lily. 'But sometimes offence is the best defence. Lots of people hide when they are scared, but some people actually attack. Have you ever been scared, and then yelled at someone?'

Mick thought to himself for a few moments as he was walking, then raised his eyebrows in surprise as a thought came to him. 'That's exactly how I was when we got robbed a few weeks ago! I was freaking out, having robbers in the house, but I ran after them and chased them out the window! Is that how Nella feels when she barks at things?'

'Exactly,' agreed Lily, smiling at the analogy. 'She isn't being naughty, she doesn't know it upsets us, she is just looking to protect herself—and probably you guys too. It makes her anxious as well, always worrying about these threats around her.'

'So how do we know when she is feeling anxious?' asked Olivia with a concerned look.

Lily pointed at Nella's mouth, open wide with her tongue hanging out. 'The most consistent sign of stress and anxiety is panting, but they only do this once they are fairly worried. They also pant to cool down, or when they are exercising—so anxiety isn't the only cause. Otherwise, they might do lots of little things like yawning, not settling, whining, not listening to you, constantly looking around, things like that. Do you notice her doing those things at home sometimes?'

'Yes!' exclaimed Tessa, waving her hand in the air. 'When we put on our shoes or jackets and leave the house, she always does that.'

Olivia gazed down at Tessa and sighed in agreement. 'Tessa's right, she does all those things as we get ready to leave, and when we come home. She was also doing that when we had storms last week, but I just thought she didn't like them...'

As they walked back through the gate and into their front yard, Nella had calmed down somewhat. She was still on edge, but when Lily offered her a treat, she was relaxed enough to take it. When they walked back into the house, she wasn't so worried about Lily intruding into their home. Nella chose to follow close behind her as they came through the door.

'I can't believe how good she's being with you now,' remarked Olivia, smiling in disbelief. 'I think she likes you!'

Lily sat down on the couch and went to get out her folder of documents. Nella climbed up next to her, turned around and casually sat her rump right in the middle of Lily's lap. She had decided that she liked Lily, she was so calm and gave her lots of treats. She also didn't force herself into Nella's space or try to touch her on the head like other strangers tended to do.

Grinning, Lily started scratching Nella's side. 'See, you're just a big baby, aren't you Nella! You act all tough, but inside you're just a scared little puppy dog.'

Nella liked the sound of Lily's voice, and turned around to try and lick her on the face.

'Come on Nella,' said Mick, feigning disapproval. 'We actually have work to do here, how's she supposed to work with you doing that!?'

Mick pulled Nella away by the collar and held her next to him on the couch. Nella was relieved that she could trust Lily now, and excited to have made a new friend. Sensing that Mick wasn't going to let her climb all over Lily, Nella stretched out on the couch in between them.

Lily slowly put her hand behind Nella's ear and gave her a scratch. 'So, where were we? Ah yes, I was just going to say that I think Nella might benefit from seeing our vet Ava for a behavioural consultation.

'Nella is experiencing a lot of stress in different situations, so it's important to have a vet look into the case. She could have some medical conditions contributing to her behaviour, or even have a mental health illness.

'She may also need medications to help her cope with things. What do you think?'

Olivia and Mick looked at each other, unsure.

'I'm not sure about medications,' Olivia blurted. 'It just doesn't feel right to me, and I don't want to change her personality.'

'Yeah, maybe if there was something natural?' added Mick, uncrossing his arms. 'Like a supplement we could try, or a special diet?'

'Well, Ava is not your average vet,' said Lily, nodding respectfully. 'She's done a lot of extra behaviour education, and she wouldn't do anything if it wasn't in Nella's best interest, I can assure you.

'How about I just leave you with her card, and you think about it. Even just seeing her for a second opinion would be a good idea. She is a vet after all, and sometimes medical issues can strongly affect a dog's behaviour.'

'Thanks,' said Mick, reaching out to take the card. 'It's actually a good idea, I guess I was just hoping this might be a bit simpler to fix.'

Lily sighed and looked at Mick sympathetically. 'There is rarely a quick fix for a dog's behaviour. Don't ever trust *anyone* who promises you that.'

Lily pulled out her notepad and pen from her bag and placed it on her lap. She started jotting down notes as she talked. 'So, I'm going to write down my recommendations for you here, so you don't forget. Until you can see Ava, I think it is better to just avoid the things that are setting Nella off. Here's what you need to do.

'Firstly, at home with the barking, I think it would be better to just block off her view of the street. She's getting overly worked up and worried, I think it's making her feel unsafe in her own home.

"Out of sight, out of mind" is my motto for this problem. You can either keep the blinds down, or get the windows frosted, or just keep her out of that room. Do you think that would work?'

'Yeah, didn't think of that,' replied Olivia, raising her eyebrows in surprise. 'Guess we could work out something pretty easy.'

Lily clicked her pen a few times and started writing again as she continued. 'Great, next thing to tackle is the walks. I don't think it makes sense to have Nella unnecessarily exposed to people or dogs on walks if it's just going to make her freak out.

'I know you want to fix her behaviour on walks, but it hasn't been improving so far and I can't see it magically getting better if we just keep doing the same thing.'

'True,' replied Mick. 'It's getting worse, not better. So do you think we *shouldn't* walk her then?'

'No, you need to try and keep walking her if you can,' she said with a sorrowful look. 'We just need to make sure the walks are enjoyable for her. She hates leaving you alone so would never consider not going, but I am not sure she even enjoys them at this point.

'She was so anxious on that walk she wouldn't even eat a treat once the man set her off. And she wasn't even sniffing the grass either. That's not normal, that's not a sign of a dog enjoying a walk.'

'So how do we walk her without her freaking out then?' asked Olivia.

'Well, we just avoid the problems for now. You need to walk her at times when there aren't as many people around, and on a route that's quiet, with less dogs. You might even have to drive for five minutes before starting if this area's too busy.'

Frowning, Mick looked up at the ceiling as he thought to himself. 'There's a reserve near here that's pretty quiet in the mornings, I sometimes go through there on my runs. Maybe we can try that.'

'Great! So, the next problem is her destroying things when you leave her. I'm worried that she could have some separation-related distress that's causing that behaviour.'

'You don't think her destroying things is just her being a naughty puppy, like teething or something?' questioned Olivia, squinting.

Lily sighed, shifted position, and explained. 'She's nine months old now, I think the teething phase is over. Her destructive behaviour could be a sign she isn't coping well with being left alone.'

Mick tilted his head suspiciously. 'I guess it could be, how would we know?'

'If you can, try to take some video footage' suggested Lily. 'To see what she does when you leave her alone. Bring it next time you see Ava or me, and we can have a look to see if she seems stressed.'

As Lily packed her bag and got up to leave, Nella followed her closely. She knew that Lily often dropped treats unexpectedly, and didn't want to miss out on any. Indeed, as the door closed behind her, Lily tossed one last small treat through the crack as it closed.

Exposure Therapy

In this chapter, we see Nella having problems barking on her walks, which is a common issue encountered by dog owners. The most common cause of this barking is fear of other dogs, although there are some less common exceptions. If you ask people why they think dogs bark at other dogs on walks, the word 'socialisation' often comes up. This leads to the explanation that the dog didn't hang out with enough other dogs when it was young, and that's the cause of all the problems. We also saw Nathan and Petra having similar thoughts about Allen earlier in the book. A lack of socialisation in puppies is certainly undesirable, but I believe it often becomes a scapegoat for all dangerous or threatening behaviours in adult dogs. I have published research in this field,[1] and the one thing that keeps getting overlooked by other researchers and the public is the *quality* of the socialisation that the puppy is receiving. If a puppy like Allen is 'socialised' as we have seen in this book, do you really think the problem is with the *amount* of socialisation he is getting?

Once a dog is having problems on walks with barking or biting, many owners look to fix the problem. When people think a lack of socialisation might have caused the problem, they often try to fix the problem by providing the dog with as much exposure to other dogs as they can. Similarly, if they think fear may be the origin of the problem, they might try to get their dog 'used' to other dogs by exposing them to dogs while feeding treats.

In all these examples, I see the same mistakes made by owners. That is, they assume their dog just needs exposure to other dogs, along with some rewards or punishment (or both). The more the better. This is a bit like how people think about socialisation of puppies, they consider the *amount* of exposure to be the key factor, rather than the *quality* of the exposure. When attempting to treat a dog's fears using exposure therapy, quality is key.

Desensitisation

Desensitisation is a classical (emotional) learning technique that allows a dog to disassociate a trigger from its emotional reaction. We can desensitise a dog (or other animal) to any trigger that causes an emotional reaction, such as separation-related anxiety, or fear of unfamiliar people. The way to achieve this is to repeatedly expose the dog to the trigger in a way that doesn't elicit the emotion. This is very confusing for most people, so don't worry if you're lost already. It will all make sense soon. I recommend thinking about the concept of a 'neutral experience' versus a 'bad experience'. Even the things that are most triggering can be experienced in a neutral way. For example, if you had a phobia of snakes, you might still be able to look at a plastic toy snake from a safe distance without being worried. If not, then you can always make the trigger less worrying. You could make the toy snake smaller, or more cartoon-like, or place it further away. Eventually, you should be able to have a 'neutral experience' with the snake. The idea of a 'bad experience' is self-evident—if you saw the snake and your heart leapt in your chest, we are calling that a 'bad experience'. This is because you experienced the emotion we are trying to desensitise against.

Let's use Nella's fear of unfamiliar dogs as our desensitisation example. When Nella sees another dog on a walk and doesn't react or get scared, this is a neutral experience. In some cases, this might only happen when they are 50m away. Every time Nella has a fearful incident on a walk, as happens when she sees another dog and barks at it, this is a bad experience. When Nella goes on a walk, we can start counting the number of neutral or bad experiences she is having. For desensitisation to be effective, most dogs need a large number of neutral experiences for every single bad experience. This is why the quality of exposure is so important, and the reason that so many people fail to see improvement. It isn't 'socialisation' or 'desensitisation' if a person is just standing there while their dog barks at other dogs from a distance. This kind of exposure is simply an unnecessary negative experience, with no benefit.

Counter conditioning

Counter conditioning is another technique we can use to train the emotions of a dog. This method aims to turn negative experiences into positive experiences. The reason this works, is that it's very difficult for the brain to simultaneously feel positive and negative emotions together in the same moment. For example, it's hard to feel sad while you are laughing, or to feel happy while you are in pain. So, we use this trick to train the brain to associate a positive emotion with a trigger that normally causes a negative emotion. This means the positive emotion can outcompete the negative emotion, thereby reducing its association with the trigger. However, counter conditioning should only be used alongside desensitisation, and should never be used on its own. This is because we want to turn a 'neutral experience' as discussed in the desensitisation section, into a 'good experience' that is enjoyable. This is much easier than turning a bad experience into a good experience.

Where it all goes wrong

Now that we have covered the right way to do things, let's explain where it all goes wrong. Firstly, people end up giving their dog too many bad experiences and not enough good experiences for the exposure to be helpful. The advanced difficulty of training the emotions of dogs is too much for many people. In other situations, the environment is too unpredictable. If you live in an area where other dogs appear out of side streets or houses without warning, it doesn't even matter how good your skills are, you're doomed to fail. We could see this happening to Nella on her walk, where people and dogs seemed to appear out of nowhere. Unfortunately, in many cases like Nella's, getting enough positive or neutral experiences to outweigh the negative experiences can be very difficult or impossible.

Another thing that people complain about when trying to fix their dog, is that 'treats don't work'. As we see with Nella, when she's worried, she doesn't have an appetite. This is an example of why you can't try to use counter conditioning if you aren't simultaneously desensitising. That is, it's too hard to turn a bad experience into a good experience using treats. The problem is not that 'treats don't work', it's that you are currently exposing the dog to a *bad* experience rather than a neutral one. Treats are best for turning a neutral experience into a good experience, but to do that, you need to have the right level of exposure to begin with. You can see in this chapter that Lily is very good at this, as she instantly moves Nella away from the scary man with the hose, before even attempting to offer her a treat.

When people fail to properly implement exposure therapy to train their dog, they often assume that this is because the methods themselves are no good. People naturally believe that the advice is bad, and if they could get better advice then they would have a solution. However, it is very rare to find a dog who is unable to respond to a perfectly implemented desensitisation and counter conditioning regime. These rare exceptions are almost always dogs that are unwell, perhaps due to severe pain, senility, cognitive defects, or severe mental health problems. If a dog isn't improving, it's almost always because the training method or environment is not ideal. This does not mean that this ideal situation is practically achievable. In some cases, like with Nella, it isn't. It takes a lot of knowledge and experience to understand this. We will explore what can be done for cases like Nella in the subsequent chapters.

CHAPTER TEN

Success?

Nathan finished the last sip of his coffee and leaned back on the couch. Petra sat next to him. She was bathed in a sunbeam that streamed through the window, warming her as she read her book. Nathan glanced down at Allen, who was lying asleep on Petra's lap. He stroked his hand down the side of Allen's body, feeling the smooth fur slide under his fingers. Petra joined in, putting her hand over Allen's head, then gently along his neck. Her fingers slid down the side of his bulky shock collar and moved on to delicately scratch his fur.

'How's the book?' asked Nathan, interrupting the peace.

Petra finished reading her sentence before replying. 'It's really good, but sad. There's this girl trying to help her friend by chasing away a guy that likes her, and she thinks he's a bad guy but he's not.

'She doesn't realise that he's actually really good, but everything he does gets misunderstood. It's so sad because he has a really good heart, but no-one sees it.'

Nathan was about to reply when he heard the sound of a dog yapping a few houses away. Petra and Nathan both looked down at Allen together, watching for his reaction as his head jerked up. The dog barked again. Allen jumped off Petra's lap and onto the floor in one leap. His hackles up, he ran towards the front room panting. Allen's heart was racing as he looked out the window to see a dog walking along the street, pulling at its leash.

As the owner yelled, 'No' at the dog and tugged back on the lead, Allen stared in horror. He desperately wanted to ward off these intruders, but he was completely defenceless. Looking up from her seat on the couch, Petra could see Allen in the front room. She saw him staring out the window, his mouth open. He was panting so widely you could see his teeth.

'I can't believe how much he has changed!' she commented. 'He's even smiling as he watches out the window now.'

Allen could take it no more, something had to be done. His mind was at its limit. Unable to bark, and in complete panic, he turned around and bit at his tail, narrowly missing it. Pausing for a moment in surprise, he realised he felt a bit better. This gave him something to do. An outlet that distracted him from the street. He did it again. Focusing on his tail felt good, it relieved him from having to worry about the stress of the outside world. It helped him disassociate from reality. He did it a third time, spinning around and biting at his tail, but this time he didn't stop. Allen kept on spinning, focusing on his tail as his mind attempted to cope with an impossibly stressful situation.

Petra's face lit up as she smiled at the sight of Allen spinning in circles. 'Nath, look he's even playing now, chasing his tail, oh it's so cute. Quick, get my phone, I want to record it!'

Nathan was now also staring at Allen. He laughed, picking up his phone and quickly setting it to record the action. Allen continued to spin in little circles for another few seconds before stopping to look out the window again. By this time, the street was quiet, the strange dog and person were gone, everything was back to normal again. Allen snapped out of his trance and let out a big sigh. When he looked around, he saw Nathan and Petra smiling at him from the couch. His tail let out a subdued wag at the sight of them, and he slowly walked back towards the couch. Head down, tail limp, he put one foot in front of the other as his mind continued to process what had just happened.

'He's such a good boy, maybe we should take him for a walk now while it's still sunny?' suggested Nathan.

'Okay, let's go quick, I am sure it's going to rain later,' replied Petra as she stood up off the couch.

As Petra was putting on her runners at the front door, she looked over at Nathan. 'Hey, do you remember how he was still barking yesterday on his walk? Even though we were correcting him with the choker?'

'Yeah, I did notice that' he replied. 'He's been so good though; I hope he isn't falling back into his old habits. Are you thinking we should try leaving his static collar on today?'

'Why not?' said Petra cheerfully. 'It worked so well with barking inside—I reckon we try it. Hopefully that way he learns it's not acceptable to bark at other dogs under any circumstances.'

Nathan gazed at Petra with a distant expression. 'Sure, it can't do any harm to give it a shot!'

As Nathan bent down with the choker chain in his hand, Allen was already panting. Allen knew what the chain meant, and the runners on his people's feet. They were going out to patrol their territory again. Allen whined and rolled onto his back, exposing his belly. He flicked his tongue out and licked his nose as Nathan slipped the chain over his neck.

Nathan carefully inspected the chain sitting next to the shock collar on Allen's neck. 'It fits okay with the static collar, just sits above it.'

Once Petra opened the door, Allen leapt up and looked outside. Steeling himself for what he knew was to come, he started walking. As he made his way down the path and through the front gate, Allen knew he couldn't pull. There was little enjoyment left in walks for him, but he couldn't imagine not going. It was his routine, his duty. As they meandered down the street, the winter sun warmed his back. Allen was at a comfortable temperature, but he was panting heavily and had an unpleasant sinking feeling in the pit of his stomach.

Before long, Allen had noticed another dog. It was on the other side of the road, walking in their direction. He stared at the dog and trembled, but didn't bark. He still feared having the chain jerk tight around his neck. He tucked his tail between his legs and kept walking, trying not to think about its presence. As they turned into the dog park, Allen heard barking coming from the fenced-in area.

The barking dog was large and brown, with short fur and a wrinkly face. It was wagging its tail in the air with its bottom sticking up as it crouched low on its front legs in a play bow. The other dog, a golden Labrador, stood panting and looking to the side. As the large brown dog ran up to the Labrador and tried to pin it to the ground, the Labrador spun around and gently bit back. The Labrador was careful to act as though the bite was playful, so as not to escalate things. It stood back again, panting and looking away, hoping the large dog would leave it alone.

'Maybe one day Allen will be playing in there like that too,' said Petra.

Nathan, who had also been watching the interaction, smiled in agreement. 'Yeah, hopefully!'

As they walked alongside the fence, a small white terrier noticed Allen. It ran up to them, barking an anxious greeting.

It had happened again. Allen was caught in an emotional checkmate. Reacting on instinct and adrenaline, he felt himself snap. Allen barked back at the dog.

Instantly, the collar around his neck calculated that a bark had been detected, and a shock was released.

Allen let out a muffled whimper as he felt the pain radiate through his neck. Stunned, he cowered and froze on the spot. Allen registered that the zapping pain could now happen on walks too. The terrier kept barking.

'Jinny! Get back here,' yelled a young lady from the other side of the park. The terrier turned her head and lowered her ears, then slowly walked back towards her owner.

When Nathan and Petra finally started walking forwards again, Allen didn't follow. Nathan looked back to see him hunched over and quivering.

'Allen, you know not to bark! Don't act all sorry now,' he mocked. 'Just don't bark next time and you won't get the static!'

'He is such a sook!' added Petra, shaking her head.

Allen picked himself up and slowly started following them along the track. His head down, putting one foot in front of the other, he disengaged from his surroundings. He didn't bother to smell the fresh scents all around him. Ruled by fear and forced into subjugation, he wouldn't have pulled on the leash if he could, what was the point?

As they continued to walk, the large brown dog chased the Labrador along the fence line, passing by no more than a few meters away.

Allen winced, but didn't react.

'Wow, that worked well, I think he got the picture,' said Petra smugly. She pulled out a small treat from her pocket. 'Here buddy, have this for being such a good boy.'

'Now we got the barking sorted, he's pretty much the perfect dog!' added Nathan.

Allen looked at the treat, but barely registered it. He had no appetite.

'Wow Allen, you are getting so fussy with your food!' complained Petra.

* * *

Tessa ran into the kitchen to see Mick preparing dinner. Nella followed shortly after, half slipping on the tiles as she turned the corner too fast.

'Dad, can I please give Nella a snack?' asked Tessa.

Nella caught up next to her, wagging her tail and panting. They had been running around in the front room together, and she was getting puffed out and hot. As she panted, the air cooled her body from the inside as she eagerly waited to see what her people would do next.

Mick's heart melted as he looked back and forward between them, both staring up at him.

'Yes sweetie, here have this,' he said, handing Tessa some dried liver.

'Nella, do you wanna sit for a treat?' asked Tessa.

Nella sat down, her tail wagging furiously. As Tessa gave her the piece of dried liver, Nella took it immediately and swallowed as fast as she could. She needed to be ready to eat the next piece, so couldn't take her time chewing this one. To her surprise, another piece didn't come.

'Good girl Nella!' said Tessa warmly, before running off back to the front room. Nella stood up and watched Tessa disappear from the kitchen, feeling disappointment that there were no more snacks. Still hopeful, Nella turned back to Mick who had resumed chopping the carrots. She wondered if he might offer her another treat. Remembering that sitting was the way to get food, she put her bottom on the ground once more and wagged her tail vigorously in an effort to get his attention.

'No more treats Nella, go see what Tessa's doing,' said Mick, smiling at her optimistic attempt.

Nella didn't understand the words, but after a few more seconds she sensed that her efforts probably wouldn't be rewarded.

'Nella, look what I found,' yelled Tessa from the front room. 'It's Lamby, she was behind the couch!'

Hearing her name, Nella stood up and trotted back towards Tessa to see what was going on. On her way, she heard the sound of a large truck pulling up outside their house. No one else noticed. Nella knew these sounds from the street could be dangerous. She ran up to the front window to look outside, ready to ward off the threat with a powerful warning bark. As she looked at the window, she remembered that she couldn't see out anymore. The window blinds were down. She tried looking around the side of the blinds, but the gap was too small. Still worried, she paced up and down, but didn't bark. Unable to see the source of the noise, she didn't get as worked up as she used to. Olivia was sitting near the window in a large, padded seat reading a magazine. She looked up to see how Nella was responding.

'I think putting the blinds down is working Mickey!' she called out to the kitchen.

'Really? Great, but I still think we're just avoiding the problem,' Mick replied. 'It"s not actually teaching her anything...'

Nella turned to see Tessa shaking a toy lamb in her direction, and quickly forgot about what might be out on the street. She jumped over to Tessa with one large bound and gently grabbed the lamb in her mouth. Tessa pulled it from side to side as Nella held on, enjoying the game, and feeling happy to be busy. It distracted her from her worries. Unfortunately for Nella, Tessa was getting tired. Before long she had crawled up onto Olivia's lap and closed her eyes. Nella was left without her playmate, and in that moment needed to decide what to do. The feeling of worry that she so often felt was starting to creep back into her belly. There was no cause of the feeling that Nella could identify, it was just a general unease. Looking down at the toy lamb, she decided it was time to help herself feel better. She whined and then picked up the lamb and started pacing around, chewing on it.

Seeing this, Olivia called out down the hall. 'I think we might need to take Nella for another walk, Mickey. She still has so much energy.'

There was a pause, and then Mick replied. 'Yeah okay, the casserole needs to go in the oven for an hour, so we might as well.'

Still feeling a little anxious, Nella lay down on the ground and started pulling at the toy's shell, trying to get at the stuffing. As she was busily trying to tear off the fabric, she was preoccupied enough to be distracted from her feelings.

Olivia stood up, hefting Tessa in her arms. 'Tessa's asleep though,' she said as she made her way into the kitchen. 'I think I might have to leave her here with you and take Nella on my own.'

'Okay,' replied Mick. 'Just lay her on the couch out here, I should probably watch the food in the oven anyway.'

As Olivia and Nella walked out their front gate, Nella pulled ahead. She rushed to the nearest tree to sniff at its base. She remembered this tree, it always had an interesting smell, quite a few of the local dogs regularly marked here. As she inhaled the scent of their urine, she concentrated, and her mind expanded with the array of scents. Once she had gone over them all in her mind, she lifted her head and looked around. The street was quiet, and she sighed in relief. They started along the path, this time going away from the local oval where Olivia knew other dogs would be. Nella was getting used to this new route, they would go three houses along the street and then cross over at the big brown tree trunk. Olivia knew that the next house along had a dog that often barked at them, so she avoided being too close to it. They crossed the road and turned down a side street.

A few minutes later, Olivia noticed another dog being walked by a lady with a pram coming towards them. Before Nella had seen them, she turned them around.

'Hey Nelly come on, let's go this way girl!'

Nella looked back, surprised, and turned to follow Olivia back the way they had come. Olivia led them down another side street to loop back to the house. They didn't encounter any more dogs the rest of the walk. Nella continued to sniff at the trees, the grass, and the bushes. She happily trotted alongside Olivia for the most part, although she did lurch her arm at times to get to the really interesting smells in a hurry.

Nella felt good; for the last few walks she hadn't had any frights. She was starting to get used to it. Her thoughts were changing, she wasn't expecting to have to bark at other dogs all the time.

Then, right as they were about to turn back into their street, a man walking a small wire-haired dog appeared from a house behind them. Olivia noticed the movement, but Nella wasn't aware yet.

'Come on Nella, let's go,' she said, skipping ahead to try and coax her forwards.

As the man closed the gate behind him and started down the path, the latch made a loud clunking noise.

Nella looked back as she started to follow Olivia, to see what had caused the sound. At first, she noticed the man, which worried her a bit, but then she noticed the scruffy little black dog walking next to him. A pang of fear shot through her, and she let out a short sharp bark followed by a soft growl.

Olivia started pulling Nella away by the leash, calling her name cheerily. The man looked back and scowled at them, shaking his head as he walked off. Olivia pulled out a treat from a pouch on her waist, and showed it to Nella as she continued to drag her backwards. Begrudgingly, Nella gave up and followed Olivia towards their house. She still tried to look back for the other dog though. As the dog was walking away from them, she realised it probably wasn't going to cause a problem, and before long they were out of sight. Still too worried to take the treat, Nella started panting from worry as Olivia guided her back through their gate and into the house.

Once inside, Olivia took off the leash and Nella did a big body shake. This shake helped her reset herself, and she often did it after something stressful had ended. As she shook, her ears made a clicking sound as they flapped back and forwards, hitting the side of her head.

This noise woke Tessa, who looked up from the couch with a sleepy expression. 'Mummy, did you go without me?' she said in a whining voice.

'Yes darling, just a short walk, it's dinner time soon.'

Tessa frowned and slid off the couch, walking up to Nella.

'So, how did she go?' asked Mick.

Olivia sighed. 'Not great,' she said in a curt voice.

'Still barking at dogs?' asked Mick.

Olivia sighed again. 'Like you said, we are just avoiding the problem, it's not teaching her anything, the dog she just barked at was a tiny little thing, she can't seriously be scared of that can she?'

Mick looked at Olivia, seeing how deflated she was. 'Well, maybe we need to go see Ava, like Lily said.'

Olivia furrowed her brow and sighed for a third time. 'Maybe, but I'm worried she will just put Nella on drugs or something. I don't want her to lose her personality, she's such a good dog with Tess.'

Morals Of Ruling And Owning Dogs

The ethics of owning and caring for a pet are complicated. When a person decides to acquire a dog, they are entering into a very unique kind of relationship. This relationship has a power dynamic that is very one-sided. If they wish, the human can have absolute control over most aspects of the dog's life. From a dog's perspective, the best they can hope for is a benevolent owner who will advocate for their best interests. The term 'guardian' can be used when describing this kind of owner. However, some behaviour professionals label each and every dog owner as a 'guardian', which I choose not to do. This is supposed to be encouraging for people to hear — that they are the protector of their dog and not simply owning an object that has no feelings. While I agree with the sentiment, my issue with this notion is that it assumes all people are guardians. Personally, I feel like that title should be *earned*, not given as a *right*. In this book, we can see that Nathan and Petra are not acting in Allen's best interests, and so I would not say they are acting as his guardians. In truth, they are misguided to the point of acting like his captors. They control his behaviour with force, and a failure of Allen to comply results in swift punishment. They cannot understand Allen's wants and needs, which means they pay no regard to them.

Even a guardian who is doing a great job of caring for their dog can still exert ultimate control over them should they wish. This means they get to decide how much freedom to give their dog in the choices and decisions that affect them. When considering the freedom of dogs in the human-dog relationship, there are two sides we must consider. On the one hand, there is the view that the human knows what's best for the dog. On the other hand, there is the view that the dog knows what's best. Depending on the circumstances, our views of who should be in control of the decisions normally change. I see many owners finding it really hard to know whether the human or the dog knows best in different situations. In some cases, they will see that the dog wants to do something, and they will let them or help them to do it. In other cases, they will deny the dog their wishes. These are important decisions, as the amount of control we give to our dog in different situations has a huge effect on their welfare. I have noticed that different people tend to lean towards either the dog or the human knowing best across many situations, similar to other political or ethical beliefs they hold. It is rare for me to encounter someone who has an extreme view one way or the other, but when I do, their dogs often struggle.

Humans know best

There are certainly plenty of situations where people know what is best for their dog and therefore decide to take control of a situation. In other words, people tend to reduce the freedom of a dog where they believe the dog doesn't know what is good for themselves. In most cases, this means the dog doesn't have a say in any major life decisions. Dogs aren't normally given a choice in whether they come with you to work, whether you get another dog or cat or have a baby. They don't get to decide whether they get desexed, or even whether they get surrendered to an animal shelter. Health decisions are often controlled by the people too, as dogs don't understand medicine. However, beyond these decisions, there is a lot of variation in how much individual people assume control of their dog.

As a general rule, having a lot of control over the life of a dog is not a bad thing, as long as that control is resulting in choices that are aligned with the interests of the dog. The problem is that the more choices we make for our dogs, the more important it is that we know what the *right* choice is for them. If an owner truly understands their dog on a deep level, large amounts of control over the dog can result in excellent welfare. The owner can set up a routine that they know their dog enjoys, and decide when to go against the dog's wishes for their own good. Unfortunately, when the owner does not understand their dog well, a strong belief that humans know best can lead to serious welfare issues. They tend to unknowingly force their dog into circumstances or routines that they don't like, and their dog's lack of control prevents them from avoiding this. This is clearly a major problem for Allen. Nathan and Petra strongly believe that they know best, and are exerting huge levels of control—but they don't understand Allen well enough to know how their decisions are affecting him. As a result, we see serious welfare consequences. Allen is even beginning to show signs of a compulsive spinning behaviour as his brain struggles to cope.

Dogs know best

Most people understand intuitively that giving dogs freedom and choice are generally good things. Through our own experience, we know that we feel happy when we get what we want. So, if we can see what our dog wants, we know that granting their wish will make them happy. People who strongly anthropomorphise their dog, or have strong views on animal rights, often lean strongly in favour of the 'dog knows best' mentality. These dogs often have pretty great lives. Their owners tend to spoil them with things they think they like or want, and take great joy out of seeing their dog happy. We will cover this more in a later chapter, when we talk about optimising the welfare of dogs. However, sometimes doing what the dog wants to do is *not* in the best interests of the dog, and herein lies a big problem.

There is a major flaw with assuming that dogs *always* know what is best for themselves. As humans, we are more intelligent than dogs, but even *we* don't always act in *our* own long-term interests. Despite knowing better, people often engage in unhealthy eating habits, smoking, exercise avoidance, or even self-sabotage. What makes us think that dogs would know what is in *their* best interests if we often don't? Obviously, it depends on the situation, so I will list a few examples below.

Many domestic dogs have problems with being overweight due to dietary excess. As the dog cannot understand that it's unhealthy to eat too much food, the owner is put in a very tough position. Then when the dog feels hungry and begs for food, some people cannot say no. They are undoubtedly doing this because they love and care for their dog, even if the dog is unhealthily obese. In the case of obesity in dogs, giving in to the wants of the dog is not in their best interest. I also see similar issues with other medical conditions in dogs. Some owners can even refuse to take their dog to the vet until they're gravely ill, because they know their dog dislikes the experience, and would choose avoid it.

We see another example explored in this book with Nella, who is fearful of strange dogs. In some cases, Nella barks at these dogs while pulling towards them on her leash. When Nathan notices her huffing and puffing and pulling towards the other dog, he naturally thinks she wants to meet them. In this situation, Nathan might believe that Nella knows best, and decide to give her what she wants. He might also be reluctant to turn her around and move her away, because that would be going against her wishes. However, as Nella continues to watch the other dog, she only becomes more fearful and continues barking. In this situation, giving Nella freedom to choose her own path actually makes her less happy. This is a very common scenario that I often see play out with dogs that bark on walks.

A similar situation I see is with dogs that sit and watch out the front window of the house all day. Many people understand that it can be nice to have a view of the outside world, and believe their dog is enjoying this. Some dogs really do enjoy it, and happily watch the birds, people and dogs go by. However, for dogs like Allen, the view itself is not enjoyable. Rather, it is a source of stress that he is forced to monitor. In this case, it is not in Allen's best interests to be looking out the window, even though he is voluntarily doing it. When I suggest this to some of my clients, they feel bad for depriving their dog of something they clearly want to do. However, this is another example where the dog does not know best.

These examples demonstrate how some of the most loving and caring owners can accidentally do things that are bad for the welfare of their dog. This happens when a dog wants something that is not in their own interests, and yet the owner believes that the dog knows best.

CHAPTER ELEVEN

Help At Hand

As Mick walked into the toy factory lunchroom, he saw Nathan sitting alone at one of the tables. Mick pulled up a chair and sat down.

'Hey buddy, how are you coping with this mess we've been landed in?'

Nathan grunted. 'They pushed another update today, fixed the processor issues we were having but now I'm getting inventory errors... Apparently, we have a surplus of three thousand elf heads!'

Mick shook his head and gave Nathan a knowing look.

'So, how's Nella going anyway?' asked Nathan, peeling his orange. 'It's been a few weeks since the trainer came, hasn't it?'

Mick's heart sank, and he glanced at Nathan sheepishly before replying. 'Hasn't changed too much. She's a bit better, but it's hard to tell.'

'Sorry to hear man,' said Nathan, frowning. 'So, the aggression hasn't been fixed yet?'

Mick took a deep breath and shook his head. 'No... still goes crazy on walks when she sees another dog. We're basically just avoiding the problem. Haven't really fixed anything...

'Then the other day she chewed up another shoe when we left her alone. So yeah, we're thinking we might have to put her on medications, like Lily said.'

Nathan raised his eyebrows in surprise as he nodded sympathetically. They fell quiet, and then continued to eat in silence for a while.

'And how's Allen going then?' asked Mick. 'You said he was a bit better last week?'

Nathan paused, unsure how to give him the news without bragging. 'Yeah, you probably don't wanna hear this mate, but he's cured. No more barking, such a well-behaved dog. Like the other day he walked right past a poodle without even looking at it.'

Mick shrugged and forced a smile. 'That's great, really great. I guess Allen just isn't as difficult as Nella, you're lucky.'

Nathan snorted before he could help himself. 'Well, I'm not sure it's all luck,' he said. 'Brooke had a pretty immediate effect on him'. After a short pause, he added 'I could give you her details if you like, for a second opinion?'

'Yeah,' agreed Mick, chewing to finish his mouthful. 'But aren't trainers all the same? Wouldn't she just find the same problems?'

Nathan raised his eyebrows before responding carefully. 'Well, I dunno... Is Lily a dog behaviourist specialist? That was what Brooke said she was. She also has like 20 years of experience...'

'No. No I don't think she was, now that you mention it' said Mick, frowning. 'She just called herself a "positive trainer". I guess it wouldn't hurt to get Brooke's details... Thanks mate. Maybe she can fix Nella too.'

Nathan wrote down the details on a piece of paper and handed it to Mick. 'She uses this static collar that made a huge difference for Allen, maybe you could get one of them too?' suggested Nathan.

Mick raised his eyebrows. 'Static? Does that hurt?'

'Just a little, but it's only to remind them that barking is a bad behaviour we don't like,' said Nathan in between mouthfuls of soup.

Mick raised his eyebrows in surprise. 'Well, that sounds pretty good, sounds like it fixes the actual problem, not just avoiding it—like we are.

'Apparently, Nella's scared of other dogs. But if we use a static collar at least we don't have to resort to drugging her up. Drugs should really only be used as a last resort in my opinion.'

Nathan nodded in agreement, before taking out a bottle of tablets from his bag. 'Reminds me, speaking of drugs, my headache is back,' he said before shaking out two tablets and swallowing them.

'And how is Petra going now you guys are trying for a baby?' asked Mick.

'Yeah good,' replied Nathan, leaning back. 'But she's off the pill now. She'd been on that thing for 10 years, we forgot how much it helped her. She used to have to put up with a lot of pain and headaches and stuff before she took it. Now that she's off the pill it's all come back unfortunately.'

Mick furrowed his brow empathetically. 'Aw no, that sucks mate, let's hope it goes away as she adjusts to everything.'

* * *

Nella loved the feeling of standing on the soft grass in her backyard. She watched Tessa as she held a ball in her hand, waiting to see where she would throw it. Mick and Olivia sat at the table sipping at their coffees, the sun highlighting the steam as it rose through the cold morning air. Tessa tossed the ball up in the air towards Nella, who leapt forwards to try and catch it in her mouth. Misjudging the distance, the ball hit her on the top of the head and bounced away. Unphased, Nella took two long strides after the ball and grabbed it in her mouth. Excited to have it once more, she spun around on the spot then took off, running a full lap around the yard. Tessa squealed with joy as Mick and Olivia watched them fondly.

'Okay Tess,' said Mick. 'I think it's time we went inside now, Nella's new trainer will be here soon.'

Tessa scrunched up her face and stared at him. 'Why does she need a trainer?'

'Because she is sometimes naughty Tess,' he replied. 'Barking at other dogs, chewing up things when we leave her alone. She needs to learn it's not okay to do those things.'

Tessa looked at Nella and then stared back at Mick. 'But I don't care, she's nice to me.'

'Come on darling, inside now,' said Olivia, laughing as she stood up and opened the back door.

They made their way into the house, with Nella eagerly following them in, ball in mouth. Her wagging tail was not at a good height for Tessa. As she walked alongside Nella, it kept knocking her in the head. Tessa, used to this problem, put out her hand to protect herself as she moved out of range. Once inside, they heard a loud knock at the door.

'Oh, she's early' said Mick, checking his watch.

Nella startled at the sound, then marched up to the door and released a booming bark.

'Come on Nella, let's go into the study,' said Olivia, trying to calm her down.

Nella, used to this routine now, reluctantly followed Olivia as she led her by the collar into the study. Olivia waited with Nella behind the closed door, feeding her treats to get her mind off the stranger. It worked to a degree, Nella was not yet stressed enough to lose her appetite, and the dried chicken was particularly delicious. As Nella heard the stranger talking to Mick and walking into the house, she was ready to accept that this person might be okay, but she still wasn't sure.

'Okay, you can come out now,' said Mick from the dining room.

Olivia slid open the study door and Nella saw Brooke for the first time. Before she could think, Nella instinctively let out a small bark at her. Nella remembered that the last time a lady sat in that seat, she had been very nice and had given her lots of treats. She watched her carefully, and tried to figure out if this new person would also be so nice.

Brooke started speaking loudly. 'Wow she's a big girl! Hi Nella, we've been a bit naughty, haven't we?'

The way Brooke was speaking worried Nella, the tone seemed confrontational to her, despite not understanding a word.

Olivia smiled and waved. 'Hi Brooke, I'm Olivia. Nella was fine with our last trainer, just took a bit to get used to her is all.'

'Yes, well I wouldn't let go of her yet,' said Brooke, nodding. 'She's a strong dog, just keep holding her for now please.'

At that point Nella sensed something wasn't quite right with this stranger. She backed up slightly, then let out another bark of fear without thinking.

'Did you want me to give her some treats to calm her down?' asked Olivia.

Brooke smiled smugly and chuckled to herself. 'Oh, is that what the other trainer told you? It's criminal really, what they teach in some of the dog training schools nowadays.'

Mick raised his eyebrows, and Olivia stood there shocked. They had liked Lily, and it was surprising to hear Brooke talking about her in such a way.

'Oh, but why shouldn't we give her a treat?' asked Olivia.

Brooke smiled smugly again. 'It's okay, I know you mean well, but that would only make things worse. She's doing the wrong thing by barking at me, so if you give her a treat now it'll just reward the behaviour and she'll do it even more!'

Mick nodded with understanding. 'Right, I thought so, but the last trainer said to do it, so we did.'

'And did it work?' asked Brooke.

Mick looked down, feeling disappointed at Nella's lack of improvement. 'No, not really, well sort of. Like she doesn't bark much anymore. But that's only because we avoid situations where it happens, so we haven't actually fixed the problem.'

Brooke sighed and rolled her eyes. 'Yes, another common mistake, how will she get used to dogs and people if you don't socialise her?'

At that moment, a slight breeze blew through the house, sending Brooke's scent in Nella's direction. Until then, she hadn't been able to smell her properly as she was on the other side of the room. As Nella inhaled the smell, a wave of realisation washed over her. Brooke was steeped in the smell of dog fear, which had rubbed on to her from an earlier appointment. This wasn't just normal fear, it was an intense version of fear combined with stress and suffering. This triggered a memory from deep within her mind. Brooke smelled a bit like the people that had broken into her home a few months earlier. Nella reacted without thinking, she had to save the family. The fur on the back of her neck stood up on end as she launched forwards, barking ferociously at Brooke.

'Get back!' screamed Brooke, jumping up from the table.

Olivia struggled to hold on to the collar. Brooke paused for a moment assessing the situation. Nella let out another bark as Olivia's grip started to come loose. Sensing the danger, Brooke suddenly turned and ran down the hallway towards the door. As Brooke opened the door, Nella finally escaped from Olivia's grasp, and charged down the hallway, barking at the top of her lungs. As Brooke slipped through the door, Nella ran up behind her. Just before Nella could follow her, Brooke slammed the door shut behind her. At this point it was too late for Nella to stop, she slipped on the tiles and slid across the floor, crashing into the door.

Tessa, who was sitting on the couch, started crying as Mick sat stunned at the table.

Olivia got up off the floor and ran up to Nella, who was now standing at the door letting out a low steady growl.

'You stay here with Nella, I'll go out and speak with Brooke,' said Mick. He slipped out the front door while Olivia held onto Nella's collar again.

Olivia tried to listen to what they were saying through the door, but with Nella's growling it was difficult to make it out. Tessa came up to Nella crying, which briefly distracted her from the stranger outside. Nella turned around and licked at the tears on her face, smelling distress in her sweat. Through the door, Olivia heard Brooke raise her voice.

'In all my years I never met such a vicious dog, I'll leave you with this and am not seeing you again until you have her wearing it.'

A moment later, Mick came back through the door looking depressed. 'She's gone,' he said, as the sound of the gate slamming shut echoed into the hallway.

Nella let out another bark, still staring at the door. Her heart continued to race. It was a horrible feeling, having someone smelling like that come inside her house.

As Olivia looked at what Mick was holding, he continued. 'She said we need to get her used to wearing these before she sees us again.'

Nella sniffed at his hand, which held a shock collar and a large black muzzle.

'What is that?' asked Olivia suspiciously, looking at the collar.

'It's a static collar,' replied Mick.

Olivia narrowed her eyes, taking in a deep breath. 'No, I don't like her, we aren't using that stuff.'

Tessa had stopped crying now, and was hugging onto Nella's neck.

'Has the nasty lady gone now?' she asked, looking up at them with glassy eyes.

'Tess! That's not a nice thing to say!' scolded Mick. 'She was trying to help, now say sorry.'

Tessa scrunched up her face and stomped her foot defiantly. 'But Nella doesn't like her, so I don't like her too.'

Olivia smirked, then glared at Mick. 'I agree with Tess. Nella sensed something, and I trust her instincts,' she said defiantly.

Mick glared back indignantly. 'She's a dog! You trust a dog over a specialist? Allen was cured by her, Lily didn't fix anything! Just listen to reason Olivia, Nella *needs* Brooke.'

Olivia scowled, turned, and walked back down the hallway.

'You're doing it again,' said Mick, calling after her. 'You're being all emotional. We need to think rationally about this Liv!'

Olivia didn't answer as she made her way onto the couch and started folding some washing. Mick started washing the dishes, a scowl on his face.

Once she had gathered her thoughts, Olivia spoke up. 'I want to go see Ava again. I remember how much Nella liked her as a puppy, and she recommended Lily who Nella also loved too.'

'What, so she can dope Nella up on drugs?' snapped Mick.

Olivia paused, before staring back at him with daggers in her eyes. 'I trust my vet Mick, if she thinks there is a good reason for drugs, we should consider it. I just want to get her opinion before we start shocking our dog.'

'It's only static, Olivia,' he retorted, scoffing.

'Ok, then let's put it around *your* neck and try it out,' said Olivia smugly.

Mick paused, he was not good with pain, and although he didn't think the collar would hurt, he was worried to try it.

'Okay, fine. We can see the vet, but there's no way we're putting Nella on drugs,' conceded Mick, in an exasperated tone.

Canine Mental Health

As we saw in this chapter, Brooke is wanting to train Nella out of her fearful behaviour using force. One of the problems with this is that Nella may not simply have a training issue, she could have a mental illness. As mentioned in the introduction to this book, the prevalence of anxiety-related mental health problems in dogs[1] and humans[2] appear to be similar. This might be surprising to many readers, but it seems very plausible to me. As discussed in the anthropomorphism chapter, the emotional regions in the brain of the human and dog are almost identical in structure and function. These brain areas are responsible for regulating fear and anxiety. Although these emotions are normal and useful for survival in both people and dogs, excessive levels of these emotions are often maladaptive. In humans, these emotions are responsible for the most common mental illnesses, which are the anxiety-spectrum disorders. Human anxiety-spectrum disorders include phobias, generalised anxiety, social anxiety, separation anxiety and more. The most common mental health conditions we see affecting dogs are also anxiety-spectrum disorders. These canine disorders include separation anxiety, fears and phobias of people and other dogs, compulsive disorders and noise phobias.[3]

Interestingly, dogs don't appear to experience all of the different mental health issues that people do, as far as we know. Human conditions including schizophrenia, psychosis and bipolar disorder are not clearly identifiable in dogs. We don't know for sure if they exist, but they are certainly not easily identifiable. As previously discussed, the main structural difference between our brain and a dog's, is that the dog brain has a much less developed cerebral cortex. This may explain why we don't often see clear signs in dogs of some conditions that affect humans. For example, a unique thing we see in humans is the presence of neurodiversity. Conditions such as autism and ADHD are well known in people, but these may not exist in dogs. I am not alone in believing that neurodiversity in humans may actually be functional and useful for the species from an evolutionary perspective.[4] Similarly, I believe that if neurodiversity were to exist in dogs, it should also have this quality. I am not sure what qualities a neurodiverse dog would have, but I see no reason why they would be the same as ADHD or autism in humans. Rather, they may exist as having other adaptations such as an extra keen sense of smell or hearing, at the expense of some other cognitive functions. Much more research is needed to identify whether such a thing exists in the dog.

Training problem or mental health condition?

If you see a stranger crying, you might not know if they are clinically depressed, grieving, or just having an emotional day. You would have to ask them to find out—and they might not know what is going on themselves if they haven't spoken with a professional. Similarly, most people cannot tell whether their dog is just struggling with training, having a normal reaction to a situation, or is suffering from a mental health condition. As dogs can't talk, you need a lot of expertise to be sure. A veterinarian with extensive training in behaviour is often needed to confirm a diagnosis. This is why Lily recommended that Nella goes to see her behaviour veterinarian.

As already mentioned, all dogs will experience the emotions of fear and anxiety many times over their life, and this does not mean they are mentally ill. The definition of what exactly constitutes a mental health condition in a dog is not always clear, although there are some texts that make an excellent attempt.[3,5,6] Some of the same requirements for diagnosing a human mental health condition also apply for dogs. For example, the condition needs to result in clinically significant distress or disability in the animal, and must not simply be an expected response to a difficult situation. For example, a dog would probably not qualify as having a mental health disorder if the only problems were with toilet training, stealing food, not sitting when asked, and pulling on the leash. However, with Nella and Allen the situation is clearly different. Both dogs suffer significant distress as a result of their fears and anxieties, which affects their daily life and welfare. Another hallmark of mental illness is their inability to learn that their worries are unfounded. Most of the negative experiences they encounter are imagined in their own head, and not caused by real-world consequences, like pain or injury. Despite repeated exposures to situations where no real harm comes to them, they do not learn to disassociate their negative emotional reactions.

What causes a dog to be mentally ill?

The causes of mental health conditions in dogs are thought to be similar to people. These factors include genetics, maternal stress, early life experiences, and chance.[7] Dogs like Allen and Nella are very likely to carry some genetic predisposition to anxiety. From the description in the book, Nella's mother seemed friendly enough and not obviously affected. However, as Mick never met Nella's father, there would be a fair chance that he was also suffering from excessive anxiety. We also don't know whether Allen or Nella's mothers were excessively stressed through pregnancy. When an animal is stressed, they release large amounts of cortisol into their bloodstream. This hormone can affect the brain of the developing foetus, effectively programming them to be more anxious and stressed when they grow up.[8] Despite all the evidence that heritable factors are the main contributors to these problems, many clients inevitably blame themselves. They fear that they did not do a good job at raising their dog, and they caused the condition. Early life experiences certainly do have a large effect on adult behaviour, but in most cases the owner is not to blame.

As we see with Allen and Nella, they both had a series of challenging early life experiences with dogs and people. While these experiences certainly contributed to their problems, they are only half the story. Most dogs are not this anxious to begin with, and put through the exact same circumstances as Allen and Nella, they would not develop a mental health condition. Furthermore, even if Allen and Nella were raised without these experiences, they were still likely to develop similar problems in the future. In many cases, I have seen a dog spontaneously develop a problem without an initial traumatic event. Another way that some people believe they are to blame for the problems in their dog, is through their own human-anxiety rubbing off on the dog.

Emotional contagion

Many people who themselves have anxiety, worry that they have somehow made their own dog anxious. They fear that their own struggle with mental health has caused their dog to also develop a mental health condition. As explained above, genetics and luck play the largest role, and even traumatic experiences can be successfully overcome by many resilient puppies. Simply living with a human who is mentally ill is not enough to cause problems in a resilient dog. However, dogs can certainly detect the presence of negative emotions in people. This could be through our behaviour, such as yelling, arguing, crying or pacing, and also through the stress-related smells we exude.[9]

There is good reason for social animals to be able to read the emotions of other animals. If you are living in a group and one of your members suddenly becomes extremely fearful, having that emotion spread to the other members of the group could save their lives. We see this in a wide variety of social species, with alarm-calls in birds being a well-known example. We also see this with people. If you are sitting in a room full of people who are laughing, you will feel much happier than if you are in a room of people who are crying. It is therefore not unfathomable that the same emotional contagion could happen between dogs and people living under the same roof.

We see examples of emotional contagion throughout this book in situations that are commonly experienced by people and their dogs. Have you ever heard a dog barking and felt on edge? This could mean the dog is probably feeling worried or unhappy in some way, and through the sound of their bark the emotion has spread to your brain. You might notice that when the same dog barks during play, it doesn't have the same effect on you. People living with dogs that have anxiety disorders often experience this—just being around their dog can make them feel stressed. I have seen this personally with many of my patients. Similarly, it isn't too far-fetched to believe that the dogs we live with will also catch some of our emotions when we are stressed. Especially when people are yelling and arguing. However, there is a difference between simply feeling anxious because the people around you are anxious, and having a mental health disorder. Emotional contagion between people and dogs is not likely to create a mental health disorder in a normal dog, but as social animals it can certainly affect their lives.

CHAPTER TWELVE

Unnatural

As Nella felt the car engine switch off; she sat up straight to look outside. Her anxious panting quickly fogged up the window in front of her nose. Something different was happening, it wasn't her normal routine, she simply didn't know what to expect. Whenever she went somewhere in the car, it seemed to put butterflies in her stomach. The feeling of her gut being pulled left, right, backwards and forwards was awfully uncomfortable.

Mick opened the rear door of the car and clicked the leash onto Nella's collar. Eager to follow her people, she jumped onto the pavement in a single bound. Scanning the car park, Nella vaguely remembered this place, it had been almost a year since she was here last. As they walked her towards the entry, she could smell hints of dog and cat in the air. Too worried to sniff the ground, she resumed panting and pulled ahead.

Olivia opened the clinic door, letting Nella walk through first. As they entered the reception area, a lady behind the counter stood up and smiled to greet them. Nella watched her suspiciously.

'This must be Nella,' she said. 'Wow she's a big girl isn't she!'

The smell of animals overwhelmed Nella. She yawned and started panting even more heavily, looking around frantically for any sign of movement.

'Yes, she has grown!' replied Olivia. 'Just to let you know, she isn't good with other dogs, or strangers.'

The lady shook her head kindly, holding up one hand as if to say they shouldn't worry. 'It's fine, we know, thanks for telling us when you made the appointment. We made sure reception would be empty for when you arrived. Let's go straight into a room now before anyone else gets here.'

As the lady opened a consulting room door, Tessa and Olivia walked in. Nella watched the strange lady from a distance, but wasn't confident enough to bark at her. When Mick tried to get Nella to follow him into the room, she stood at the entry and refused to move. Nella didn't like the smells in here, and was worried about what might be in the room. She could sense sickness as well as the faint scent of stress and fear from the other patients that morning.

The receptionist put her hand in a large jar of treats and handed a few to Mick. 'Here, see if this helps.'

Nella watched the lady reaching towards Mick and stepped back suspiciously, she was now even further from the door.

'Hey Nelly, want a snack?' said Mick, showing her a large brown treat.

Nella refused to even sniff at the dried liver. It was right in front of her face, but she didn't feel safe enough to eat right now. She didn't understand what was happening, it was all very strange and confronting.

Mick sighed in resignation, then started to push Nella from the other side. As she slid along the floor into the consulting room, Nella held her ears right back. She looked around with large, worried eyes, unsure what to do.

Olivia started laughing, then quickly covered her mouth with her hand. 'Nothing is easy with you, is it Nella?'

Nella had sat down as she was being pushed along, so Olivia had to help rotate her out of the way in order to close the door behind her. As they waited for Ava, Nella slowly surveyed the room. She had a few good memories from inside this room, but they had mostly faded with time. Tessa took a treat from Mick and showed it to Nella again. She just sat there, not moving, and briefly sniffed the treat before snapping her head around to stare at the door.

'What was that?' asked Mick.

Olivia shrugged. 'I guess she must have heard something?'

A few moments later, there was a gentle knock on the door, it slowly opened just a crack.

Nella jumped up from her position and moved to the side of the room, standing behind Olivia. As she watched the door, her head lowered as she tried to make herself smaller. She had stopped panting for now, but was feeling acutely fearful of whatever was on the other side of the door.

Ava slowly poked her head through the crack. Her dark hair was pulled back from her face and tucked behind a pair of black-rimmed glasses.

'Hi, it's just me,' she said. 'Can I come in Nella?'

Nella stood frozen, watching her suspiciously.

Olivia was sitting with Tessa in her lap, she smiled back at Ava. 'Hi, yes come in. She'll just hide behind us, I think.'

Ava slowly opened the door and carefully entered the room without making any sudden movements. Despite this, Nella could take it no longer. She felt cornered and had to do something. She let out a flurry of deep rumbling barks, which echoed throughout the clinic.

Ava didn't react outwardly, although inside she was a bit shaken. Nella was a big dog, and she was intimidating. Ava softly closed the door behind her and squatted down on the floor. Nella was worried by the stranger entering the room, but seeing her lower to the ground made her slightly less threatening.

Ava tilted her head, looking at Nella confused. 'Is this the same dog? She's all grown up now!'

Tessa put on her serious voice and held up her hand. 'Nella weighs the same as two of me.'

'And you must be Tessa?' asked Ava, grinning back at her.

'Yeah, this is Tess,' responded Mick in a warm tone. He put his arm around her and pointed towards Ava. 'That's Nella's vet, Ava. Nella used to love her when she was a puppy.'

'Yes, we got along great,' replied Ava, glancing briefly at Nella. 'But she obviously doesn't remember me now. Maybe she was too young to remember.'

Seeing Ava glance at her, Nella felt her heart jump in her chest again. Having this strange person stare directly at her was extremely threatening. But as it only lasted half a second, she didn't feel the need to react.

'Now that she's older,' continued Ava. 'I can see she's still a bit nervous, despite being so much bigger. Hopefully she remembers me, and it helps warm her up a bit later.'

Nella hadn't sensed Ava's scent properly yet, so hadn't made the connection between her and the friendly vet she met as a puppy. As Ava slowly got up and walked over to her seat, a breeze in the room sent her smell in Nella's direction. Ava was also wearing the same perfume she had worn last time as well. Nella stretched her head forwards and sniffed in Ava's direction to figure out what to think of her. Nella did remember the smell, and although the memory was faint, it helped. She felt more willing to trust Ava, although she didn't right now.

As Ava started clicking away on the computer, she continued talking. 'So, we have two whole hours blocked out for this consultation, which is far longer than we normally spend for a standard consultation.

'As you know, I have done a lot of extra animal behaviour study, and it's just not possible to figure out what to do in any less time.'

'That's great,' replied Olivia. 'We need to get to the bottom of this, urgently. Lily recommended we see you too.'

'Yes, I heard,' agreed Ava. 'She told me all about the difficulties you've been having, but I still have a few more questions, if that's okay?'

As Ava proceeded to ask a long list of questions about Nella, she tossed a small liver treat across the room. Nella saw it bounce along the ground towards her, and sniffed at it out of curiosity. Once she realised it was food, she yawned widely. Nella was starting to feel anxious again, she wasn't under immediate threat, but she didn't know what to do. She yawned a second time, and licked at her nose in worry. Still without appetite, Nella sat back down and ignored the treat.

Before long, Tessa had become restless. She slid off Olivia's lap and started playing with Nella's fur. Nella gave her a small gentle lick, and then looked back up and watched Ava speaking.

'So, does Nella act like a relaxed dog at home? By that I mean, does she often curl up near you and have a snooze or just watch the world go by?'

Mick glanced at Olivia, before looking at Ava. 'Well sometimes—not much though. She's a bit hyper, can't sit still for two seconds most of the time! She's normally playing or following us around. It's like she has ADHD.'

'Yeah,' agreed Olivia. 'As soon as we go anywhere, she follows us, she even cries when I have a shower because she can't see me! She pretty much only sleeps if Tessa's sleeping.'

Ava nodded, smiling gently, and continued. 'So, if everyone was home with Nella for a whole day on the weekend, and you were all inside because it was raining, how many hours would she be asleep?'

Mick looked up at the ceiling, calculating the hours in his head. 'Well, she would be up at 7 when we get up, then she might lie down and rest for an hour just after lunch when Tess has her nap, and then she is back to sleep at around 11 when we turn in.'

Ava raised her eyebrows, then scribbled on some paper for a few moments. 'So, it seems like she only sleeps properly for about 9 hours a day then!'

'Isn't that enough sleep?' said Olivia, looking concerned. 'She doesn't seem tired; she always has so much energy.'

Ava thought to herself for a moment before replying. 'It's certainly less than average. But I'm not too surprised.

'Most dogs will sleep for at least 12–14 hours a day, large dogs like Nella even more. Even when they're not sleeping, they would be spending quite a few hours just loafing around relaxing, not doing much.'

'But she's free to rest as much as she wants,' said Mick, frowning. 'How do we get her to sleep more?'

Ava shook her head in understanding. 'It's not your fault, I think she might just be a bit too anxious to relax enough and sleep a normal amount. When you're worried, it's hard to do nothing.

'Anxious dogs have to find ways to keep themselves busy, to take their minds off what they are worrying about. The things they do to keep busy are often the things that other dogs do as well, so it can sometimes be hard to tell them apart. But an anxious dog doesn't do these things because they want to.

'Anxious dogs often do things because they *have* to, to make themselves feel better. Do you notice her showing signs of anxiety around the house?'

'I'm not sure,' said Olivia, a concerned look on her face. 'She does pant and yawn which Lily said are signs of anxiety, is that right?'

'Yes, that's right, but also hypervigilance and the inability to settle and relax are signs too.'

'Yeah, that sounds like Nella,' agreed Mick. 'She's often panting or pacing or whining, I often say to Olivia that Nella might be anxious when she does that.'

Olivia gave Mick a look of disbelief, but held back her tongue.

'But I think she's also just being a sook,' continued Mick. 'Like wanting attention or treats or something.'

'Yeah maybe,' said Olivia suspiciously. 'But none of the other dogs I ever had did that. I honestly thought it was just a wolfhound thing, could that be it?'

Ava met Olivia's gaze with a sorrowful look on her face. 'No, sorry,' she answered. 'It's not normal for wolfhounds, or any breed. It does sound like anxiety.

'But remember, anxiety itself is normal in small amounts, just like for people too. I get a bit anxious crossing a busy road, but that's a good thing. It stops me from accidentally walking in front of a bus!

'Anxiety helps keep dogs safe too, like if they were in the wild and there were some dangerous animals around, anxiety would help keep them vigilant and alive.'

'Yeah,' agreed Olivia. 'It's just a problem when there's too much I guess?'

Ava nodded sadly. 'Yes, some dogs have much more anxiety than normal. The same thing with some people as well. In humans, too much anxiety can cause phobias, social problems, OCD... And it's becoming more common too.'

Meanwhile, Nella's nerves were finally calming down a little. She was starting to get used to the room. It didn't seem like much was going to change any time soon, which comforted her. Change was worrisome. When the scent of liver wafted into her nose, she started to get her appetite back. Just as Ava was about to continue talking, Nella lowered her head to the ground. She carefully sniffed at the treat in front of her, then quietly licked it into her mouth.

Ava paused, noticing what had happened from the corner of her eye. Even though she never stared at Nella directly, Ava had been carefully observing her every move. She collected a handful of treats from her desk before continuing.

'The problem with anxiety is when there's too much, it prevents an animal from living a happy and functional life.'

Ava tossed another treat over to Nella. She promptly lent down to take it, before looking back up at Ava expectantly.

'The other issue is that excessive anxiety can be self-reinforcing, and so it prevents an animal from learning. When you leave Nella alone, nothing bad happens. But she can't learn it's okay because she's too anxious.

'The same thing on walks. When she sees other dogs, nothing bad actually happens—but she isn't learning that. She just keeps on worrying about them despite the lack of evidence that they're dangerous!'

Mick furrowed his brow and put on his thinking face. 'But maybe she just hasn't learned that barking at other dogs is bad?'

Ava paused, thinking to herself before responding. 'It's an interesting idea, but unfortunately dogs aren't that smart. To make moral judgements between right and wrong requires a lot of brain power. Dogs learn to do something, or to stop doing something, based entirely on the consequences.'

'Right, yeah didn't think of that,' said Mick, raising his eyebrows.

Ava continued. 'It's actually quite hard to imagine what it'd be like to have the IQ of a dog. People don't realise how smart they are compared to animals.

'By the time children acquire morals, they're already far smarter than any dog on earth. Now, I'm not calling Nella *stupid* to insult her, I'm just saying that we underestimate how smart humans are compared to dogs.'

'I like it when dogs do dumb things though, it's cute,' said Olivia with a big grin on her face.

Mick chuckled in agreement.

The sound of laughter in the room helped Nella relax further. She normally heard laughter at home when things were safe and secure. She took a few steps away from her people to get the treat that had fallen in the middle of the room. Then a switch flicked in her head, a memory was triggered from when she was a puppy. Nella remembered doing something like this before, with Ava in this very room. She started feeling like she wanted to be friends with her after all. As Ava continued tossing her treats, Nella got closer and closer, and started slowly wagging her tail.

Olivia looked down at the ground, then glanced up at Ava. A realisation came over her. 'So, if Nella's feeling worried all the time, is it because of us doing something wrong with her?'

Ava shook her head slowly, having heard this question many times before. 'No, I don't think so in this case. You aren't hitting her or yelling at her, are you?'

Meanwhile, Tessa had walked up to Nella and grabbed her tail, gently pulling at the wispy fur. Nella didn't mind, she was just waiting for the next treat. She took another step closer to Ava.

'Daddy sometimes yells at her,' said Tessa. 'But only when she's naughty and I wouldn't let anyone hit her, ever.'

Tessa put her arms around Nella's neck, who was now sitting just in front of Ava, waiting for another snack.

Mick furrowed his brow, looking a little embarrassed.

'It's not often though,' added Olivia, sticking up for him. 'And it's not like he's screaming at her.'

Ava gestured in understanding, holding her hand out in front of her. 'No no, it's okay. The odd yell wouldn't cause a normal dog to have an anxiety disorder. But I think after today you won't want to yell at her anyway.

'When she does those things that get you upset, she's probably feeling worried, and as you know being yelled at does not help relieve anxiety.'

Mick nodded slowly, a distant expression on his face. 'Yeah, it just gets under my skin. I'll try not to do it again... But what about static collars? Are they as bad as yelling? The other trainer told us to use one.'

Ava stared directly at Mick, her face deadly serious. 'No, they are much worse. They work on the same principles, but static shock collars cause pain as well as fear.'

Ava slowly reached the back of her hand towards Nella, who sniffed it carefully. There was something she liked about Ava's scent. She stepped forwards and leaned her body into her. Ava smiled as she started to gently stroke Nella's fur. She was careful to only touch her exactly at the part of her body that Nella was pushing into her.

'The way I think of it,' said Ava, 'is that all the issues that you brought to me today, all the things she does wrong, they are not my main priority.

'What I really care about is that she's happy. Nella is currently sick; she has a mental health condition. If I can make her less anxious and stressed and fearful, I will have done my job. The good thing is, if I can achieve those goals, you'll notice that she starts behaving much better.

'All of these behaviours that worry you, like barking at dogs, chasing the trainer, destroying things when left alone—they all require a lot of effort for Nella to do. If she was happy, calm and relaxed, she really couldn't be bothered doing any of them!'

Olivia looked at Nella and felt her heart swell with love. 'Yeah, of course we want that too, we just want her to be happy.'

As Ava continued to stroke Nella, she sat down and put her front paw up Ava's lap. She looked up into Ava's eyes, no longer afraid.

'It looks like I have won her over again!' said Ava, smiling warmly. 'She was a bit harder this time, compared to when she was a puppy.'

'I think Nella likes you' agreed Tessa, looking up at Ava.

Noticing all the attention on her, Nella whined softly and started pacing around the room. The treats had stopped and now she didn't know what to do. She resumed panting.

'Is this what she's like at home?' asked Ava, watching Nella.

Mick looked at Nella pacing around the room. 'Like what?' he asked.

Ava pointed at Nella's mouth, saying, 'Like this—panting, breathing fast with her mouth open.'

Olivia frowned, squinting her eyes in confusion. 'Oh, but I thought that was normal, I thought she was only panting when her tongue is poking out.'

'See how her mouth is open?' explained Ava. 'Sometimes it can be hard to pick up, but if you look at her chest too, you can see she's breathing very fast right now.'

'I hadn't noticed that either,' added Mick, frowning. 'She does that quite a lot now I think of it. I just thought she was excited.'

Ava pulled out a folder and started rummaging through it. 'Okay, now we have gone over the extent of the problem, we need to talk about our solution.'

'Yeah,' agreed Mick. 'Lily tried to show us what to do on walks, but she said Nella was super anxious. So apparently, we need to avoid everything that makes her bark. But the problem is, I don't see how that fixes things—like how will she get used to it?'

'I wish there was a simple way to explain it,' said Ava, sighing. 'It's just not how the brain works. I have been occasionally exposed to spiders my whole life, but I'm still dreadfully scared of them. These things don't always just go away with regular exposure.

'The key is to have her experience the things she is afraid of without her actually feeling any strong emotions. That can be very hard to do, as she will need to experience a really tiny dose of the real thing. Every time she freaks out from something, you take 10 steps back with any improvement you've made.'

'Is that why she needs to be medicated?' asked Olivia.

Ava pulled out a sheet of paper from her folder before replying. 'Yes, some medications might help, but we need to decide on that together.'

Mick sighed in relief, then glanced at Olivia. 'We decided we wanted to stick with something natural if possible. Like, we don't believe in just drugging up animals to make them behave.'

Ava paused for a moment, then sighed. She had heard this many times before. 'Do you think that's what I do? Vets like me care more about animal welfare than almost anyone on earth, we just have a different understanding of it.

'There's actually a lot to unpack from what you just said. Now where do I start...'

Ava slid off her chair and moved to the centre of the room, squatting down. Nella came up to her and she started stroking her chest as she spoke.

'Let's start with the idea of unnatural drugs. The problem with this, is that I think we are treating quite an unnatural condition. Dogs and humans evolved to live in a natural world that is very different to where we find ourselves now. Could you imagine if you lived in a clan of hunter-gatherers, living naturally in the wild with Nella. Would she have any of the problems she has now?

'She certainly wouldn't have separation anxiety, because she would never be left alone. In fact, if she got lost from you, she might not survive. Leaving her alone is unnatural.

'You would also have a territory where unfamiliar animals or dogs or people could represent a real threat. They wouldn't regularly be trespassing on your land. It would be natural and useful for her to bark at these things, to alert you and the clan of their presence.

'So, if you want the completely natural solution to this, you'll need to abandon your unnatural lives, are you willing to do that?'

Mick was staring at the wall, silent, thinking, when Olivia replied. 'Well, no. Obviously we have to go to work. But can't we just teach her to adapt to our situation?'

'That's not how brains work,' replied Ava. 'They can adapt to a degree, but when there's also lots of anxiety it gets really difficult. The brain struggles when the environment is too far removed from what it's designed for.

'What's amazing is just how well most dogs cope with things. That's what I find hard to understand. Nella's reactions are perfectly reasonable if you ask me. The real problem is how she's forced to feel in these situations.'

Mick glanced at Olivia and seemed uncomfortable. 'I guess when you explain it like that, it all makes sense. But we don't want to turn her into some kind of sedated zombie dog...'

'Agreed,' said Ava. 'So sometimes when you have an unnatural situation, you need unnatural solutions. But simply sedating her or suppressing her behaviours is not a solution.

'Just so you know, I don't use drugs on every dog that misbehaves. I only use them when I think the animal is dealing with a lot of negative emotions, like fear and anxiety. Secondly, do either of you take any tablets yourselves?'

'Well yeah, sometimes,' replied Mick defensively. He didn't understand why this was relevant, it wasn't like he was on antidepressants.

'But I only take them when I need to. Like I take aspirin for my headaches.'

Olivia realised she was also recently taking tablets too, and was starting to make the connection. 'I was on the contraceptive pill. So yeah, I guess I used to as well,' she admitted.

'Good,' said Ava agreeably. 'Because as you know, medications can be very useful, but they are unnatural as you said.

'So Mick, you're happy to treat your physical pain in your head when it's hurting, but what about mental pain?

'When you ask someone what the worst times of their life have been, they don't normally tell you about when they were in the most physical pain. They talk about the time they were the saddest, or when they were suffering mentally the most.

'People are often happy to treat painful diseases of the body with medications—but why not painful diseases of the mind? Especially since it can be much worse?'

Mick frowned, he understood where this was going but didn't like the logical conclusion. It frustrated him, he had strong beliefs, and they were being seriously challenged. Not willing to concede, he changed the subject.

'Yeah, but the problem is it might change her personality. We love Nella how she is; we don't want her to be a different dog, that's the real issue.'

Ava nodded slowly, pretending like it was a good point and that she hadn't heard this argument a thousand times before.

'Well yes, it might change her personality. It will make her less anxious, hopefully. And that's a part of her personality that she doesn't need and doesn't feel nice. It's also the part of her personality that causes all the behaviours that you don't approve of.'

Ava stared directly at Mick and put on her serious voice.

'So let me explain, you and I really want the same thing. If we used medications and they had bad side effects, I would recommend we stop them, because I want her to be happy, not feeling sick or like a zombie.

'However, it's important to think about what the side-effects are and what the intended effects are. Some dogs can feel bad on the medications, and no one would want that. In other dogs the medications work perfectly, and their anxiety is reduced a bit.

'If Nella goes on medications, and they work well for her, it might mean that she doesn't feel so worried all the time and she might actually start to sleep a more normal amount. You might notice this and think she was drugged up and sedated, but really, she might be happily relaxing.

'However, the medications don't always work well. It depends on the dog. So, it's important you watch her closely. You need to let me know if anything in her behaviour or health changes. I will also reassess her a few months after starting, that way we can be sure she's coping well with them.'

Olivia sighed, then looked over at Mick. 'Don't you think it's worth a shot honey?' she said.

Mick shuffled his feet and agreed. 'I guess it's worth trying, but how long does she have to be on them? Are they safe for long term use?'

Ava smiled; she was glad to see they were coming around. 'Yes, they are almost always safe when used carefully, but it's very important to monitor their health closely to make sure.

'If she has any negative effects we would stop them, and it's highly unlikely to cause any permanent damage in a healthy dog. 'Now, in regards to keeping her on them long term. That's for you to decide. But remember to have her best interests in mind. Nella can't decide for herself whether she wants to be treated naturally or with pharmaceuticals—she just notices how she feels every day.

'Olivia, you mentioned you were on the pill, so was I. We both take them long term for as long as we want the effect. When we stop taking the pill, we go back to normal.

'So, I would say that if Nella's responding well to the drugs and she's happy because of them, you should continue to give them to her as long as you want her to be happy...'

Tessa, who had been distracted by looking at a dog chart on the wall, had just started to pay attention to what Ava was saying.

'I want Nella to be happy that's why I play with her,' she said, smiling at Ava.

Hearing her speak, Nella walked over to Tessa and started licking at her face. Tessa turned away and giggled, pushing her away.

'So, I guess she's on them for life then?' asked Mick, still feeling concerned.

Ava smiled at Tessa, then looked back at Mick. 'We can certainly try stopping her in a few years' time, and she could do well. In my experience though, dogs like Nella do exactly what we'd expect, they go back to being anxious.

'She's wired differently, Mick. Like Olivia said, she doesn't act like the other dogs you had before her. Her brain is permanently designed to worry about things that might go wrong and be on the lookout for threats.'

Nella walked back up to Ava and sat down, looking at her intently. She had been waiting for a treat for a few minutes now.

Ava had forgotten to keep giving them. Nella was starting to feel frustrated at being stuck in this room with nothing to do.

'I guess we'd better try the meds then,' said Olivia, glancing over at Mick. He returned her gaze, nodding.

'So how will we know if it's helping her then?' asked Mick.

'That's an important question Mick,' replied Ava. 'I think that if it's working, she'll be happier. Less anxious, less fearful, less worried, and with minimal side effects.

'You'll need to watch her behaviour to monitor how it changes too. I'd like you to keep a diary of how she goes each day so we can look back on it and see her progress.

'But you can't just let the tablets do all the heavy lifting. I'd like you to see Lily again so you can keep up her training.'

Nella really wanted more food. She had been sitting next to Ava for a long time now and was overcome with impatience. She sneezed at Ava in frustration, then shuffled from side to side and continued to stare at her expectantly.

Ava smiled back warmly and gave her another treat.

Natural Behaviour

In this chapter we learned that Nella appears to be suffering from a canine mental health condition. It might seem like a bit of a coincidence that both Allen and Nella appear to be similarly affected. However, as about one in five dogs has an anxiety disorder, it's not really that unlikely.[1] Many people worry about the rising rates of mental health disorders in humans and blame the doctors, saying they are over-diagnosing the conditions. People often have the same reaction when they hear that dogs are being diagnosed with anxiety in ever greater numbers. The same stigma that people had—and still have—against treating human mental health is present today with animal mental health treatment also. I believe that part of this stigma is caused by the desire of people to live 'natural lives'—that you shouldn't have to take a pill to be happy. I completely agree with this sentiment, but this line of thinking misses half the problem. I agree that 'natural lives' are good, but when you can't necessarily achieve this, we shouldn't be denying medicine to help treat mental pain and suffering.

As a veterinarian that treats multiple species, I see a similar pattern with behavioural welfare and mental health in all the species I treat. As a general rule, the more 'unnatural' the environment the animal is living in, the more behavioural issues they seem to get. The brain of each species of animal is designed to live in a very specific ecological niche.[2] To survive in their niche, these species have to detect the optimal conditions for survival, and to strive for these conditions to be maintained. Over many millions of years, their brains have developed a set of specific behaviours that are designed to maintain the life of the animal within these ideal conditions. I see with any species that is taken by people and put into an 'unnatural' environment, that a certain number of those animals really struggle to cope. Their brain is designed for a very different world to what life has offered up for them. This mismatch between their expected environment and the one they are served up inevitably leads to a lot of stress and negative emotions. One example of this is when people keep caged parrots as pets. If they are not able to fly, bond and mate with another bird of their choosing, a certain percent of parrots develop feather plucking. They get so stressed they pull out all their feathers with their beak. This very sad example of a parrot mental illness is not uncommon. Similarly, if our dogs lived a more natural canine lifestyle, we would also see far fewer behaviour problems.

What is the 'natural' environment of a dog?

The definition of a 'natural' environment for dogs I use here is the set of conditions in which they have evolved and in which they thrive both physically and mentally. Domestic dogs have been living with humans for at least 15,000 years—well before the agricultural revolution.[3] They were domesticated from a now-extinct species of wolf by our hunter-gatherer ancestors. As the dog was domesticated, its lifestyle and behaviour changed.[4] As the lifestyle of humans has changed over time, so too has the environment of our dogs. The modern western lifestyle of most people is now far removed from the environment in which the dogs originally evolved. Many of the issues I see causing mental illness in dogs would probably not exist in dogs living with human hunter-gatherers. To clarify, I am not saying that the problem with modern human existence is that it is unnatural, but that our current existence does not mimic the existence that our dogs' brains are designed for. The reasoning for this assertion is explored below with two different examples.

Separation anxiety is a common mental health problem in dogs today, but I don't think a dog on its own is a natural circumstance. I have never met a healthy dog that actually wants to be isolated from their family members all day. Even wild dogs living in urban environments will preferentially choose to live and sleep as close to humans as they can.[5] It is hard to imagine how ancient dogs living a natural way of life would have been much different, living separated from people against their will. Why would they be? Would we purposefully isolate our dogs from us if we didn't have to? This is why I believe that having a dog separated from their family is as unnatural as caging a bird. This doesn't mean I think it is cruel to keep a dog on its own, but that it makes perfect sense to me why some dogs cannot handle this unnatural circumstance.

Territorial barking is another common issue in dogs today, along with barking directed at unfamiliar dogs or people. All these behaviours can be seen as a desire for the dog to live in an environment with a safe territory where no strangers intrude. Could these behaviour issues also be a consequence of dogs being forced to live in an 'unnatural' environment? The first domesticated dogs would have had a relatively large territory (compared to suburban backyards), as do wild dogs living today.[6] When a puppy was born, they wouldn't need to be socialised with *unfamiliar* dogs and people on walks, because they hardly ever encountered these things. The puppy would stay in their own territory, as it would be unsafe to roam into the territories of other dogs.[7] Yet we expect our dogs to be walked in communal territories like parks and footpaths on a daily basis. This environment is so unnatural for our dogs, that to get them to accept it, we have to put significant effort into regular socialisation and training from a young age.

Fixing a dog naturally

If you want your dog to have a happier and more natural life, the best way is to change your *own* lifestyle. You need to get back in touch with some aspects of the ancient human way of life. This is not a reference to how you eat, or the origin of the fibres in your clothing. I am talking about what you actually spend your day doing, where you live, and what your dog is doing with you. For many dogs, including Allen and Nella, changing these things to be more 'natural' would go a long way to solving most of their problems. It would probably also help with the mental health of people too. Some ways in which you and your dog can live a life that is more aligned to our ancestral origins are explored below.

The first thing to consider is your location. Most modern homes do not have the same amount of land as is natural for a dog's territory.[6] This wouldn't have been an issue for dogs when they were first domesticated by our ancestors.[4] Ideally, you would live on a property where your fence is very far away, so that you couldn't see or hear any person walking by. If Allen or Nella were in this situation, they would feel much more secure. They would hardly ever need to guard their territory. This would be a large improvement over their current situation where they are being spooked multiple times every day.

Another thing you could change is the where, and how, you work. Ancient humans didn't leave home each day and work in an office—they lived off the land or settled in a village. You could spend most of your day outside, working on your property with your dog by your side. If you never left your property, there would be no more separation anxiety, and you wouldn't need your dog to socialise with unfamiliar dogs either. Could you imagine how different the story of Allen and Nella would be if this was how their days went by? Hanging out with their people in the garden all day, and going for the odd stroll around their private property? Although moving to the country and living off the land is a completely impractical solution for most people, it does help highlight how many of the issues we see in dogs are directly caused by the environment we live in.

Although making these changes would help most of the dogs I see, I need to write a brief disclaimer. Living in this way would not be enough for some. The behaviour of an animal is determined by their genetics, their environment, and past learned experiences. Simply fixing the environment will not always be enough. Dogs that have very high levels of fear or anxiety due to genetics or traumatic past experiences may continue to be anxious, even in their ideal environment. They could end up having problems with aggression towards other dogs living in the family, or towards the children or farm animals. Medications are often needed to help these dogs live a happy and fulfilling life. Although the unnatural environment our dogs exist in is only part of the picture, I believe it plays a much greater role than most people realise.

Nature vs reality

As a species, humans are living in an increasingly technological world. Many of us understandably yearn for aspects of a pre-industrial existence, that embraces all the comforting elements of nature. This longing for what we feel is a 'natural' human experience often pervades our choices and morality. Many people also seek a more natural existence for their dog. They do this in all sorts of ways, such as choosing to feed their pets raw food diets that are supposed to mimic their pre-domestication diet. However, most people don't even attempt to have their dog's environment mimic that of the ancestral dog as discussed above. Rather, they put them into unnatural situations on a daily basis, like leaving them isolated for hours, or having them meet a series of unfamiliar dogs on a walk for only a few minutes each in a communal territory with uncertain ownership. The fact that *most* of our dogs manage to cope with an unnatural lifestyle amazes me, and is a testament to how well we have domesticated them.

As we saw in this chapter, people can be very worried about using unnatural behaviour-modifying medications on their pets, as it goes against their desire for a less artificial existence. However, I see this as a necessary evil. This is what we can expect if we want to mould our dogs into our artificial human existence. It isn't fair for us to bring our pets into our lives without their consent, force them to live unnatural lives according to what they are designed for, and then prevent them from taking unnatural medicine when they suffer as a result.

CHAPTER THIRTEEN

Happy Dogs

Allen stood perfectly still as he watched Nathan pull out a green padded chair and sit next to Petra. They were seated at a wooden table outside a small cafe, located a few streets from their house. Nathan reached over and handed a menu to Petra.

'Isn't it nice being able to bring Allen here now,' commented Nathan. 'Remember how bad he used to be at cafes?'

Petra glanced down at Allen, who had moved between her legs for extra safety.

'Yeah, he's improved so much,' agreed Petra. 'He hardly even needs corrections anymore.'

Allen stared up at Nathan, confused that they weren't continuing down the street as they normally did on a walk. He felt himself starting to pant again. Their waiter soon appeared; he was a well-groomed, middle-aged man who cheerfully took their order. Allen retreated back under the table, trying to keep as far back from him as he could.

Just as the waiter was leaving the table, he noticed Allen. He stopped himself mid-stride and smiled tenderly.

'Oh my,' he said fondly. 'I didn't realise you have a little dog, he's so quiet. Do you mind if I give him a wee pat?'

Petra smiled and indicated he could, flattered by the attention.

'Good boy Allen, want to say hello to the man?' she said in her baby voice.

The waiter squatted down next to the table. Smiling, he moved his hand in towards Allen, who was cowering in place next to Petra's feet. As Allen saw the hand coming in towards him, he knew he couldn't react. He steeled himself for what was to come and stayed perfectly still. The waiter managed to touch the side of his back as Allen looked away, his heart pounding in his chest.

Noticing he didn't seem interested, the waiter stood back up. 'Fabulous dog,' he commented, grinning as he left the table.

A few minutes later, a young couple strolled over to a nearby table. As they took their seats, Nathan noticed they had a dog with them. They were with a golden Labrador who was pulling on her lead quite forcefully. She was trying to get to a scrap of food, left on the ground by an earlier customer.

When Allen noticed the dog he shuddered, things were not going well. His already elevated heart rate spiked even faster, and he could hear his pulse in his ears. Worrying what this dog might be about to do, Allen moved further behind Petra's legs for protection.

The Labrador soon noticed Allen, hidden under the table. Curious, she tried to smell him from a distance. As she pulled in his direction, her nose twitching in the air, she caught a whiff of his scent. The smell told her he was stressed, very stressed. Recoiling, she snorted a short burst of air out her nose to try and clear the unpleasant odour.

'Freya, come back here darling,' said the female owner as her long black hair flew across her face from a sudden gust of wind.

Freya turned around and reluctantly walked closer to her people. She stood there, looking around as they browsed their menus and discussed what they wanted. Freya wasn't bothered by seeing other dogs or people, but she wasn't happy. She often went to cafes with her people, and the same thing always happened. Freya shuffled on her feet and whined a few times softly.

The male owner looked down. Bending his tall body around the table, he checked to see she was okay.

'What's wrong?' he asked, staring inquisitively.

Freya looked at him and wagged her tail as she sat down on the cold, hard concrete. She let out another soft whine.

'You just want attention! Good girl Freya, stay there,' he said. He sat back up and rolled his eyes dramatically.

The lady laughed at his expression, then gazed lovingly down at Freya. 'I think she wants to eat all that food she can smell too!'

Freya snorted, then stood back up and whined again, but this time she was ignored.

The waiter emerged from the café, this time holding two plates of food. As he walked over to Allen's table, he noticed the plastic bulge on the static collar around Allen's neck.

'Here's your food, please enjoy! That isn't a shock collar on your dog, is it?' he asked, frowning.

'Not exactly,' replied Nathan, confused. 'It's a static collar, for his training.'

'Right...' said the waiter in a clearly disapproving tone, before quickly turning and heading back inside.

'What was that all about?' said Nathan, raising his eyebrows at Petra.

'Never mind,' said Petra, picking up her cutlery and digging into her toast. 'So, are we seeing Nella at the park later?'

'Yeah absolutely, I was thinking we could just walk there after this.'

As Petra finished her next mouthful, she reached down and stroked Allen on the head. 'It's been ages since we saw them last, what's been going on?'

'It has,' agreed Nathan. 'They've still been having problems with Nella. Apparently, she chased Brooke out the door of their house and so they went to their vet instead.'

Petra swallowed quickly, nearly choking on her food. 'Brooke? She was so nice!'

Freya whined again, particularly loud this time.

'Yeah,' confirmed Nathan, glancing over at Freya. 'The vet put her on drugs for the last few months, and they've been waiting for them to work while they train her to be around other dogs.'

Petra opened her mouth in shock. 'Wow! Just wow. That's a bit much if you ask me,' her tone turned disapproving as she added, 'they should just fix the problem like we did with Allen. And then they wouldn't need the drugs!'

'I know!' said Nathan, feeling outraged. 'It's so sad. It's not right to drug up dogs just to make them behave. I might suggest they give Brooke another call when we see them later.'

'Well, I guess they don't know any better,' replied Petra sighing. 'But it's like drugging a baby, it's just so wrong!'

Allen stood up under the table, his legs sore from sitting on the hard concrete. As he shifted uncomfortably, he felt like whining, but was too afraid to make a sound.

'I still can't believe what a perfect dog Allen turned out to be,' commented Nathan.

Feeling proud, Petra took a crust of her toast off her plate and reached under the table to offer it to Allen. He sniffed at it out of interest, but didn't respond further. Even though it smelt delicious, he was far too stressed to have an appetite at the moment.

'What a fusspot!' said Nathan, who had been watching the whole thing. 'He loves our bread at home, but for some reason this one isn't good enough!'

As the morning sun filtered through the trees, the two couples sat at their tables with their dogs. Even though they were quiet, the dogs didn't go unnoticed by the people around them. When an old lady carrying her shopping walked past the café, she watched them both, smiling to herself. She thought how wonderful it looked and wished her own dogs would be so well behaved.

Freya started shifting on her feet then sighed and gingerly sat down once more on the concrete. She tried to rest as she watched her people sitting in their comfortable padded chairs. She wanted to enjoy the morning too, but there was just nowhere to lie. The ground was too cold and hard, she needed her bed.

* * *

Nella lay on the edge of the couch, carefully positioned to catch a ray of sunshine streaming through the window. Her breathing was slow and steady as she drifted in and out of sleep. When a loud motorbike slowly hummed past the front of her house, she lifted her head to look down the hallway. Her heart skipped a beat for a moment, until she realised it was probably nothing to worry about. Her sleepy eyes slowly forced themselves open as she slid onto the floor and walked over to her bowl for a drink. Nella was content watching time go by, but was still looking forward to when her people would come back home. She used her tongue to flick the water from the bowl up into her mouth before swallowing, enjoying the sensation. Nella saw one of Tessa's shoes on the ground at the base of the stairs and walked up to it. She pawed it once, wishing Tessa was there, then walked back over to the couch. Feeling relaxed, Nella was keen to lay back down in her sunbeam before it moved across the room. As she curled up and rested her head on her paws, she let out a big sigh as she closed her eyes.

A few minutes later, Nella heard an engine noise outside the house and lifted her head again. This noise was familiar—it had exactly the pitch and vibration of what she normally heard before her people arrived home. Feeling pleasantly expectant, she got up off the couch and wandered over to the door. Before long the lock was clicking, and the front door was swinging open in front of her.

Nella started vigorously wagging her tail and poked her head through the door to greet her people. As they walked inside, they stroked and rubbed her body and head as they spoke to her in comforting tones.

'Wow, she seems calm!' exclaimed Olivia, smiling at Nella warmly.

Mick walked ahead down the hallway and into the lounge. 'Oh look, Tess left one of her shoes out, and it's whole!'

Tessa ran up to her shoe and picked it up. 'Look she didn't eat my shoe, Mum,' she said excitedly as she showed it to Olivia.

Olivia smiled in mock disapproval. 'Yes Tess, that's very good but you know you still shouldn't leave your shoes out like that!'

'I gotta say,' said Mick as he put down his bag and collapsed on the couch. 'I'm glad we tried these medications on her, she just seems happier.'

Olivia nodded smugly. 'I told you Ava was good.'

Mick quickly sat up and checked his phone. 'I forgot! We need to leave soon—remember we're meeting Nath and Petra at the park this morning?'

'Yes honey, I hadn't forgotten. I just need to change outfits, give me two minutes.'

Tessa found a short rope toy lying on the floor and picked it up. 'Nelly, look! I got ropey!' she squealed, running into the front room of the house.

Nella saw Tessa running with the rope snaking behind her and excitedly bounded in pursuit. Her tail wagging gently, she tried to get the rope off Tessa, who was attempting to hide it behind her back.

'Nella, want to go for a walk?' asked Mick, holding up her leash.

Nella snapped her head around to look at Mick and froze for a second, before walking towards him with her tail swishing wildly.

As they all left the house, Nella set about finding things to sniff at. She loved checking all the new smells. Each time they went on a walk, new smells would appear and the old ones

would change or fade. Just outside the house, she smelled
something interesting in a patch of grass. On closer inspection,
she quickly identified it. It was the same dog pee she had smelt
there yesterday, she quickly moved on. As they wandered down
the street, Nella noticed another dog coming towards them. It
was the small black scruffy dog with the elderly man that lived a
few houses down. Nella's heart jumped for a moment, but she
was starting to get used to other dogs now.

Olivia was also on the lookout for other dogs, and noticed it
too. She quickly stepped into action, and produced a small piece
of dried liver for Nella. Before she even had the treat out, Nella
was already looking up at her waiting.

'Good girl Nelly,' she encouraged.

As had happened now many times over the last few months,
Nella took the treat from Olivia while she ignored the strange
dog. The enjoyment of the treat, paired with the sight of the
other dog, reinforced a connection in her mind. She had now
become used to getting delicious morsels of food when she saw
other dogs, and it happened whether she barked at them or not.
This led her to immediately look at Olivia for her treat as soon
as she saw a dog. This new routine was a lot more enjoyable than
barking.

As they continued walking, Nella chewed on the piece of
liver and looked back at Olivia for more. Olivia kept giving her
treat after treat as they passed by the small dog on the footpath.

Once it was out of sight, Nella sensed an interesting smell of
something rotten and pulled towards a patch of grass.

'Good girl Nella,' said Mick. He was smiling, happy with her
reaction to the little black dog. 'You're gonna meet Allen soon,
maybe you could even learn to be his friend?'

Then, a loud crunching sound started coming from Nella's
mouth.

'Nella! What are you eating!' exclaimed Olivia. She pulled up
Nella's head to see a slimy piece of chewed muck fall out onto
the ground.

'It's a chicken bone,' said Mick, shaking his head with disgust. 'Why do people think it's okay to throw them on the sidewalk!'

Olivia pulled Nella on down the path, sighing deeply. 'Not again, I hope we don't have to take you back to the vet Nelly, you silly girl!'

While Nella swallowed the last of the old chicken bone, she sensed the disapproval from her people. Nella held her ears low and looked up at Olivia, hoping she would reaffirm their bond. As usual, Olivia's heart melted at the sight of her. She smiled at her big eyes and floppy ears, giving her a gentle pat on the neck.

'It's okay Nelly, just don't eat gross stuff alright?'

As they continued down the path, a small white dog appeared on the other side of the road. Despite the long fur covering his eyes, he managed to catch sight of Nella's large grey silhouette. He pulled against the leash and barked at her loudly. He barked at a lot of things, he was always feeling anxious, and this was his way of dealing with it. Right now, he was frustrated that he couldn't get to Nella to interact and play. He loved big dogs but hated being restricted by his leash. His owner, a tall, elegant lady, gently pulled back on the leash and kept walking. He couldn't help himself, turning his head to watch them as he was dragged away, he barked again out of frustration. Olivia gave Nella another piece of the dried liver as she watched the other dog warily.

Due to the dog's small size, Nella wasn't too worried, but she was glad they were moving away. As the dog let out a final bark from the distance, she dropped her head back to the path. She had found another strange scent that needed exploring.

Optimising Welfare

We can see in this chapter that when Nella is feeling happier and more relaxed, her behaviour becomes more acceptable to the people around her. It is in both our interests and the interests of our dogs for them to live a stress-free life. Avoiding negative experiences, like those Allen is subjected to, will clearly help achieve this objective. However, avoiding negative experiences is only half the solution. To provide exceptional welfare for our dogs, we need to be giving them regular enjoyable experiences as well. This is not a controversial opinion, and there are many books out there that provide excellent examples of positive things to do for your dog. In this section, I will focus on a few lesser-known and non-obvious examples of things we can do that can have a huge impact on the happiness of our dog.

Health

The health of our dogs is clearly going to impact their welfare, as we see with the back pain that Allen experiences. Most people take their dog to the veterinarian when they are unwell, and also for a yearly check-up. As a veterinarian myself, I have been involved in this routine for over a decade. The first thing worth mentioning is how often I hear people say that they only go to the vet if they notice a problem. As dogs can't talk, they can't tell you if they are feeling a bit off or are in pain. A veterinarian can pick up things by glancing at a dog in the waiting room before they even touch them, things that an owner didn't even realise were an issue. This is why regular 'health' check-ups are so important. It is also vital that the dog owner carefully observes their dog at home to try and guide the vet to any potential issues.

Out of all the health conditions that dogs can get, the one strange thing I see that is often overlooked and under-treated is anal gland discomfort.

The anal glands are two small fluid-filled sacs on the inside of the dog anus. These glands mark faeces when they toilet. When the dog is frightened, they also express themselves similar to a skunk. The fluid that comes out is disgusting by all accounts, it is brown and usually smells like decomposing fish. It is common for pet dogs to have problems with these glands, where they get impacted (blocked and full), and are unable to express themselves. This can be very uncomfortable for the dog, due to the pressure on the glands and the surrounding tissue.

One of the strangest things about blocked anal glands is the wide variety of signs a dog can display in response. Behaviours can include scooting their bottom on the ground, suddenly flicking their head around to look at their bottom, sitting down for excessive periods of time with their bottom touching the floor, hiding somewhere in the house (often under a bed), licking at their bottom, biting at their hind legs, and even licking their bedding excessively where they are cleaning up the leaked excretions. If the owner doesn't notice this issue, the dog is forced to just put up with it forever. This problem is often missed as it isn't life-threatening, and the signs can be subtle. This is why I think anal glands are responsible for a lot of low-level discomfort in dogs. There are many happy, healthy dogs out there with uncomfortable anal glands that never get treatment. I don't know why so many dogs get this issue, but I do know it is very commonly overlooked. To optimise the welfare of our dogs, we need to go beyond treating the serious diseases they get, and start treating their minor discomforts, such as anal gland issues. This means visiting the vet regularly, asking if they can find anything that might be making the dog uncomfortable, and paying attention to their advice. These minor issues also affect their behaviour, as we have seen in this book. Allen has mild back pain that is not noticed by his people. It only flares up occasionally, but when they try to lift him, this pain is sometimes enough to cause him to bite. Over my career, I have seen many situations where dogs have developed defensive behaviours when their owners try to pick them up, due to an incorrect and painful lifting technique.

Individual preferences for touch

As we have already discussed in this book, different dogs like different things. By assuming that all dogs like something, we can unintentionally force some dogs into things they don't like. If we want to optimise the welfare of a dog, we need to know what they like—as an individual. Studies that examine a group of dogs to find out if *all* dogs like this or that are missing the point of individual preferences. As mentioned in the first chapter, the preference for physical affection from people is wildly variable between dogs. Some dogs love being touched by all people in all situations, but this is not the norm. A fact that most people don't realise is that many dogs *don't* like to be touched by people. When people ignore their preference, the dog either puts up with it, withdraws, growls, or bites. This is the case with Allen, where fear is the main reason why he does not want to be touched by strangers. For other dogs, the reason they don't enjoy touch can be more physical, where it just feels uncomfortable to be stroked. Sometimes, their preference for touch depends on the situation or the person. Like a dog that enjoys a cuddle in the evening in front of the television, but not in the middle of a walk. Other dogs like being touched by their owner, but not by strangers. Plenty of dogs like being touched in a specific location like the lower back or chest, but dislike being touched on top of their head or their paws.

How might someone know if or where a dog likes to be touched? This is a very important question that is not asked enough. Too many people reach over and touch the top of the head of every dog they meet, without any regard for the feelings of the dog. The way to find out if a dog wants you to touch them is to simply watch their body language. I have seen owners say their dog likes being patted, then immediately reach over their dog's head to pat them only to have the dog flinch and pull their head down or to the side in avoidance. After pointing this out it seems obvious to them, however they never noticed it before because they didn't realise it was even possible for a dog to not like a pat from a person. Generally, if a dog is leaning into your affection and remaining calm, still and quiet, they are probably enjoying it. If you keep your hand still, you will find that many dogs will move their body along your hand until you are touching their favourite location to be touched.

A basic human right is the requirement for consent before being touched by another person. I believe dogs also deserve to have some sort of right over their own body, even though they are very different animals to us. The dogs I see are much more comfortable when they are given the right to consent or refuse touch from a person. Throughout this book, we can see examples of dogs being touched with or without their consent, and the different experiences associated with this. Only touching a dog in the manner and location that they want to be touched is excellent for dog welfare. If I am ever in doubt, I don't touch the dog at all, as I believe they deserve the right to consent.

In this chapter, Allen would have been much happier to *not* be touched by the waiter who reached in under the table. So how can we avoid this kind of thing from happening? If you think a dog might want your affection, you can do a consent check with them. To do this, you can try to gently touch the part of them that is closest to you (or already touching you). As a tip, if you want them to consent, don't go for the top of the head! You are more likely to be successful with the chest, neck or lower back.

Once you are touching them, you must carefully watch their reaction. This is where you can see if they are consenting or not. To have their consent, the dog needs to have done something to show you they want you to continue. If they appear to be either tense, fearful, threatening, ignoring you or withdrawing away, then you should immediately stop. As with people in relationships, once you know each other well, you can learn the kinds of touch they will be likely to consent to. However, a dog is also allowed to change their mind. Consenting once does not give implicit consent going forwards. There are many reasons why this might occur; even simply not being in the mood to be touched. You should always keep an eye out for signs that a dog is maintaining consent.

Communication of needs

If a dog can communicate with their owner to let them know what they want, it helps them to live a much happier life. Sadly, I see many issues with owners who cannot understand when their dog is asking for things that they would happily give them if only they understood. One common problem I see is around the ability of a dog to gain access to the toilet. Some dogs are locked inside or live in an apartment block where their owner needs to take them out for toilet trips. When a dog can't ask for toilet access in a way their owner understands, this leads to a lot of distress. They end up feeling more and more uncomfortable as they feel their urges becoming stronger and stronger. Allen experiences this problem in chapter 4, when he barks at Nathan for want of a toilet. He has no way of asking to get access to the toilet, his attempts are not understood. Nathan incorrectly assumes Allen wants to get onto the couch, so he is then forced to toilet inside as there is no other option.

In this chapter we also saw an example of a communication breakdown with Freya the Labrador and her people, when she was whining at the café due to a feeling of discomfort. She wasn't suffering or in a bad state of welfare, but she was clearly not content either. I regularly see dogs at cafés without a bed, and can often tell that they are in want of some comfort. Their owners normally have no idea at all! A dog wouldn't often pick hard ground to lie on. If no bedding was available, then they would often rather choose some soft grass or dirt that affords more padding. As with anything that involves a personal preference, there will be a few exceptions: lying down on a cold hard surface can sometimes be useful for cooling off.

I see similar issues with dog beds inside the house, but in locations that the dog would rather change. When I come into someone's home, the dog bed is often at least a few meters away from where the owners are sitting at the table or couch. Some dogs get quite upset that there isn't somewhere soft to lie next to their person. When I see this, and point out that the dog is lying on the hard floor and keeps moving around with discomfort, most people hadn't considered it. By simply moving their bed next to where we are sitting, many dogs quickly jump in and happily fall asleep. By simply moving your dog's bed to within a few meters of your location, you can make them that little bit happier in life.

CHAPTER FOURTEEN

Obey Your Master

Tessa pointed ahead at a long black dog with floppy ears, standing in the distance.

'Is that Allen, Daddy?'

Mick looked up from the path and squinted at the outline of the dog waiting next to two people.

'Yep, sure is!'

As they made their way into the parklands, Olivia realised she was feeling nervous. Their previous meeting as puppies did not go well. Nella had improved a lot, but she did occasionally react.

As they came closer, Nella suddenly stopped. She stood frozen for a second, recognising another dog was in view. She tensed up further when Petra and Nathan started waving at them. She couldn't recognise any of them, but realised the dog was quite small. She was okay with small dogs now, they weren't so frightening as the larger ones. She even felt a little interested in meeting him. Nella looked up at Olivia, expecting a treat to appear.

'Oh, your treat, sorry Nelly!' apologised Olivia, quickly handing her some liver.

As they approached, Allen stood still, staring at Nella and her family. He started panting heavily, the sheer size of Nella was very intimidating. He was feeling exhausted, they had been out of the house for almost two hours now. Allen had expected they would go home after the café. He had been unpleasantly surprised when they turned into the park.

'Hi guys,' said Nathan as they came within earshot, smiling at them.

Nathan walked forwards, with Petra holding Allen on his leash. As they greeted each other, Nella shied away from the two strange adults and tentatively approached Allen. She was anxious, to be sure, but interested in meeting him.

As Nella slowly approached, Petra became nervous. 'Is Nella going to be okay with Allen? She's awfully big...'

Allen pulled back on the leash, sensing that Nella was coming for him.

'She should be fine,' replied Olivia, smiling at Nella as she slowly advanced. 'She's really improved a lot the last few months.'

Mick looked down at Allen and noticed him breathing heavily. 'Wow, Allen's panting a lot, is he okay?'

Nathan looked at Allen, surprised by the concern. 'Yeah, I think he's just happy to be out! He's doing great. We just had breakfast with him at the cafe over there.'

Nathan pointed back the way they had come.

Allen felt trapped, he knew he couldn't react. All he could do was crouch down, lower his head and look away from Nella.

Nella carefully sniffed at Allen, but didn't crowd him. She could tell he wasn't interested in her, and he smelled very stressed.

Olivia was also suspicious that Allen wasn't feeling completely comfortable. She pulled Nella back away a few steps, giving him some space.

'So how was that place?' asked Mick. 'We've been meaning to try some new cafes in the area.'

'Great, yeah great,' replied Nathan. 'I got the big breakfast, even had oyster mushrooms... Coffee's good too.'

Nella turned further away from Allen, and leant down to sniff at the edge of the path. Relieved, Allen stood back up and moved himself behind Petra's legs, still panting heavily.

Soon everyone had started walking along the path together. Nella resumed her sniffing while Allen stayed close to Petra.

'Allen is so well behaved,' commented Olivia, looking down at him smiling.

Just when Petra was about to reply, Nella jerked on the leash. Olivia was not expecting this. Being mid-stride, she stumbled, and the leash fell out of her hand. Unrestrained, Nella pounced into a thick bush growing beside the path. The bush shook and there was the sound of branches snapping as Nella forced her way through. Shortly after, a light-grey rabbit darted out, running straight past Allen.

Seeing the rabbit running, Allen felt a strong predatory urge to chase. As it ran away through the grass, the feeling ignited, consuming him. He instantly switched from having subdued resignation to panicked determination. He pulled backwards against the leash, trying to escape, but was no match for Petra's strength. However, as he pulled a second time, his head now facing Petra, the choker chain somehow slipped free of his neck. He found himself suddenly released.

By this stage, Nella had turned and was in hot pursuit of the rabbit. When it disappeared inside another bush, Nella crashed into it seconds later.

As Allen charged in their direction, the rabbit shot out again, racing through an open field. Both dogs turned to chase after it, running with all of their energy.

The people were slow to come to their senses, but now the shock of what was happening had started to wear off.

'Allen! Get back here right now!' screamed Nathan, running towards him.

Allen heard the screaming faintly, in the back of his consciousness. However, as he was used to being yelled at, it was something that hardly bothered him anymore. It was definitely not as bad as being shocked.

Petra reached into her pocket to get out the shock-remote, but fumbled it onto the ground. The rabbit turned, running towards the edge of the park. Mick could see they were heading towards a road, and had calculated what might be about to happen. His heart racing, Mick also yelled, but at Nella.

'NELLAAAAA!' he screamed, at the top of his lungs.'

Unlike Allen, Nella was not used to being yelled at. Hearing her name shouted out in this way was new to her, she was shocked, scared and surprised all at once. She knew something must be wrong, something important. Nella immediately stopped chasing the rabbit, settling into a walk. She looked over at Mick, worried about what had happened. As she watched Mick running towards her, the rabbit continued to run towards the road. Just as Allen had almost caught up to the rabbit, Petra finally managed to pick up the shock-remote from the ground. She frantically pressed the button.

Allen yelped in pain as he ran onto the road after the rabbit, his neck on fire. However, it didn't stop him. He was becoming used to the pain, and the adrenaline was clouding his perception. He felt free. It was liberating to act the part of the predator—this was something his brain had been designed for. As he ran across the road, he felt the collar searing his neck for a second time.

Just then, with the worst possible timing, a black van swept past and connected with Allen's body. There was a loud thud as he rolled under the van, which immediately skidded to a halt.

Screaming, Petra ran up to Allen's body. He was still breathing, but lay still on the road with a spot of blood dripping from his nose. Mick had managed to grab Nella's leash, and Tessa was starting to cry. A young man stepped out of the van; he held his hands to the side of his face as he slowly walked over. Petra picked up Allen's body from the road, wailing.

'Can you drive us to the vet?' she asked the young man.

He paused for a second, then nodded. 'Sure, I didn't see him, sorry…'

Nathan and Petra climbed into the van with Allen in their arms.

'I hope he's okay mate,' Mick called out. 'Call me to let us know how you go, our vet's probably the closest, it's just on the other side of the supermarket.'

* * *

The black van pulled into the parking lot of Nella's veterinary clinic. Petra and Nathan burst out, past a surprised client who was making their way out the reception door. Gasping and sobbing, they tried to explain to a shocked receptionist what had happened. Not making much sense, the receptionist struggled to understand them, but could see Allen was hurt.

'So, he was hit by a car?' she asked.

'Yes, yes, just do anything,' cried Petra, tears rolling down her face.

Hearing the commotion, Ava stepped out of the consult room and immediately sensed the emergency. She abandoned her current case and rushed up to the receptionist.

'It's a hit by car,' she explained, with urgency in her voice.

Ava reached out and took Allen's limp body from Petra's arms. 'Cindy will take your details, I'll get him straight out the back and start assessing him, just wait here.'

Ava ran out to the back of the clinic, with Allen cradled in her arms. Allen lifted his head, looking confused, but he wasn't aware of what was happening.

Cindy took their details. When she asked about Allen's general health, Nathan became inpatient.

'So, is he going to be okay? Do many dogs survive being hit by a van?'

Cindy paused and sighed, unable to give a good answer. 'We'll do everything we can, Ava should have an update for you in a few minutes.'

At the back of the clinic in the treatment area, Ava was assessing Allen's gums. 'They're pale, I think he's losing blood, we need to do an x-ray, now!'

Allen was rushed into a dimly lit room and onto a table. Ava noticed the black shock collar around his neck. Recognising what it was, she grabbed a pair of scissors without thinking. She quickly snipped it off his neck, paying no regard to whether it might be damaged in the process. Then, as she pushed it off the table it smashed open on the floor.

'We can't have that piece of rubbish interfering with our images,' she said with disgust.

Once they had carefully rushed through the first set of x-rays, they had to wait for them to process. With a moment to spare, Ava sat on the table next to Allen. As he lay there half-conscious, she stroked his head tenderly. A single tear fell from each of her eyes and landed on his back. She shook her head slowly. 'What have they done to you my dear, what have they done?'

Feeling the moisture land on his back, Allen roused. Light-headed and weak, looked up at her. Squinting, Allen could see the light from the doorway forming a halo around her silhouette.

As the image of the x-ray appeared on the screen, Ava peered closely at it. Sighing, she whispered to herself. 'Looks like my dinner plans are going to be cancelled again tonight.'

Ava quickly directed the nurse to prepare Allen for surgery, then walked back out to reception to relay the news.

Petra locked eyes onto Ava as she came into the waiting room. 'Is he okay?' she asked, her voice quavering.

Ava furrowed her brow, preparing to deliver the bad news. 'He's lost a lot of blood, I think he's bleeding internally into his abdomen. That means he might have a ruptured spleen. He has some broken ribs as well.'

Petra put her hand up over her mouth as she gasped.

'So can you fix it?' asked Nathan, wrapping his arm around Petra.

Ava shook her head, not feeling hopeful. 'Maybe, he needs surgery for me to remove his spleen to stop the bleeding. If that goes well and there's nothing else wrong, then he might be okay. We can only try.'

Petra burst into tears again, her makeup running. 'Yes, do it, I don't care how much it costs, he's my baby. Just please try to save him.'

* * *

Later that evening, Ava called Nathan and Petra in from the busy reception. As they came through the consulting room door, Ava started talking.

'I'm sure you're dying to hear how he's going, and I am happy to say he's still stable. The surgery went as well as we could have hoped.'

As relief swept through Petra, she suddenly realised how exhausted she was. She collapsed into the chair and managed to smile at Ava. 'That's such good news, thank you so much.'

Nathan let out a big sigh, and was about to add his thanks.

'But he's not out of the woods yet,' continued Ava. 'He'll need to stay in hospital for a few days to recover, he's been through a lot. And there's still a risk of other injuries that we can't yet see. Overall, though, it's good news.'

Nathan tried to put on a cheerful face. 'Well, that was a close one, hopefully he learns not to chase rabbits after this!'

Ava paused, choosing her words carefully before continuing.

'I also noticed that he had a shock collar. Unfortunately, it was damaged as we were rushing him into surgery.'

Petra raised her eyebrows, surprised. She had thought it quite sturdy.

'Oh, really?' she replied. 'Maybe it got damaged when he was hit. Well never mind, we can easily buy another.'

Ava let out a deep breath. 'About that, if Allen makes it through this, I would like you to promise me something.'

Nathan and Petra looked at each other.

'Okay, what's that then?' asked Petra.

Ava replied slowly. 'I want you to come in for a behaviour consultation with me, so we can chat about the use of shock collars on dogs. I don't think you understand how they work, because if you did, I don't think you'd be using one.'

Ethical Punishment?

In this book, we have seen how humans can get a dog to behave in ways they consider 'appropriate'. Allen is ruled with fear and domination, often turning him into a compliant subject. Nella is ruled with empathy and love, often turning her into a willing companion. The way in which we rule over our dogs is a choice made by every dog owner. After reading this book, you are now equipped with the knowledge to answer this question: How will you rule over your dog? Will you use fear and domination, or empathy and love?

The issues raised in this book make it clear why the people that truly understand dog behaviour *never* recommend using aversive methods for training. This means never hitting, shocking, water-squirting, yelling or even saying 'no' in a firm tone. Although the alternative methods of controlling the behaviour of a dog may be more difficult for us to understand and implement, they are the only ethical option. Where positive reward-based training methods fail to change the behaviour of the dog, it is not a failure of the methods themselves. As we saw with Nella, it is a sign that the methods are being used incorrectly, or the dog is too fearful or anxious in that environment. Using reward-based training for treating mental illness in dogs is a bit like surgery for treating skin cancer—it is a large part of the treatment, but it isn't everything. Where the cancer is very serious, surgery alone may not be enough. This does not mean that surgery is not a useful tool. A failure of surgery to fix a cancer in a patient does not mean that 'surgery doesn't work', rather it is a reflection of the nature and severity of the disease. Just like with serious cancer, in some cases a dog will be so badly affected by a mental health condition that reward-based training is unable to fix the problem. This isn't because reward-based training 'doesn't work', it's simply a reflection of the severity of the condition. In these situations, medications can certainly help in a lot of cases, but they are not a silver bullet. There are some very sad cases where medications are not enough, and where the level of psychological suffering is so great that euthanasia is tragically the only humane option.

When Nella was running towards the road and Mick yelled out at her, she stopped. This appears on the face of it to contradict the central message of this book. Controlling the behaviour of a dog through fear or intimidation is not ethical. However, in this circumstance it might have saved Nella's life. I believe that Mick did the right thing here, as calling Nella in a friendly tone with a treat would not have worked. She was far too focused on the rabbit. This is a difficult contradiction that is not often addressed by ethical dog behaviour professionals such as myself. To be clear, the only reason that shouting worked to stop Nella from running on the road was that it really surprised her, she wasn't used to having a person yell at her. So, when exactly is it okay, if ever, to use aversive methods to control the behaviour of a dog?

Ethical punishment?

This is a complicated topic, but it is important to be addressed. I do not believe that aversive punishment can ever be ethical. However, I do believe we can ethically use force to control the behaviour of a dog in very specific circumstances. The distinction between these two sentences is the use of the word 'punishment'. Punishment implies that the dog will learn from the situation to repeat the behaviour less. As we saw with Allen, using aversive punishment to teach him to learn how to behave to avoid that punishment was extremely harmful. This is why it's never okay to use fear or pain to teach. However, when Mick yells at Nella in this chapter, it saves her life and prevents a great deal of suffering. So why do I think that was okay, how is this a consistent message?

Firstly, when Mick yelled at Nella, it wasn't technically a punishment (according to learning theory). This is because she didn't *learn* anything from it. If the same thing happened again the next day, Nella would not stop chasing the rabbit as she approached the road, she never made that connection. Rather than punishment, I would call Mick's yelling an aversive stimulus. This means that the sound of Mick's voice was unpleasant and worrying for Nella, which was why she stopped. Obviously, it would have been better for Nella to never be in that situation to begin with, so the yelling wasn't needed. Repeatedly putting a dog into a situation where you have to yell or shock them to save their life is not ethical.

Secondly, Nella's behaviour that Mick was trying to control (chasing the rabbit) was not motivated by negative emotions. Nella was experiencing the thrill and pleasure of play and predatory chase when Mick yelled at her. This is a very important distinction! I do not think it is ever okay to use an aversive stimulus to control the behaviour of a dog if they are doing that behaviour due to negative emotions like fear or anxiety. Just to be clear, most of the behaviours that are difficult to control fall into this category. For example, when Nathan is yelling at Allen for barking at the window: he is barking because he is scared, and then being yelled at by Nathan makes him feel fearful or threatened, so this is not okay.

Finally, when Nella was being yelled at, it was uncomfortable for her, but far preferable to the pain and suffering of being hit by a car. This aversive stimulus had an immediate net-positive effect on Nella's welfare. This leaves us with three things that I believe must ALL be satisfied for us to ethically use an aversive stimulus to control the behaviour of a dog.

1. The aim of the aversive stimulus should not be to train or teach the dog, but to control their immediate behaviour when reward-based techniques are not working, AND

2. The behaviour being controlled should not be motivated by negative emotions such as fear or anxiety, AND

3. The intended and likely outcome of the aversive stimulus should have an immediate net-positive effect on the welfare of the dog.

So, as we can see from this list, there is almost never a situation where it's ethical to use force like this to control the behaviour of a dog. This is why behaviour professionals like me just never recommend its use. The example in this chapter was a very rare exception, that would not ever occur during the lifetime of most dogs. Unfortunately, in almost all cases where punishment is used to train a dog, all three of these rules are being broken, every single time the punishment is administered.

The benefits of compassion

There is something magical that happens when you truly understand your dog and never use force to control their behaviour. Over time, they learn to trust you completely. They get used to doing the things you ask, because they expect good things to happen to them afterwards. They also don't have any fearful memories of you angrily shouting at them, which can really damage their bond with you. I raise my own dogs in this way, never needing to raise my voice at them or to teach them right from wrong. They live a simple yet happy existence under my roof. When I see the love and trust in their eyes as they look back at me, there is no greater reward I could receive. I truly hope that everyone who reads this book will aspire to have a similar relationship with their dogs too.

A short note from the author

I wrote this book in an attempt to spread a message through society—a message that I hope will make a lasting change in the way that difficult dogs are understood and treated by the people that love them. You too can help spread this message, by recommending, reviewing, and sharing this book.

References

Chapter 1. Anthropomorphism

1. Asif, N. (2022). Minimal theory of mind–a Millikanian Approach. *Synthese*, 200(2), 1-26.
2. LeDoux, J. E. (2012). Evolution of human emotion: a view through fear. *Progress in Brain Research*, 195, 431-442.

Chapter 2. Breeding dogs

1. Harris, A., & Seckl, J. (2011). Glucocorticoids, prenatal stress and the programming of disease. *Hormones and Behavior*, 59(3), 279-289.
2. Murphree, O. D., Peters, J. E., & Dykman, R. A. (1969). Behavioural comparisons of nervous, stable, and crossbred pointers at ages 2, 3, 6, 9, and 12 months. *Conditional Reflex: a Pavlovian Journal of Research & Therapy*, 4(1), 20-23.
3. Maejima, M., Inoue-Murayama, M., Tonosaki, K., Matsuura, N., Kato, S., Saito, Y., ... & Ito, S. I. (2007). Traits and genotypes may predict the successful training of drug detection dogs. *Applied Animal Behaviour Science*, 107(3-4), 287-298.
4. Hammond, A., Rowland, T., Mills, D. S., & Pilot, M. (2022). Comparison of behavioural tendencies between 'dangerous dogs' and other domestic dog breeds–Evolutionary context and practical implications. *Evolutionary Applications*, 15(11), 1806-1819.

5. Wauthier, L. M., & Williams, J. M. (2018). Using the mini C-BARQ to investigate the effects of puppy farming on dog behaviour. *Applied Animal Behaviour Science*, 206, 75-86.
6. Westgarth, C., Reevell, K., & Barclay, R. (2012). Association between prospective owner viewing of the parents of a puppy and later referral for behavioural problems. *Veterinary Record*, 170(20), 517-517.
7. Czerwinski, V. H., Smith, B. P., Hynd, P. I., & Hazel, S. J. (2016). The influence of maternal care on stress-related behaviors in domestic dogs: What can we learn from the rodent literature?. *Journal of Veterinary Behavior*, 14, 52-59.
8. Pierantoni, L., Albertini, M., & Pirrone, F. (2011). Prevalence of owner-reported behaviours in dogs separated from the litter at two different ages. *Veterinary Record*, 169(18), 468-468.

Chapter 3. Interpreting dog behaviour

1. Golden, O., & Hanlon, A. J. (2018). Towards the development of day one competences in veterinary behaviour medicine: survey of veterinary professionals experience in companion animal practice in Ireland. *Irish Veterinary Journal*, 71(1), 1-9.
2. Flint, H. E., Coe, J. B., Pearl, D. L., Serpell, J. A., & Niel, L. (2018). Effect of training for dog fear identification on dog owner ratings of fear in familiar and unfamiliar dogs. *Applied Animal Behaviour Science*, 208, 66-74.
3. Wormald, D., Lawrence, A. J., Carter, G., & Fisher, A. D. (2016). Analysis of correlations between early social exposure and reported aggression in the dog. *Journal of Veterinary Behavior*, 15, 31-36.

Chapter 6. Unfamiliar territory

1. Kavoi, B. M., & Jameela, H. (2011). Comparative morphometry of the olfactory bulb, tract and stria in the

human, dog and goat. *International Journal of Morphology*, 29(3), 939-946.

2. D'Aniello, B., Semin, G. R., Alterisio, A., Aria, M., & Scandurra, A. (2018). Interspecies transmission of emotional information via chemosignals: from humans to dogs (Canis lupus familiaris). *Animal cognition*, 21, 67-78.

3. Cafazzo, S., Natoli, E., & Valsecchi, P. (2012). Scent-marking behaviour in a pack of free-ranging domestic dogs. *Ethology*, 118(10), 955-966.

4. Dürr, S., Dhand, N. K., Bombara, C., Molloy, S., & Ward, M. P. (2017). What influences the home range size of free-roaming domestic dogs? *Epidemiology & Infection*, 145(7), 1339-1350.

Chapter 8. Punishment works

1. Hierarchy of Procedures for Humane and Effective Practice. International Association of Animal Behavior Consultants. https://m.iaabc.org/about/lima/hierarchy. Accessed Jan 2023.

Chapter 9. Exposure therapy

1. Wormald, D., Lawrence, A. J., Carter, G., & Fisher, A. D. (2016). Analysis of correlations between early social exposure and reported aggression in the dog. *Journal of Veterinary Behavior*, 15, 31-36.

Chapter 11. Canine mental health

1. Tiira, K., Sulkama, S., & Lohi, H. (2016). Prevalence, comorbidity, and behavioral variation in canine anxiety. *Journal of Veterinary Behavior*, 16, 36-44.

2. Bandelow, B., & Michaelis, S. (2015). Epidemiology of anxiety disorders in the 21st century. *Dialogues in Clinical Neuroscience*, Sep;17(3):327-35

3. Overall, K. (2013). Manual of Clinical Behavioral Medicine for Dogs and Cats-E-Book. Elsevier Health Sciences.
4. Sonuga-Barke, E., & Thapar, A. (2021). The neurodiversity concept: is it helpful for clinicians and scientists? *The Lancet Psychiatry*, 8(7), 559-561.
5. Horwitz, D., & Mills, D. (2009). BSAVA manual of canine and feline behavioural medicine.
6. Landsberg, G., Hunthausen, W., & Ackerman, L. (2011). Behavior problems of the dog and cat. Elsevier Health Sciences.
7. Wormald, D. (2016). Exploring predisposing factors to anxiety-related behaviour problems in dogs (Doctoral dissertation, University of Melbourne).
8. Abbott, P. W., Gumusoglu, S. B., Bittle, J., Beversdorf, D. Q., & Stevens, H. E. (2018). Prenatal stress and genetic risk: How prenatal stress interacts with genetics to alter risk for psychiatric illness. *Psychoneuroendocrinology*, 90, 9-21.
9. D'Aniello, B., Semin, G.R., Alterisio, A. et al. (2018). Interspecies transmission of emotional information via chemosignals: from humans to dogs (Canis lupus familiaris). *Animal Cognition* 21, 67–78.

Chapter 12. Natural behaviour

1. Tiira, K., Sulkama, S., & Lohi, H. (2016). Prevalence, comorbidity, and behavioral variation in canine anxiety. *Journal of Veterinary Behavior*, 16, 36-44.
2. Gygax, L., & Hillmann, E. (2018). 'Naturalness' and its relation to animal welfare from an ethological perspective. *Agriculture*, 8(9), 136.
3. Perri, A. (2016). A wolf in dog's clothing: Initial dog domestication and Pleistocene wolf variation. *Journal of Archaeological Science*, 68, 1-4.
4. Serpell, James, ed. (2016) The domestic dog. Cambridge University Press.

5. Sen Majumder, S., Paul, M., Sau, S., & Bhadra, A. (2016). Denning habits of free-ranging dogs reveal preference for human proximity. *Scientific Reports*, 6(1), 1-8.

6. Dürr, S., Dhand, N. K., Bombara, C., Molloy, S., & Ward, M. P. (2017). What influences the home range size of free-roaming domestic dogs? *Epidemiology & Infection*, 145(7), 1339-1350.

7. Cafazzo, S., Natoli, E., & Valsecchi, P. (2012). Scent-marking behaviour in a pack of free-ranging domestic dogs. *Ethology*, 118(10), 955-966.

About The Author

Dr Dennis Wormald earned his Bachelor of Veterinary Science and PhD on canine anxiety from the University of Melbourne, Australia. He also has a biomedical science degree with a neuroscience major, and research experience in addiction neuroscience at the Florey Institute of Neuroscience and Mental Health. Dr Wormald is also a member by examination of the Veterinary Behaviour Chapter of the Australian and New Zealand College of Veterinary Scientists.

Dennis enjoys working as a veterinarian doing private veterinary referral behaviour consulting for dogs in Melbourne, Australia. He is also the founder of ABAdog, an online dog behaviour education business. This startup currently services over 50 veterinary clinics across Australia, providing custom dog behaviour advice for their patients (see www.abadog.com).